Overcoming the Stigma of Intimate Partner Abuse

Overcoming the Stigma of Intimate Partner Abuse addresses the impact of the shame surrounding intimate partner violence and the importance of actively challenging this stigma. Through examples of survivors who have triumphed over past abuse, the book presents a new way to understand the dynamics of abusive relationships as well as demonstrates the strength, resourcefulness, and resilience of victims and survivors. *Overcoming the Stigma of Intimate Partner Abuse* offers professionals, survivors, and communities an action plan to end stigma, support survivors, advocate for better response systems, raise awareness about abuse, and prevent violence.

Christine E. Murray, PhD, LPC, LMFT, associate professor, Department of Counseling and Educational Development, University of North Carolina at Greensboro, and co-founder of See the Triumph.

Allison Crowe, PhD, LPC, NCC, assistant professor of counselor education, Department of Interdisciplinary Professions, College of Education, East Carolina University; co-founder, See the Triumph.

Overcoming the Stigma of Intimate Partner Abuse

Christine E. Murray, PhD, LPC, LMFT
Allison Crowe, PhD, LPC, NCC

NEW YORK AND LONDON

First published 2017
by Routledge
711 Third Avenue, New York, NY 10017

and by Routledge
2 Park Square, Milton Park, Abingdon, Oxon, OX14 4RN

Routledge is an imprint of the Taylor & Francis Group, an informa business

© 2017 Taylor & Francis

The right of Christine E. Murray and Allison Crowe to be identified as authors of this work has been asserted by them in accordance with sections 77 and 78 of the Copyright, Designs and Patents Act 1988.

All rights reserved. No part of this book may be reprinted or reproduced or utilised in any form or by any electronic, mechanical, or other means, now known or hereafter invented, including photocopying and recording, or in any information storage or retrieval system, without permission in writing from the publishers.

Trademark notice: Product or corporate names may be trademarks or registered trademarks, and are used only for identification and explanation without intent to infringe.

Library of Congress Cataloging-in-Publication Data
A catalog record for this book has been requested

ISBN: 978-1-138-12131-7 (hbk)
ISBN: 978-1-138-12132-4 (pbk)
ISBN: 978-1-315-65103-3 (ebk)

Typeset in Sabon
by Apex CoVantage, LLC

This book is dedicated to my sons. You inspire me to work toward a world that is safe and peaceful.
~ Christine E. Murray

I dedicate this book to my parents, who taught me how to be an advocate, and to my husband and daughter, who remind me every day how lucky I am to be loved.
~ Allison Crowe

Contents

Acknowledgments   xiii

PART 1
Introduction   1

1   **Understanding Abusive Relationships**   3
     The Research Basis for This Book   6
     Understanding Abusive Relationships   8
     What Is Intimate Partner Violence?   9
     Who Does Intimate Partner Violence Affect?   10
     A Closer Look at the Dynamics of Abusive
        Relationships   12
        The Cycle of Violence   12
        The Power and Control Wheel   13
        Individualized Experiences of Intimate Partner
           Violence   14
     The Story Is Not Over Yet   25

2   **The Added Complexity of Stigma**   29
     Stigma   31
     Nikki's Story   33
     Stigma From Professionals   35
     Sam's Story   37
     Added Stigmas   40
        Same-Sex Relationships: Taylor's Story   41
        Male Victims of Abuse: Joseph's Story   46
     Consequences of Stigma   47
     Overcoming Stigma Related to IPV   48
     Conclusion   50

PART 2
Understanding Stigma 53

3 **Stigma as a Function of the Abuse: How Abusers Perpetuate Stigma** 55
   Abusers' Tactics and Stigma 58
   Perpetrators' Tactics of Abuse 62
   Control Tactics 62
   Isolation 64
   Verbal Denigration 66
   Humiliation 68
   The Overlaps Between Perpetrator Stigma and Emotional Abuse 69
   Victim-Blaming 69
   "Crazy-Making" 71
   Blocking Access to Potentially Helpful Resources 72
   Why Perpetrators Often Escape Accountability for Their Abusive Actions 73
   How Perpetrators Fail to Accept Responsibility for Their Abusive Actions 73
   How Friends, Family Members, and Communities Can Fail to Hold Perpetrators Accountable 75
   Unique Challenges Resulting From Stigma Perpetuated by Perpetrators 76

4 **Stigma From Within: When Stigma Is Internalized** 81
   The Stigma Internalization Process 85
   A Closer Look at the Impact of Internalized Stigma 88
   Cassie's Story 89
   The Added Challenges of Internalized Stigma 92
   Understanding Internalized Stigma to Support Victims and Survivors 96

5 **How Stigma Impacts Victims and Survivors When They Seek Help** 100
   Stigma From Friends, Family Members, and Other Sources of Informal Support 105
   Stigma From Professionals 108
   Law Enforcement 111
   Court System 112
   Medical Professionals 112
   Mental Health Professionals 113
   Domestic Violence Agencies 113

Religious Organizations 114
Employment and Education 114
Factors That Can Contribute to Stigmatizing
  Responses Among Professionals 116
  Lack of Training 116
  Lack of Resources, Support, or Validation 118
  Personal Biases, Assumptions, and Struggles 118
The Harmful Nature of Stigmatizing Responses
  From Professionals 119

6 **Stigma in Society: Stereotypes of Abuse and Victims
    at the Societal Level** 122
   Naomi's Story 123
   Common Stereotypes About Intimate Partner
     Violence and the People Who Experience It 124
     *Stereotypes About Who Does, and Who Does Not,
       Experience Intimate Partner Violence* 125
     *Stereotypes That It Is Easy to Leave an Abusive
       Relationship and That Victims Are Somehow
       to Blame for the Abuse They Experienced* 126
     *Stereotypes That Victims and Survivors Are Not
       as Valuable as Other People* 127
     *Stereotypes That Victims and Survivors Are Impaired
       in Their Work and Parenting Abilities* 128
     *Stereotypes That Abuse Should Not Be Discussed
       Openly and Publicly* 129
   Stigma That Occurs Within Cultural Groups 129
     Cultural-Group Norms 130
     Religious-Group Norms 132
   Multiple Levels of Stigma 135
   Stigma in the Media 136
     *Problematic Practices of Reporting Violence
       in the Media* 138
   Conclusion 139

PART 3
Overcoming Stigma 143

7 **Holding Perpetrators Accountable for Their Abuse and
    the Stigma They Perpetuate** 145
   How Perpetrators Escape Accountability 146
     1. People Become Too Afraid to Help 146

x   Contents

    2. Professionals Failing to Take Action 147
    3. Minimal Legal Consequences 149
    4. Professionals Reinforcing Stigmatizing Messages
       About Intimate Partner Violence 151
  What Happens When Perpetrators *Are* Held Accountable? 152
    Alana's Story 152
    Jody's Story 155
  How to Hold Perpetrators Accountable 156
    1. Ask the Right Questions 156
    2. Friends, Family Members, and Community Groups
       Can Hold Offenders Accountable and Make Clear
       That Abusive Behaviors Will Not Be Tolerated 157
    3. Community Response Systems Should Maintain
       a Clear Stance That Perpetrators Must Be Held
       Accountable for the Abuse They Perpetuate 160
  Understanding Batterer Intervention Programs 162
  How Holding Offenders Accountable Ultimately
    Supports Survivors 165

8   **It's Not Your Fault**   169
  How Victims and Survivors Can Counter the Stigma
    They Face at Every Level 170
    Strategies for Overcoming Internalized Stigma 170
    Strategies for Overcoming Perpetrator Stigma 174
    Strategies for Overcoming Stigma in Communities 176
    Survivors as Advocates for Social Change 178
  Turning Points 180
  Overcoming Abuse and the Stigma That Surrounds It 182
    Ava's Story 182
    Mona's Story 185
  The Processes Involved in Overcoming Abuse 187
    Intrapersonal Processes 188
    Interpersonal Processes 190
  Conclusion 191

9   **Creating Responsive Systems for**
    Victims and Survivors Who Seek Help   192
  Lina's Story 193
  Madeline's Story 196
  Tiara's Story 198
  How Communities Failed Lina, Madeline, and Tiara 199

The True "Frontlines" of Community Responses
   to Intimate Partner Violence 201
   1. Do Not Judge 202
   *2. Ask the Survivor What Kind of Help You Can
      Provide 203*
   *3. Know Your Limits When Helping a Friend in
      an Abusive Relationship 204*
   *4. Offer to Provide Practical Support That Will
      Promote Their Safety 205*
   *5. Tell Them That They Deserve to Be Treated
      With Dignity, Respect, and Love 205*
Creating Non-stigmatizing Organizations and
   Resources to Better Serve Victims and Survivors
   of Intimate Partner Violence 206
   *1. Developing Positive Collaborations With Other
      Professionals in Their Communities 207*
   *2. Identify and Address Community-Based Barriers
      That Victims and Survivors May Face When
      Seeking Help 208*
   *3. Create Supportive, Non-stigmatizing Environments
      That Reflect the Best Practices in Trauma-Informed
      Care 209*
   *4. Challenge Personal and Organizational Biases
      and Practices That May Directly or Indirectly
      Perpetuate Stigma and Make It More Difficult for
      Victims and Survivors to Receive the Help They Need 209*
   *5. Educate and Train Professionals to Understand the
      Dynamics of Abusive Relationships and Support
      Survivors, Examine Their Own Biases and
      Assumptions, and Seek Support for Themselves
      to Avoid Feelings of Helplessness 210*
The Power of Positive, Non-stigmatizing Support for
   Victims and Survivors 211

**10 Ending the Stigma Surrounding Intimate Partner
    Violence in Society   214**
Rationale for Ending the Stigma Surrounding
   Intimate Partner Violence in Society 217
   *Ending Stigma to Provide Better Support to
      Victims and Survivors 218*
   Ending Stigma to Hold Perpetrators More Accountable 221

*Ending Stigma to Stop the Silence That Allows
   Abuse to Continue* 223
Advocating to Promote Positive Social Change to
   End Stigma, Support Survivors, and Hold Offenders
   Accountable 224
   *Community-Based Advocacy for Strengthening
      Local Response Systems* 225
   Media Advocacy 227
   *Creating Spaces for Survivors to Share Their
      Stories in Safe Ways* 228
Challenging Common Stereotypes and Biases
   About Intimate Partner Violence 230
Conclusion: A Vision for a Stigma-Free World 231

Index   241

Acknowledgments

Christine E. Murray: First, I want to thank Allison Crowe for her collaboration over the past several years. I truly enjoy your partnership and appreciate all that you bring to our work together. It is an honor to work with you. Second, I am grateful beyond words can express for the survivors of intimate partner violence who have participated in our research studies. Your stories are so inspiring, and it means so much to us that you entrust those stories to us. We have heard your wish to have your stories help, educate, and inspire others. The courage we have heard from you inspires us to continue working toward the day when nobody has to walk through any experiences of abuse and certainly not feel alone in those experiences if they do occur. Third, I am so thankful for the many dedicated professionals who work every day "in the trenches" to provide support and resources to victims and survivors of abuse. I have learned so much from many of you and have a deep respect for the work you are doing. I know that the work you do is so challenging, but I hope that you never have any doubts about the positive impact you can make on so many lives. Fourth, I express my gratitude for the students in my graduate and undergraduate classes on family violence and adult violence and victimization. Your questions and insights over the years have helped me to clarify my own views and perspectives on the topic of intimate partner violence, and I love seeing your growing passion for helping and supporting others, both in your personal and professional lives. Fifth, I remain grateful for the ongoing support of my colleagues, especially in the UNCG Department of Counseling and Educational Development. Sixth, and finally, my heart remains full of appreciation for the love and support of my family members and friends. It would take an entire book to express my appreciation for you all fully, so in this space, I will simply say thank you for helping me to know what safe, healthy, and supportive relationships are. To all who are reading this book, I hope that the stories you read in the book lead you to consider ways that you can take action in your own communities to help change the world so that we can end the stigma surrounding intimate partner violence. We can do it, together!

Allison Crowe: I want to offer a huge thank you to Christine Murray, who makes all of this possible. I have learned so much from collaborating with you through the years and look forward to what else we can accomplish together. You are a tremendous advocate and leader. I am grateful to my colleagues at ECU who support my work and also know when to pull me out of my office for a laugh. You make coming to work something to look forward to. I am thankful for my parents, who never once doubted that I was capable of whatever I set my mind to. Your validation and support taught be to be self-assured and confident in my abilities. To my husband, Terry, and daughter, June, you are the best things that have ever happened to me. The greatest part of my day is coming home to you. Thank you for all of the love and support. Finally, to the survivors who shared their stories for this book, I am humbled beyond words at your courage, resourcefulness, and perseverance. You inspire me every day to keep working toward a world that is free from violence. Never doubt that you can make a difference in others' lives through telling your story.

Part 1
Introduction

1 Understanding Abusive Relationships

Alana is a bright, professional, educated woman who has a successful career that allows her to make the most of her many talents and interests. She is currently married to a man she describes as "lovely" and "in no way abusive at all." However, several years before we met Alana as a participant in our research, she faced horrific abuse at the hands of an ex-boyfriend. Her story is both unique—as every survivor of past abuse has a unique story to tell—and all too common, as it reflects many of the typical dynamics that are involved in abusive intimate relationships.

Alana was in college when she met her ex-boyfriend, Jay, who was several years older and already established in his professional career. They met at a forum on women's issues, so naturally she placed a lot of trust in him from the first time they met. Alana thought it was a good sign. He was professional, stable, sensitive, and supported women's rights. In the beginning of their relationship, Jay could be very, very nice in lots of ways. In fact, during their early days of dating, Jay was nothing but safe, healthy, and respectful. But things began to change after about a year of dating. He began to become jealous and upset. Alana had grown up witnessing physically violent altercations between her parents, so when the violent incidents first began in her relationship with Jay, they didn't seem strange or a cause for alarm. Jay would sometimes push or slap her, but to Alana that didn't seem bad. Having witnessed this behavior in her home growing up had normalized it for Alana. Coupled with the fact that the incidents were not frequent, she passed it off as not ideal, but not the worst scenario either.

The physical violence escalated soon after the couple moved in together. Alana explained how moving in with him actually was the catalyst for the abuse.

> "When I moved into his place, it felt very much like I was invading his space. I guess nobody likes to have their routine messed with, and it was hard for him. Maybe a month into living together was when he first got really much angrier and abusive than he had before. Afterward, he suddenly got so upset, said it's really hard for him to kind

of keep himself together, but that he's trying really hard and that it really is hard for him, and, you know, that it was a one-time thing, and he only had done it once before and . . . he just kept saying that it was really hard for him."

Over time, the violence became more frequent, with incidents occurring every couple days. Most of the time, it was hitting and slapping, but Alana also described some extremely severe incidents of violence. For example, one time when Jay had been drinking, he violently raped her. After the rape (and in the days leading up to Alana leaving him), Jay kept Alana locked in the bedroom and didn't allow her to leave the house. He even went so far as to tie her up so she wouldn't escape. During this time, there was one day when Jay didn't lock Alana in the house, and she escaped while he was at work. For Alana, this was a quick decision, and not one she had been planning for a long time. She left with only a few belongings and went to stay with a friend before staying with a family member. Although Jay tried to contact Alana a few times after she left, overall, she had minimal contact with him, and he moved on and accepted that the relationship was over relatively quickly.

Another level of complexity that added to the challenges that Alana faced was the stigma she experienced as a result of the abuse. We'll delve deeply into understanding stigma in the next chapter, but Alana's story is useful for beginning to explore stigma and its impact on victims and survivors of abuse. Some of the main aspects of stigma that impacted Alana were blame, isolation, and fear of being judged. Blame played out in Alana's efforts to seek help from others in her life. When we asked her about how isolation impacted her she said,

"I felt like I had gotten myself into it, and so I needed to get myself out of it. It felt like I couldn't figure out a way to get myself out of it after my really dumb attempts hadn't worked, and so then it just seemed like there had to be some external something would have to happen. But I couldn't think of anyone who I could explain it to right or in that way. That could make it okay, because I hadn't done the right things all along. To ask for help seemed like I didn't deserve it at that point, because it had been happening for so long."

Fear of being judged also impacted how Alana anticipated others would respond to her. She said, "It felt so fundamental, like okay, I'm bad at math or I'm good at my work, and it just seems like that was me fundamentally, like that was who, what I was, or what I believe in." This led her to keep the abuse secret from many people. She was afraid that, if others found out, "people would think that I was really just gross and kind of stupid for all of that."

Even years after the relationship ended, Alana continued to feel the impacts of the abuse. First, she noted, "I'm not great at trusting people."

She also panics when she is around someone who is expressing anger. In those moments, she says, "I feel like I'm looking through a tunnel, I feel like I can't see straight." Alana also continued to struggle with blaming herself for the abuse she experienced. For example, she said,

> "I could think, well he's not acting right. I felt very much like, not necessarily that I caused him to act that way, but the fact that I didn't leave the first time it happened seemed like, God, well then, I can't leave now. It felt very much like because I hadn't gotten out of it right at the start, then I was somehow complicit or something, in that way, in it. And that I was kind of like choosing that, and if I was the kind of person who would choose that, then I didn't deserve to not be in it."

One of the most striking aspects of Alana's story is that she didn't view her abuse as serious enough to warrant the support of agencies that are designed to support people who have experienced domestic violence. When asked if she had sought services from a domestic violence agency, Alana said,

> "When I was in college, we had done women's rallies, and so there were programs and shelters and that kind of thing that I knew about, but it didn't seem like I was the right person. Like, the people who would go there would be so hurt, that it seems like it'd be like wasting their time. You know, because there were people who were really in terrible, terrible situations who would have nowhere else to go than there. And it also felt like it would be so greedy to go there. It just seemed like it'd be wasting their time, or taking up space that somebody else needed."

* * * * * * *

Alana, whose name, along with Jay's, has been changed,[1] is one of the hundreds of survivors of intimate partner violence (IPV) who have participated in our research over the past several years. In fact, she was one of the first participants in our very first studies—and even today, after we've been doing this research for several years, her story stands out as one that has had a major impact on our understanding of abusive relationships and the toll they take on victims and survivors. In this book, we aim to delve deeply into the complexity of intimate partner violence (also commonly referred to as domestic violence) and how this form of abuse is complicated even further by the stigma that surrounds it.

It is a common, and harmful, stereotype that victims of intimate partner violence move from one abusive relationship to another, never getting out of the cycle of victimization and abuse. While this pattern may hold true for some people, for many other survivors, it does not. In this book, we turn to the lived experiences of survivors in order to present a new view of survival during, and triumph following, intimate partner violence victimization. This first chapter addresses the dynamics of abusive relationships, and then we delve deeply into exploring how stigma complicates these dynamics and impacts victims and survivors. The second half of the book will offer key insights into ending this stigma and provide empowering future directions for overcoming stigma—for survivors themselves, for friends, for family, and for professionals who want to support them, as well as for communities and society.

The Research Basis for This Book

Before we delve into discussing the dynamics of abusive relationships, we want to provide some background information about the research behind this book, which is the source of the stories and quotes from survivors of past abuse that you'll find throughout this book. This book is grounded firmly in our ongoing research program through which we focus on understanding the stigma surrounding intimate partner violence. At the time of writing this book, hundreds of survivors of past abuse have shared their stories with us through interviews and surveys. We won't go too in depth into the research methodologies we've used in those studies, and interested readers can turn to the articles where we've reported the findings for more information about the technical details of the research.[2] In addition to our research with survivors, you'll also read insights from another study we conducted that involved a national panel of experts from advocacy organizations that work to address domestic and sexual violence. For all of our studies with survivors of abuse, the participants were adults over the age of 18 or 21 (the specific age requirements varied across different studies) who were previously in at least one relationship in which a partner abused them. All participants in these studies were required to have been out of any abusive relationships for at least one or two years and report that they hadn't experienced any abusive victimization for at least one or two years (again, the length requirements varied across studies).

Our research has evolved over the years as our understanding of the stigma surrounding intimate partner violence has expanded. When we began our research in 2010, we were unable to locate any previous research that had applied the concept of stigma to experiences of intimate partner violence. We've since learned of a few other researchers studying this phenomenon, but at the time, we were interested in learning whether the concept of stigma—which had been studied extensively in social psychological research on other populations—applied to intimate partner violence. To gain an initial perspective on this topic, our first study involved individual interviews with 12 female survivors of domestic violence. These in-depth interviews lasted between one to two hours each. We asked participants to discuss in detail their experiences of abuse, how they experienced stigma related to their abuse, and how they overcame the stigma associated with their abuse. From these original interview participants, we heard a resounding "yes" that the concept of stigma applied to their experiences of intimate partner violence, and so we wanted to see if and how a larger and more diverse sample of survivors would similarly resonate with the application of the concept of stigma to their experiences.

Therefore, our second study involved an electronic survey of survivors of intimate partner violence. To date, 312 survivors have completed this survey.[3] In this survey, participants described their personal backgrounds, the nature of their abusive relationships, ways they experienced stigma related to their abuse, how they overcame that stigma, and messages they would want to send to individuals who are currently involved in abusive relationships. In a follow-up study, we conducted a second survey with survivors of abusive relationships. The focus of this study was how they overcame past abuse and the turning points that led to the end of their past abusive relationships. The sample for this second survey included 123 survivors. We've also done additional research involving small samples of immigrants who are survivors of past IPV and survivors of teen dating violence. Most recently, we have worked on a study of health and wellness among survivors, which included 130 participants. Thus, across our research studies with survivors of abuse, we have heard from over 500 survivors of abuse to date, and their experiences with abuse and the stories they shared with us—both through the interviews and surveys—are weaved into this book to provide readers with a deeper understanding of the lived experiences of survivors of abuse.

In addition to our research with survivors, we used a research method called a modified Delphi study, which involves working with a panel of experts. For this study, we defined experts as national leaders in the movement to end domestic and sexual violence in the United States.[4] A total of 16 leaders participated, and the research process resulted in a total of 14 consensus statements on which the panel members agreed on the following subjects: the social context of the stigma surrounding domestic and sexual violence, the impact of the stigma on resources for victims and survivors, and strategies for eradicating the stigma surrounding domestic and sexual violence. Therefore, in addition to the insights provided by survivors, the findings of this expert panel study informed our work on this book.

The survivors who've participated in our research shared very detailed stories with us about their experiences of abuse, stigma, and recovery following the end of their abuse relationships. Many of these survivors specifically told us that they were sharing their stories with us because they wanted their stories to help other people learn from their experiences. Aside from the first 12 participants in our interview study, all of our other research has been conducted anonymously, meaning that participants were never asked to tell us their names or other identifying information about themselves. However, we are very sensitive to the need to respect the privacy and safety of the survivors who shared their stories with us. As such, throughout this book, we have made extensive efforts to disguise any potentially identifying details about participants in our research.

Even when survivors shared their stories anonymously, they often shared their stories in such detail that someone familiar with them (e.g., a friend or family member or a professional who worked with them in the aftermath of the abuse) might recognize their identities based on the details provided. Therefore, we have made every effort possible to disguise any potentially identifying details about the survivors whose stories and statements we share in this book. In all cases, the names used to identify survivors and other people in their lives, including their abusers, have been changed, and we removed and/or altered identifying details to protect their privacy. When statements are presented as quotes from survivors, we made every effort to preserve their original wording as they reported their experiences to us. However, in some cases, we made minor alterations to these statements in order to protect their privacy as well to enhance the readability of their statements (e.g., we removed words like "um," "you know," and "well"). However, we worked hard to retain the original meaning and intent of participants' statements and stories. Now, after we've shared some background information about the research behind this book, let's turn our attention back to Alana's story to give a glimpse into what we want to highlight next—the dynamics of abusive relationships.

Understanding Abusive Relationships

Think back to Alana's story, which you read at the start of this chapter. Were there aspects of her relationship with Jay that were similar to other stories about domestic violence that you've heard, experienced, or seen in the media? Were there other aspects that were surprising to you? Perhaps the types of abuse that Alana experienced—physical, sexual, and emotional—are familiar to you, including the fact that Jay was controlling and jealous. Maybe you've heard before that abusers often start off as charmers and that abuse starts slowly and escalates over time. These are commonly discussed dynamics of abusive relationships that are often taught in community outreach efforts to raise awareness about domestic violence. And, indeed, they are patterns that we heard from many of the survivors who participated in our research.

However, perhaps you were surprised to read some of the details of Jay's abuse, such as his violent rape of Alana. Did you anticipate that Jay would go so far as to tie Alana up in the bedroom and lock her in the house so she couldn't escape, virtually holding her hostage in her own home? Even if you knew before that abusive relationships could involve such horrific acts of violence, would you have anticipated that, in the face of such extensive abuse, Alana didn't view herself as worthy of receiving support from agencies that are designed to support victims and survivors of abuse?

Before we began to do research on the stigma surrounding intimate partner violence, both of us had years of previous research, teaching, and clinical counseling experience that involved working with people impacted by this form of abuse. So we were very familiar with the dynamics of abusive relationships and had heard many stories of abuse through our prior work. And still, through the many stories that poured in from participants in our research, we continued to hear stories that challenged the definitions we'd learned before about abuse, and we heard unique stories that often surprised us and challenged us to expand upon anything we thought we knew before about abuse.

One truth we've learned through our work—and one we hope to convey in the pages of this book—is that intimate partner violence is both a *common experience* that often involves some typical dynamics and a *unique experience* that is *always* experienced in an individualized way. We made a decision early in our research that we would take the stance of believing the participants in our research, even and especially when their stories seemed so extreme as to be difficult to believe. Even in this stance of believing, we acknowledge that the participants in our research share their stories from their own perspective, and others involved in the situation may have described certain facts and experiences in a different way. However, we believe that honoring survivors of abuse by believing them is one key step to ending the stigma surrounding abuse. Of course, it is possible that someone may fabricate a story of abuse, and this does happen, although this happens very, very rarely. On the whole, when someone reports abuse, they are almost certainly telling the truth. In the context of our research, we simply cannot imagine any reasons why someone would lie or fabricate abuse for any reason related to participating in a research study for survivors of past abuse, especially when they are sharing their stories anonymously, as the vast majority of participants in our studies have done. While it is true that participants in our surveys had an option to enter a drawing for a $50 store gift card, very few participants actually entered the drawings, and even those who did knew their chances of receiving the gift card were low. Furthermore, sharing one's story of past abuse has the potential to unearth past traumatic memories and difficult emotions. With that in mind, we believe we can say with confidence that the stories we heard from participants in our studies are credible.

What Is Intimate Partner Violence?

We use the term *intimate partner violence* as an umbrella term to describe any form of physical, sexual, emotional, psychological, verbal, and/or financial abuse that occurs in a current or former intimate relationship.[5] Although the typical focus in our society is on intimate partner violence perpetrated by males against female victims, it can take many forms, including violence in same-gender relationships and violence perpetrated by female partners against male victims. Furthermore, intimate partner violence may occur in virtually all forms of intimate relationships, including dating, cohabiting, married, separated, and divorced couples. It's important to consider abuse between former partners, because in many cases, the relationship may end, but the abuse does not. Throughout the pages of this book, you'll see many examples of the vast diversity of the types of relationships in which intimate partner violence can occur.

We want to share additional background on some of the terms you'll read in this book. In this book, we use the term *perpetrator* to describe a person who uses violent and abusive behaviors to control his or her partner. In addition, we use the term *victim* to describe people who are currently being victimized by an abusive partner, and we use the term *survivor* to describe those who have previously been abused but who no longer are in that abusive situation. However, we acknowledge that both of these terms are limited in that they define people in relation to their experiences of abuse, and the term *survivor* also could be used to reflect the courage and strength that is required of a person who is currently being abused. Furthermore, in many cases, the line between an abusive relationship occurring and ending is very blurry. For example, a survivor may have left an abusive relationship, but the perpetrator continues to hurt the survivor, such as through ongoing threats, emotional abuse, manipulation, or using the court system as a control mechanism.

Despite the limitations of these terms for fully capturing the experiences of people who have experienced intimate partner violence, we believe that distinguishing between *victims* and *survivors* based on whether the abuse is still ongoing is generally useful and reflects the current language used by many survivors and professionals. Overall, though, we encourage readers to move beyond labeling any individual with sole respect to their experiences of intimate partner violence. Let us always remember that no person is defined solely by those experiences—we must also consider who survivors are as individuals, friends, family members, workers, neighbors, and community members. The more people use labels to identify those who have experienced intimate partner violence, the easier it becomes to separate and distance themselves from them. As we'll see throughout this book, intimate partner violence could impact nearly anyone and everyone.

Who Does Intimate Partner Violence Affect?

Although many people often want to believe that intimate partner violence occurs only among certain "types" of people, this assumption simply does not hold up in previous research or in the stories of the survivors that you'll read in this book. In truth, intimate partner violence occurs across all social and demographic categories in staggering rates. In 2011, the U.S. Centers for Disease Control and Prevention published the results of their *National Intimate Partner and Sexual Violence Survey*.[6] According to this survey, approximately 36% of women and 29% of men in the United States have experienced physical violence, sexual assault, and/or stalking within an intimate relationship at one point. This is roughly one-third of the adult population of the United States!

It's important to consider gender in our discussion of who is impacted by intimate partner violence. Although the rates of victimization were not vastly different between women and men in the *National Intimate Partner and Sexual Violence Survey*, other research suggests that, in heterosexual relationships, violence perpetrated by men against women tends to be more severe and have more negative consequences than violence perpetrated by women against men.[7] Although general population surveys often show that rates of intimate partner violence are relatively similar between men and women, the more severe forms of violence that may lead victims and survivors to seek services tend to be experienced at higher rates by women.[8] Therefore, gender is an important consideration in understanding intimate partner violence, and indeed the vast majority of the participants in our research—at least 90% of them—have been women.[9] But, with that said, we must always remember that violence may occur—and be very severe and have many negative consequences—in all types of relationships, including violence perpetrated by females against male partners, in same-sex relationships, and in the relationships of people who are transgendered.

In the *National Intimate Partner and Sexual Violence Survey*, the rates of emotional/psychological abuse were even higher, with just under half of both women and men having experienced this form of intimate partner abuse. These statistics show that intimate partner violence is pervasive and widespread in the United States, and we know that rates of intimate partner violence and other forms of abuse are high in countries around the world. With such high rates of abuse, it is likely that nearly every adult in the United States and beyond knows someone who has personally been affected by intimate partner violence.

Take a moment to let these statistics sink in. This means that when we discuss the topic of intimate partner violence, we're talking about a pervasive social problem that impacts nearly half of the population of adults in the United States. And yet, somehow this critical issue has remained a marginalized topic about which many people—even today—simply do not know or do not acknowledge the full extent of the problem. Later in this book, we'll explore how stigma impacts societal views surrounding intimate partner violence as well as some of the ways that we can work to break this societal stigma so that more people will feel equipped to take action to promote safe, nonviolent relationships. Before we get there, though, it's important to dig deeper into the dynamics of abusive relationships so that we can really grasp the complexities of intimate partner violence. When we fail to grasp this complexity, it's all too easy to write off abusive relationships as "somebody else's problem." But as we'll see in the next section, a closer look at the dynamics of abusive relationships helps to expand how people understand intimate partner violence and how it impacts victims and survivors. The more deeply we understand a complicated experience such as intimate partner violence, the more we can appreciate the lived experiences of those who have survived it.

A Closer Look at the Dynamics of Abusive Relationships

Advocates and previous researchers have identified common patterns that often occur in abusive relationships. We begin this section by examining two descriptions of these patterns—the Cycle of Violence and the Power and Control Wheel—before we turn to more individualized experiences of intimate partner violence that emerge when we look more deeply at the stories of survivors.

The Cycle of Violence

In one of the seminal books about domestic violence, Lenore Walker[10] described the Cycle of Violence, which involves three main phases that may occur in abusive relationships. The first phase is the Tension-Building phase, in which there is a gradual increase in tension and discord between the partners. In the Tension-Building phase, relatively minor incidents of violence may occur, although significant emotional abuse may happen during this phase as well. It's common for victims in this phase to feel very much on edge, as they must choose their words and actions very carefully for fear of what their partners may do. The second phase is the Acute-Battering phase. This phase is when the most severe violence may occur, often akin to an explosion by the perpetrator. There is no set time line on how long the Acute-Battering phase may last. It may be over in a matter of minutes, but it also could extend over many days or, in extreme cases, weeks. The third phase happens after the Acute-Battering phase and is called the Honeymoon phase. During the Honeymoon phase, the abuser often becomes very apologetic and makes grand, romantic gestures to win back the victim's affections and to convince him or her that the violence won't happen again. The abuser may even make some initial attempts to change, such as going to a counseling session or reading a book about anger management. But in an abusive relationship, the Honeymoon phase doesn't last. Eventually tension begins to build, and the cycle begins anew.

The Cycle of Violence theory resonates with many victims and survivors, as well as the professionals who work with them. Many survivors, upon learning about this Cycle, can easily identify their own relationships within that pattern. Learning about this Cycle can help victims and survivors gain insights into their relationships and feel reassured that they are not alone in what they have experienced because many others have also experienced this Cycle as well. In addition, understanding this Cycle is extremely useful for understanding how victims can become trapped in abusive relationships, especially when we start to understand just how convincing perpetrators can be during the Honeymoon phase. Not only can perpetrators manipulate their victims during this phase, but they also prey upon their victims' positive feelings and attachment to the relationship. It's common for victims in this phase to question their own judgment during the Honeymoon phase, and they may begin to think, "What they did to me really wasn't all that bad," or "I really want this relationship to work, so I'm going to give my partner the benefit of the doubt that they can change." As the Cycle of Violence plays out repeatedly over time, victims become more and more entrapped in their relationships, and the severity of the violence during both the Tension-Building and Acute-Battering phases continues to increase.

The Cycle of Violence is a useful description of some common dynamics in abusive relationships. However, the Cycle of Violence does not always play out neatly and predictably, as every relationship is unique, and it is often difficult to determine what phase someone is in when they are in the thick of the relationship. This Cycle also can change over time, especially once violence becomes increasingly entrenched in a couple's relationship. For example, the Honeymoon phase ultimately may become obsolete once the perpetrator has gained full control over the victim. For example, consider a perpetrator who has completely isolated the victim from friends and family members, convinced the victim that he or she is worthless through emotional abuse, and rendered the victim completely financially dependent on the perpetrator. At this point, the perpetrator likely has no need to use the behaviors that occur in the Honeymoon phase to keep the victim in the relationship. Over time, this perpetrator has established control and realized that the victim is going to stay in the relationship, no matter what. Thus, over time, abusive relationships may not include the Honeymoon phase and simply move between the Tension-Building phase and the Acute-Battering phase.

The Power and Control Wheel

Another widely used tool for education about intimate partner violence is the Power and Control Wheel, which was developed by the Domestic Abuse Intervention Program in Duluth, Minnesota, to describe the ways that male perpetrators in heterosexual relationships abuse their female partners.[11] This Wheel provides a useful framework for understanding the power and control dynamics that underlie abusive relationships, and it serves as a valuable reminder that abusive relationships really are defined by these power and control dynamics, not just by any particular acts of violence. The Power and Control Wheel situates physical and sexual violence within intimate relationships as occurring within an ongoing pattern of power and control tactics used by perpetrators against victims. In particular, there are eight categories of these tactics: (1) using coercion and threats; (2) using intimidation; (3) using emotional abuse; (4) using isolation; (5) minimizing, denying, and blaming; (6) using children; (7) using male privilege; and (8) using economic abuse. Within each category, the Wheel presents a list of specific behaviors that may occur, and these behaviors include everything from "making light of the abuse" to "displaying weapons." In fact, there are over 30 examples of abusive behaviors depicted on the Wheel, which serves as a powerful reminder that there are many, many forms that abuse can take in intimate relationships.

We have seen firsthand the impact of learning about the Power and Control Wheel for victims and survivors of abusive relationships by sharing the Wheel with clients in our counseling work. Often, when clients first read through the Wheel, it is clear that lightbulbs go off in their minds as they begin to recognize the patterns of power and control dynamics in their own relationships. Advocates remind people when talking about the Power and Control Wheel that all of the categories depicted in the Wheel may not apply to any given relationship. In fact, some relationships may be abusive if they demonstrate only one category, while all eight categories can be found in other abusive relationships. Overall, the Power and Control Wheel illustrates our point that abusive relationships have both *common* and *unique* experiences—the power and control dynamics involved in these relationships are common, but how they are expressed in each relationship can look very different.

Individualized Experiences of Intimate Partner Violence

We can't underscore enough the importance of understanding the common dynamics that often occur in abusive relationships. Understanding these patterns is critical for helping people to identify abusive relationships in their own lives and the lives of their loved ones. These common dynamics are also important for helping professionals to develop programming and to support victims and survivors, and they can be used to help formulate safety plans that identify strategies that can be used to promote their safety. And, as we discussed earlier, learning about these common patterns can help victims and survivors understand their experiences and realize that they are not alone.

And yet, what happens when people's experiences don't line up neatly with the typical or common definitions of intimate partner violence? When people hold overly rigid definitions of what an abusive relationship is supposed to look like, they may fail to recognize a potentially abusive relationship, or, as we saw with Alana's story at the start of this chapter, people may not reach out for help because they don't think their own experiences meet the "qualifications" for getting the help and support they need. For these reasons, alongside our attention to the commonly discussed patterns of abusive relationships, we must also remember and honor the unique experiences that each person may have.

To illustrate the many unique forms that intimate partner violence can take, this section highlights some additional examples from survivors who participated in our research. Let's take an in-depth look at their stories, in their own words. As with Alana's story at the start of this chapter, some of the details provided in this section, and throughout the rest of the book, are graphic and disturbing. We urge readers to practice self-care when reading this book and take care of yourselves in whatever way you need to do so. Examples of how to do this may include reading this book in small chunks of time, planning time after reading for debriefing and clearing your mind, keeping a journal to write down your emotional reactions while reading this book, and reading the book with a friend and talking about the difficult and emotional topics with that person. It is normal and natural to feel upset upon hearing stories of the horrific abuse that some survivors have experienced, so please consider how you can best move through these stories in a way that feels safe and comfortable to you.

Let's turn now to examining six of the complex dynamics of abuse as seen through the words and experiences of some of the courageous survivors who have shared their stories with us through our research.

First, Abuse Often Develops Gradually Over Time

As we've discussed already, abusers don't typically show their true colors right from the first date! In fact, often they are very charming, sweet, and romantic at the start of relationships, and this is one of the ways that they can manipulate their partners into getting into a deeper level of relationship. For example, consider the following quote from a survivor in our research:

> "He was nice until he moved in, and very charismatic. He was several years older than me, and I was very young and naive. Once he moved in, it was awful—he became controlling and abusive. Eventually when I tried to break up with him, he held me with a gun to my head for hours in the middle of the night while his friend begged for my life."

Even when the violence first appears, it often begins with more subtle forms of abuse, such as emotional or psychological abuse. Another survivor in our research said,

> "I was in the relationship for a long time. I married him as a teenager; we had a child. It started with verbal and emotional abuse, then

> some physical abuse, and then when we were a year into the relationship, he raped me. We separated shortly, and I returned for several 'wrong' reasons. The verbal and emotional abuse continued, the physical abuse mostly stopped; there were a few more incidences of sexual abuse for many years. Then, when I was in my early 30s, well, my whole life changed; the way I thought about myself changed, and I suddenly had the courage to do the hard stuff. I have no regrets."

As this survivor's experiences show, the relationship may begin without any abuse and then gradually emotional abuse appears, potentially followed by physical and/or sexual abuse. Over time, the abuse dynamics can change, such as how this survivor eventually stopped facing much physical abuse. These twists and turns in abusive relationships can make it especially complicated for people to recognize when their relationships are abusive because it's likely they also have some periods of calm and nonviolence over the course of their relationships.

Overall, the dynamics of abusive relationships can change a lot over time, and every abusive relationship will show some unique changes and fluctuations in abuse. However, the escalation pattern is very common and reflects that Cycle of Violence theory we discussed earlier. As another survivor said,

> "It was extremely insidious how the abuse began: belittling, embarrassing me in public, calling me heinous names; then the repeated apologies, the jewelry, the flowers, the romance. As I say today, 'Abuse doesn't usually begin with a slap,' and that was certainly my experience."

Second, Abusive Partners Can Ensnare Their Partners Through a Complex Set of Control Tactics

The Power and Control Wheel, which we discussed earlier, demonstrates the diversity of controlling behaviors that abuse perpetrators may use to monitor their partners and usurp their power. We heard many examples of controlling behaviors through our research, and we'll highlight some of those examples here.

A common control tactic used by perpetrators in abusive relationships is controlling their partners' choices. For example, one survivor said the following about her relationship: "It was a very controlling, manipulative relationship. He controlled everything from what I wore, to what I ate and drank, to how I talked. He controlled how I should interact with my children and my family." Another survivor said,

> "One look from my ex was all that it took for me to know that I was in trouble. In public he would whisper in my ear, 'Whore . . . slut . . .'

over and over and over. Tears of shame would burn my eyes, but I fought with all that I was to put a smile on my face and keep walking. Money was controlled, and my every single move was controlled."

Especially for younger people with limited relationship experiences, this control tactic can be mistaken for their partner's affection, as can be seen in the following quote from a survivor who was abused during her teenage years:

"My relationship in high school was, I thought, at the time, perfect. When he would tell me what I could and could not wear, what and when to eat, how to act around his friends, etc., I thought he loved me and just wanted me to be perfect for him."

A second way that abuse perpetrators exert control over their partners is by devaluing them and making them think that they're at fault for all of the problems in the relationship. As one survivor said, "He was controlling, verbally put me down, and wanted to be in control of me by making me think I was nothing. He constantly put me down." Another shared that her abuser devalued her by taking advantage of her love and concern for him:

"I was totally confused. One day, he was the sweetest person around the world, and next day, he was a monster. I also found out that he had alcohol issues. He also had a trauma history list and he never received counseling, family support, etc. I felt sorry for him, but the love was gone; I think I was just trying to fix him."

Another survivor said,

"The abuse consisted of constant accusations that I was sleeping with every man that looked at me. He tried to constantly mess up any plans that I made personally and to convince me that I was selfish for wanting to do anything that he didn't generate. He never hit me physically, but he broke my things, including my back door."

Perpetrators may even go so far as to blame their victims for their own unfaithfulness to the relationship, as is reflected in the following survivor's experiences: "Once he started cheating on me and justifying it by saying, 'I'm a man and I have needs that you aren't meeting.' I thought something was wrong with me and tried everything in my power to change his mind." This type of control tactic is especially complex for victims, in that the manipulation is confusing and can cloud one's judgment.

Another common control tactic used by abuse perpetrators is isolating their victims so that they have limited access to their support networks.

This can be seen in the following quotes from participants in our research: (1) "I was completely isolated from anyone, except work. I went to work in the morning and straight home and into the house at night. He had total power. I was afraid all the time. He separated me from all human contact except work. I had no friends and no contact with family. As a result, I was excluded from all social activities." (2) "When living with someone that abused me, when he was suicidal, and life was a walking time bomb. You can't call the police, knowing that if you do, you will have to explain to your children, your parents, your friends the very secret that you have been hiding all along." (3) "I lived with a male who was psychologically abusive. He attempted to isolate me from my friends and family, did not work when we were together, and would threaten to commit suicide to play on my emotions and control me." (4) "I was kept from having anything to do with my family, including my children. I still wonder to this day why I stayed in that relationship for so long. I feel very fortunate to be alive. My self-esteem was practically gone, and I was severely depressed."

Perpetrators may also use social systems and status in their efforts to control their victims. For example, norms in cultural groups and religious communities can serve to reinforce perpetrators' power over their partners. As one survivor said,

> "Religion played an active role. His family was well known in the community; thus, he hid behind the church. Little did I know that this pattern had been a role in his family for many generations. My children and I had to leave our church."

In other cases, the social status of the perpetrator can make it difficult for a victim to get help, as the perpetrator's abusive behaviors may be very different than the image he or she projects in the community, such as is reflected in the following quote from a participant: "He was a business owner and presented himself to the public in a good light. I was very much controlled. I was put down and talked to horribly every day." Other perpetrators control their partners by using their social and professional connections to limit their victims' ability to access help, as was the case for the survivor who said, "His best friends in town were the Chief of Police and director at the local hospital. I was stuck in a situation I didn't know how to get out of and nowhere to turn for help."

An extreme form of controlling one's partner, which we already discussed as part of Alana's story at the start of this chapter, is physically trapping him or her in a location, thereby completely restricting freedom of choice. Although this was a less common form of control that we heard about in our research, Alana was not the only survivor who shared with us that her partner had physically trapped her. Examples from other survivors are found in the following two quotes: "My abuser beat me and then held me in the home for almost two days. He threatened to take my child and is now using her against me in family court." And,

> "My first abusive ex was over two decades older than me, and he was a hoarder. He trapped me in his house, beat me, choked me, isolated me from friends and family, and was always looking for excuses to become violent. When there was no stress on him or excuse for him to be upset, he got even more angry. I was violently restrained from ever leaving the house or getting medical attention I needed for concussions he gave me and told me, 'Don't call the cops. Don't ruin my life by calling the cops.' He always acted like nothing ever happened. My family was not allowed to visit, and I was only allowed to visit if he was with me."

The control tactics that perpetrators use are often individualized and unique to the circumstances of their particular relationship. For example, a victim who has compromised health could be controlled by being denied access to medical care, as we heard in the following statement by a survivor: "He never hit me, but he did deny me medical or dental care. When I left, my health was really bad, and it took months of emergency treatment, followed by surgeries, to begin to restore my health." The important point to remember is this: abusive partners can take virtually any aspect of their victims' lives and exert control over it. And, in many cases, areas of victims' lives that are most important to them are most vulnerable to becoming embedded with control. Whether it be in relation to their victims' children, employment or education, relationships with friends and family members, and general sense of self-worth, perpetrators are most threatened by any aspects of their victims' lives that offer them alternatives to the relationship, and so they clamp down on their control over those areas until they've won the overall battle for control in the relationship.

Third, There Is No Single Form of Violence That Defines Abusive Relationships

The violence that occurs in abusive relationships can take many, many different forms. In fact, from the hundreds of stories we've heard from survivors who participated in our research, we have seen that there is virtually a limitless number of ways that perpetrators can abuse their victims. Take a moment to read through the following statements from participants in our research about the various types of abuse they experienced:

- "He threatened to kill me. He was searching our apartment for weapons he had brought home the day before. When I found them, I hid all the knives. He said if he didn't find them, he'd kill me with

a fork and held it to my throat. This was after he had already started hitting me and throwing me around the living room. He left to our bedroom, and I grabbed for the phone to call the police. This was the first time I'd ever been brave enough to do so. He caught me and pulled the phone from the wall."
- "He threatened my life, stalked me, tried to hit me with his car while I backed out of my driveway, and threatened to take his own life. It was an unforgettably vivid period of my life."
- "This partner tried to set me on fire with WD-40 and a lighter. He was ultimately placed in a mental institution, which he kept calling me from and would not stop, even when the police themselves said to him, in person, not to have any further contact with me. Also, he caused property damage to my apartment complex. I had to pay for the damage and filed charges."
- "I ran away to a secluded, safe place after him strangling me to death. I lost all my bodily organs, and 911 brought me back to life."
- "My boyfriend and I were driving around town. He became angry because I forgot to do something, and he started driving erratically and dangerously. I asked him to take me back to my house. He dumped me out on the street, and I thought he was going to hit me with the car."
- "He blamed me for the failure of our marriage and asked for divorce, but I later discovered he had been in a long relationship with another woman and he had possibly fathered a child with her."
- "He held a knife to my throat."
- "Once he had pulled a gun to my head in a rage, I decided it was enough and I was able to move in with my family member."
- "I was involved in a relationship where I was verbally abused, and it lasted a few years, off and on. I finally had to threaten him with a restraining order. He came to my house drunk and threatened to beat me up and hurt my family. He urinated on my door when I wouldn't let him in. I ended up moving and called the police."
- "The onset was great with a lot of positive influence, but within a year, he became manipulative, emotionally abusive, and put me at risk for STDs because of his multiple high-risk partners. He nearly choked me once, and that was when I decided to end it."
- "He was a very angry person, not just towards me. I also suspect that he was not mentally well. He suffered violent hallucinations and lucid daydreams. Sometimes they involved me. I started to become afraid for myself."
- "He was arrested after smashing my head against the cement for trying to leave him, and then got into a physical fight with my parent."
- "He got mad at me one morning because I didn't know where his shaving cream was and threw a hard object at my face. His mother showed up and saw me crying and bleeding."

- "My first abusive relationship was by far the worst, as far as physical abuse goes. He beat me, raped me, and burned me. He stole my money and my car. He lived off me financially."

As these survivors' statements demonstrate, abuse perpetrators have a vast array of weapons in their arsenal of ways to inflict harm upon their partners. The severity of their violence can be relatively nonlethal, such as a slap in the face, but it also can be life threatening. The severity of the actual acts of violence doesn't have a one-to-one correlation with the harm it inflicts on victims and survivors, as even emotional abuse, which is generally not life threatening, can leave lasting scars that are difficult to heal. Keep in mind that, for the most part, the statements presented all reflect single incidents of abuse or summaries of a few experiences that occurred over time in those survivors' relationships. This is significant, because we know that abusive relationships often occur in long-term patterns that occur over an extended period of time. Over the course of an abusive relationship, a victim may experience abuse in many forms, leading to a cycle of terror that instills ongoing fear and threats of harm, further trapping the victim in the relationship and making it extremely difficult to leave.

Fourth, Sexual Assault and Abuse Are Common in Abusive Relationships

Further extending the idea that there are a vast number of ways that perpetrators can abuse their partners in abusive relationships, we want to underscore that sexual abuse is an often under-recognized form of abuse within intimate relationships. By sexual assault, we are referring to any form of forced, coerced, or nonconsensual sexual activity, including rape, unwanted touching, forcing someone to engage in sexual activities they do not want to perform, and coercing someone to engage in pornography.[12] When many people think of rape, the first thing that comes to mind is rape by strangers, or the idea of an assailant jumping out from behind a bush to attack. This is indeed a very scary form of sexual assault, and its occurrence represents a significant, ongoing social problem that we as a society need to continue to address and work toward preventing.

However, statistics about sexual assault show us that most sexual assault is perpetrated by someone the victim knows, including people with whom they are involved in an intimate relationship. For example, among female rape victims in the *National Intimate Partner and Sexual Violence Survey* by the Centers for Disease Control and Prevention, 51.1% had been assaulted by intimate partners, and 40.8% were assaults by an acquaintance.[13] It was not until relatively recently that marital rape was considered to be illegal.[14] Even today, it's not uncommon to hear media reports in which prominent people, such as politicians, make statements suggesting that marital rape doesn't occur.[15]

Sexual assault within the context of an intimate relationship can be very confusing for victims, and it can be difficult to identify as a sexual violation. Only recently have advocates begun to call attention to the need for enthusiastic consent in sexual activity,[16] including among couples in committed relationships. Therefore, in many cases, people may have difficulty identifying when they have been sexually assaulted by a relationship partner because they may struggle with questions of whether or not they consented to sexual activity, especially because communicating about sexuality can be extremely challenging for many couples.[17] For example, a partner may feel that because they agreed to engage in intercourse or any other form of sexual activity at a previous time they have granted permission to their partner to engage in this activity again. Other people may feel that they don't want to engage in a particular sexual activity, but they do not feel comfortable speaking up about their desires because they are afraid of how their partner may react. Unfortunately, even today, many people believe that being in an intimate relationship with someone grants their partners full access to their bodies, thus failing to recognize that each person has the right to make choices and to set boundaries about all aspects of his or her sexuality, even in the context of an intimate relationship.

Sexual assault is a clear violation of the trust and intimacy required of a safe, healthy intimate relationship. Similar to abusive behaviors in general, sexual abuse can take many forms in abusive relationships. For example, one survivor who participated in our research said, "I was forced to have sex every single day whether I was sick or tired or not." Sexual abuse often is intertwined with emotional and physical abuse, as is reflected in the following two quotes:

> "When I look back on the relationship, sexual coercion, abuse, assault, and rape had been present from the early days, but I did not recognize it. Verbal and emotional abuse evolved into occasional physical abuse. Ultimately, I made the decision to leave for good when he raped me, although it took years for me to name it as rape, and he threatened to harm our child."

And, "I got a permanent restraining order and moved thousands of miles away as a result of an especially violent rape, which resulted in permanent physical injury, followed by several more months of escalation, threats, and sheer terror." Sexual abuse in intimate relationships also can take the form of a perpetrator infecting the victim with a sexually transmitted infection (e.g., "I put him in jail and he filed for divorce after he found out he had given me HIV") as well as by reproductive coercion, which the American College of Obstetricians and Gynecologists defines as "behavior intended to maintain power and control in a relationship related to reproductive health," which may include intentionally impregnating one's partner and interfering with pregnancy and/or contraceptive methods.[18] An extreme example of reproductive coercion can be found in the following quote from a participant in our research: "My abuser took pride in raping me enough to ensure a pregnancy only to beat me enough to lose it later. Just to do it all again. To this day, I do not know how I survived the relationship."

Fifth, Abusive Behaviors and Fear Often Continue Long After a Relationship Officially Ends

As we'll discuss throughout this book, many people often wonder why victims don't "just leave" abusive relationships, which implies that leaving an abusive relationship will automatically end the abusive behaviors. Although sometimes this does happen, and some perpetrators do stop engaging in abusive behaviors once the relationship ends, we know that the end of an abusive relationship does not always lead immediately to the end of the abusive behaviors. Rather, an abusive partner often continues to control and harm his or her victim after the relationship ends. In fact, the end of the relationship often prompts an escalation of the violence, and it is widely known that the time of leaving an abusive relationship can be one of the most dangerous times for victims of abuse. Of course, it is possible to leave an abusive relationship, as can be seen clearly in the lives of the survivors who've participated in our research—all of whom were required to have been out of any abusive relationships for one to two years. However, leaving an abusive relationship must be done safely—ideally in partnership with trained professionals and a network of supportive resources that are activated to ensure that the relationship can end in a safe manner.

The stories of many survivors in our research demonstrate that the journey to ending an abusive relationship can be long and arduous, and perpetrators often continue to engage in abusive behaviors, even after the relationship has ended. One survivor said,

> "After leaving over 13 times and him forcing or coercing me to come home, or I would come home from work and he would have moved into my home, I had given up. I accepted the fact that I must have done something really bad in my life, so I stayed with him. Once he started telling me how he could bury me alive in a local construction site and no one would ever find me, I fled the state with my child. For several months, I called my family from payphones each week to let them know we were okay, but I would never tell them where I was. I remember collapsing at social services, breaking down in tears, begging them not to contact him about child support because I knew that he would find and kill me."

Some perpetrators use their children to continue to harass and abuse their former victims, as one research participant shared with us: "I eventually left him and moved in with my family. He continued to verbally and emotionally abuse me by using my children when he would come to get them on weekends." Other perpetrators continue to abuse their partners by stalking them. As one survivor said,

> "I left him after he 'blew up' in front of me, my mom, and my child. I went back for a couple of months, but only with the agreement he moved in with me at my parents. I made him leave after a few months. After this, he stalked and harassed me for years."

Another shared, "It took me almost 3 years of not being with him to get him to leave me alone. I literally was stalked at my job."

Survivors of abusive relationships may continue to fear what their perpetrators could do to them, although abuse eventually may come to an end, especially if perpetrators are cut off from having any access to them. For example, consider the following story of triumph over abuse from one of the survivors who participated in our research:

> "When the end came, I took off walking with only the clothes on my back and my purse, and all the while I kept repeating to myself, 'I'm done . . . I'm done . . . I'm done.' I stood my ground this time—this made the seventh time I had left—determined to get out for good. I had to flee the state because I was in fear for my life. He wouldn't leave me alone and was stalking me. Finally, a court date came up, and I was granted a protective order. I am so glad he is no longer in my life."

Sixth, Abusive Relationships Can Have a Profound Impact on Children in Many Different Ways

Children who witness the abusive relationships of their parents or other adults in their lives can be impacted in many ways. Clearly, children may be impacted if the perpetrator also directs abuse at them. This may occur in the form of child maltreatment, but it also could occur during pregnancy. For example, one survivor said,

> "I experienced the worst time of my life; I was beaten, raped, locked in a closet, hung out of a three-story building, and beat at the very end of my pregnancy, which left damage to my newborn and myself. I was poisoned and had a nervous breakdown. This drama left me insecure, with no self-esteem, and many more things."

Children also can feel the impact of intimate partner violence if they see it happening before their own eyes, as the following quote illustrates:

"Although the physical violence was only to me, my children suffered deep emotional trauma from his violent outbursts." Beyond seeing abuse happen directly, children are impacted by witnessing it, even if they are not in the same room. Another survivor said, "I prayed that my children would not hear the beatings, scared, and shamed . . . I woke up every morning with a smile on my face hoping that it covered anything that happened the night before." Even if children do not see or hear abuse directly, they often can sense that something is wrong, especially if they observe the physical or emotional impacts of the abuse on their parent.

Summary of the Dynamics of Abusive Relationships

We share the stories and survivors' statements not to shock or upset you, although certainly you may be feeling those emotions (and others) after reading them. Rather, we share them with you because they demonstrate the complexity of abusive relationships as well as how each relationship can look so unique. Keep in mind that the quotes represent only a small part of these survivors' stories—each one could likely write a book or more about their experiences that would delve even further into the unique aspects of their stories. We do hope that these stories, and the others you'll read throughout the rest of the book, help you develop an even greater appreciation for the challenges faced by victims and survivors of abuse, as this appreciation can help to increase your empathy and motivation for helping to support them.

The Story Is Not Over Yet

Survivors' stories don't end with the abuse they experienced. In fact, we heard from survivors in our research that the abuse was but just one part of their stories. It is an important part of the story and one that should be honored. But the real power in their stories can be found in what happens *after* the abuse. Reflect back on Alana's story and the other stories you just read from other survivors and consider the emotional, relationship, physical, economic, and other challenges and barriers that can arise in the aftermath of the abuse they experienced. Take a moment to think about the strength and courage required to overcome those challenges on a daily basis. You'll see more of that strength and courage shine through as you move forward in this book. Even situations that can feel extremely hopeless can turn into great triumphs. For example, let's return to Alana's story, which was far from over after she left her relationship with Jay.

In the years since Alana's relationship with Jay ended, she worked hard to regain her sense of self, foster positive connections to her community, and pursue opportunities to be involved in meaningful work. Alana's marriage has been a source of healing with the support of her husband, although Alana shared that it was difficult to tell her current husband about her experiences with abuse before they were married. However, he responded in a loving and supportive way, which surprised Alana initially. She shared,

> "I told him a little bit and his response was, 'That is so awful, I'm really sorry.' He didn't go running and screaming. We've never talked about any kind of detail, but he just in that moment of not recoiling, seemed good. There were some other things that he had saw that had happened that he didn't he never treated it like I was bad or gross or anything like that, so it just made it seem like, oh, okay, it's not a thing."

Therapy also was valuable for Alana as she processed her experiences with abuse, addressed its lingering impacts, and came to understand that she was not responsible for Jay's abuse of her.

In the pages of this book, you'll read many more stories of survivors like Alana who have walked through the tragedy of abuse and dealt with the stigma that surrounds it, but moved into the triumph of recovery and strength. We believe that survivors of abuse are unsung heroes, and we hope you'll be inspired and encouraged by their strength and power as you learn more about their experiences. Whether you have experienced abuse yourself, now or in the past, or whether someone you care about is being or has been abused, or whether you're a professional who works with individuals impacted by intimate partner violence, and even if you fall into all of these categories, we hope that this book deepens your understanding of the experiences of survivors of abuse and inspires you to take action to support victims and survivors, hold offenders accountable, and prevent future violence in your life, your community, and society.

Notes

1 Alana and Jay's names, along with potentially identifying details about them, have been altered to protect the privacy and safety of the participants in our research. Throughout the entire book, all names of participants have been changed, and potentially identifying details have been altered to protect the safety and privacy of participants in our research.
2 For more information about the technical aspects of the methodology of our research studies, readers may consult the following articles:

- Murray, C. E., Crowe, A., & Overstreet, N. (2015). Sources and components of stigma experienced by survivors of intimate partner violence. *Journal of Interpersonal Violence*, 1–22. DOI: 10.1177/0886260515609565.
- Flasch, P., Murray, C. E., & Crowe, A. (2015). Overcoming abuse: A phenomenological investigation of the journey to recovery from past intimate partner violence. *Journal of Interpersonal Violence*, 1–29. DOI: 10.1177/0886260515599161.
- Murray, C. E., Crowe, A., & Akers, W. (2016). How can we end the stigma surrounding domestic and sexual violence? A modified Delphi study with

national advocacy leaders. *Journal of Family Violence*, 31, 271–287. DOI: 10.1007/s10896-015-9768-9.
- Murray, C.E., King, K., & Crowe, A. (2016). Understanding and addressing teen dating violence: Implications for family counselors. *The Family Journal*, 24(1), 52–59. DOI: 10.1177/1066480715615668.
- Murray, C.E., King, K., Crowe, A., & Flasch, P. (2015). Survivors of intimate partner violence as advocates for social change. *Journal of Social Action in Counseling and Psychology*, 7, 84–100. Retrieved September 11, 2015, from http://www.psysr.org/jsacp/murray-v7n1-2015_84-100.pdf.
- Murray, C.E., Crowe, A., & Flasch, P. (2015). Turning points: Critical incidents in survivors' decisions to end abusive relationships. *The Family Journal*, 23, 228–238. DOI: 10.1177/1066480715573705.
- Murray, C.E., Crowe, A., & Brinkley, J. (2015). The stigma surrounding intimate partner violence: A cluster analysis study. *Partner Abuse*, 6, 320–336.
- Crowe, A., & Murray, C.E. (2015). Stigma from professional helpers toward survivors of intimate partner violence. *Partner Abuse*, 6(2), 157–179.

3 This original survey remains open to new participants, and additional information can be found at http://www.seethetriumph.org/participate-in-our-research.html.
4 Murray, C.E., Crowe, A., & Akers, W. (2016). How can we end the stigma surrounding domestic and sexual violence? A modified Delphi study with national advocacy leaders. *Journal of Family Violence*, 31, 271–287. DOI: 10.1007/s10896-015-9768-9.
5 Murray, C.E., & Graves, K.N. (2012). *Responding to family violence*. New York: Routledge.
6 For more information about the CDC's *National Intimate Partner and Sexual Violence Survey*, please visit the following website: http://www.cdc.gov/violenceprevention/nisvs/index.html.
7 Research studies addressing gender patterns in intimate partner violence include the following:

- Ehrensaft, M.K. (2008). Intimate partner violence: Persistence of myths and implications for intervention. *Children and Youth Services Review*, 30, 276–286.
- Holtzworth-Munroe, A. (2005). Male versus female intimate partner violence: Putting controversial findings into context. *Journal of Marriage and Family*, 67, 1120–1125.
- Holtzworth-Munroe, A., Smutzler, N., & Bates, L. (1997). A brief review of the research on husband violence: Part III: Sociodemographic factors, relationship factors, and differing consequences of husband and wife violence. *Aggression and Violent Behavior*, 2, 285–307.
- Kernsmith, P. (2005). Exerting power or striking back: A gendered comparison of motivations for domestic violence perpetration. *Violence and Victims*, 20(2), 173–185.

8 Michael Johnson, a researcher at Pennsylvania State University, has identified different types of intimate partner violence, such as intimate terrorism and situational couple violence, which show different patterns based on gender. Two useful resources for learning more about this work are as follows:

- Johnson, M.P. (2006). Gender symmetry and asymmetry in domestic violence. *Violence Against Women*, 12, 1003–1018.

- Johnson, M.P. (2009). Differentiating among types of domestic violence: Implications for healthy marriages. In H.E. Peters & C.M. Kamp Dush (Eds.), *Marriage and family: Perspectives and complexities* (pp. 281–297). New York: Columbia University Press.
9 Note: All of our studies, aside from the initial interview that included 12 participants, have been open to participants of any gender and used survey instruments that were written in gender-neutral language.
10 Walker, L. (1984). *The battered woman syndrome*. New York: Springer.
11 A gallery of Power and Control Wheels is available at the following website: http://www.theduluthmodel.org/training/wheels.html.
12 Murray, C.E., & Graves, K.N. (2012). *Responding to family violence*. New York: Routledge.
13 For more information about the CDC's *National Intimate Partner and Sexual Violence Survey*, please visit the following website: http://www.cdc.gov/violenceprevention/nisvs/index.html.
14 For an overview of marital rape and the history of its legality, please see Bergen, R.K., & Barnhill, E. (2011). Marital rape: New research and directions. National Online Resource Center on Violence Against Women. Retrieved October 28, 2015, from http://www.vawnet.org/applied-research-papers/print-document.php?doc_id=248.
15 For more on this topic, please see our past See the Triumph blog post on the topic: http://www.seethetriumph.org/blog/married-or-not-rape-is-rape.
16 See our past See the Triumph blog post on this topic: http://www.seethetriumph.org/blog/enthusiastic-consent-go-for-the-yes.
17 Murray, C.E., Pope, A.L., & Willis, B. (2016). *Sexuality counseling*. Thousand Oaks, CA: SAGE.
18 The statement from the American College of Obstetricians and Gynecologists cited here can be found at the following website in paragraph 1: http://www.acog.org/Resources-And-Publications/Committee-Opinions/Committee-on-Health-Care-for-Underserved-Women/Reproductive-and-Sexual-Coercion/.

2 The Added Complexity of Stigma

Anna was a single mother in her early 50s whose children were in high school and college. She had homeschooled her children and was very invested in her roles as mother and teacher. Anna had a fascinating story. At the time of our interview with her, she felt as though she was just entering a new, exciting phase of life. She was getting ready to finish homeschooling the youngest of her children, which would afford her with new opportunities. So much of her life up until then had been dictated by what her kids needed. Now she wanted to care for herself in the same way that she had been doing for her family throughout the years. She was excited about the idea of taking classes at the local community college, starting a new hobby, or volunteering. In the meantime, she was working in a temporary position while she was trying to figure out what she wanted to do to get more financially stable. She loved cooking, singing, arts and crafts, and creative writing.

Anna had been married to her abuser and father of her three kids, Rick, for almost a decade. He worked in his local community as a first responder. She described their marriage as unhealthy and abusive from the start. He sexually and emotionally abused her, although she didn't necessarily know that it was abuse at the time their relationship started. Sex was not special or sacred; it was something Rick was entitled to. She remembered a neighbor telling her that it was normal when Rick was unfaithful to her.

> "He had married me because then he could have sex whenever he wanted to. You know, when I was pregnant with my first daughter, he hooked up with someone else, and I talked to my neighbor about this, and her response was 'Oh, he's just a little nervous about becoming a father. You know, they do things like that.' I thought there was something wrong with *me* because I didn't think that it was OK."

For many years, Rick had everyone fooled. As a first responder in his community, he was well respected by his coworkers, neighbors, and friends. His abusive behavior was masked, and Anna described this as a Dr. Jekyll/Mr. Hyde personality, where no one knew how nasty he was but her. Eventually, however, Rick's "true colors" started to show, and people in her community started to believe her when she felt brave enough to disclose the abuse. Even so, she spoke of how difficult it was to tell her story for fear of being labeled and blamed: "Especially when you've got this man who has status, and has it all together, I mean, my blessing was that Rick showed his other side. But how many times does that happen?"

Anna wanted to leave Rick and end the marriage many times, but he threatened her emotionally and physically, and she felt pressured to stay with him for the sake of the family,

> "You know, just still trying to preserve this essence of family. And he used to always threaten me too, that if I left he would disappear from the kids' lives. And that kept me because of that strong family, family, family."

The day Anna finally left was when she saw that he was starting to abuse and manipulate the children. She said this about her decision:

> "But, he started to do it to them . . . the mind-fuck games. And I said, 'No way, there is no way you are going to ruin these children's lives. I don't know how I'm gonna do it, but I'm leaving.'"

Anna talked about the struggles she faced due to the past abuse. She felt as though she was in a very different phase of life when compared to other 50-year-old women she knew. Anna was finally feeling healthy and stable, and she was just starting to really live her life. This came up when asked whether or not she felt a sense of isolation in her life. "So being at my age, there is a sense of isolation, because I'm ready to start living my life and most of the folks that I know—they're winding down. And I'm just getting geared up." Anna described the stressors that were involved in leaving her abusive relationship, for example, figuring out how to become financially stable since she had been a stay-at-home mother married to the breadwinner of the family.

> "As more and more women are garnering the courage to leave these relationships, people expect them to leave and then just—'OK! You left!'—Well, there's so much more to it. There's the financial piece, there's the constant conversation of healing that has to go on."

She also spoke of the work it takes to repair the whole family:

> "So the stigma, yes, I think people expect 'Oh, OK, well you left the abusive situation so now it's all over and done.' That's when the

work only begins. Especially if you want to pull your children out of the hole with you. And I was very committed to that."

* * * * * * *

Stigma

We began this chapter with Anna's story as a way to introduce a phenomenon that is inherent in the lives of women and men who are experiencing or overcoming abuse—stigma. Stigma occurs when groups of people are marginalized based on negative labeling and stereotyping, discriminated against, and lose status in relation to more powerful groups. Stigma encompasses a variety of components and sources that combine to make it an extremely damaging experience. The consequences of stigma are many, and researchers agree that stigma can be as damaging as the issue that is being stigmatized. Blame, isolation, negative emotions, and loss of status are a few of the components that combine as part of the stigma experience. When we looked into a variety of disciplines to understand the concept of stigma, we found a lot of previous research on the stigma surrounding other challenging life experiences, such as mental illness and HIV/AIDS. However, before we started our research, we had not seen the term stigma applied to victims and survivors of abuse, even though it was a concept that has long been studied in other populations and in other disciplines. As we began to delve into our research and learned more about the work of other researchers who also began studying this topic around the same time, we confirmed that people who had been abused within intimate relationships experienced stigma in several ways, such as by mental health professionals pathologizing their presenting symptoms, by members of their communities judging them, and by abusers labeling them with damaging self-images (e.g., stupid or slut). When we heard from the survivors who participated in our research, the concept of stigma resonated strongly with them. Therefore, we knew we needed to learn more about what the experience of stigma is like for people who have faced intimate partner violence victimization, especially because we hoped that understanding this stigma would offer clues for how we could work toward ending it.

Initially, we considered the following for categories of stigma, based on the work of other researchers on stigma related to other issues:[1]

- Blame: Survivors may be blamed or viewed as somehow responsible for the abuse they experienced.
- Isolation: Survivors may be isolated and separated from others because they were abused.
- Negative emotions: Survivors feel shame, guilt, embarrassment, or other painful emotions that can result in secrecy.

32 Introduction

- Loss of status: Survivors may lose standing and/or power within social networks and systems as a result of having experienced abuse.

These four categories provided a useful framework for our earlier work, but as we delved deeper into analyzing and understanding the stories of the survivors who participated in our research, we realized that they were only part of the story. First, these four categories did encompass much of the stigma that our research participants experienced. However, some of their experiences with stigma didn't fit neatly into the aforementioned four categories. Second, and perhaps more importantly, we realized that these different categories of stigma could be experienced from different sources and that the source of the stigma mattered. It mattered in how survivors make decisions about whether or not to end their relationships. It mattered in their decisions about whether and from whom to seek help and support. And, it mattered in how they came to view themselves over time in relation to the abusive relationship. Therefore, in order to capture more fully the experiences of stigma related to intimate partner violence, we partnered with another researcher, Nicole Overstreet at Clark University, to develop a model that accounted for both the types of stigma that survivors experienced and the sources from which they faced stigma. This work, involving the analyses of data from 279 survivors who participated in our research, resulted in our proposed Integrated IPV Stigmatization Model (see Figure 2.1).[2]

As is depicted in the Integrated IPV Stigmatization Model, the major components of stigma experienced by victims and survivors of intimate partner violence include blame, isolation, negative emotions, and loss of status. We also included an "other stigma" category to reflect that some experiences of stigma do not fall neatly into one of these four categories.

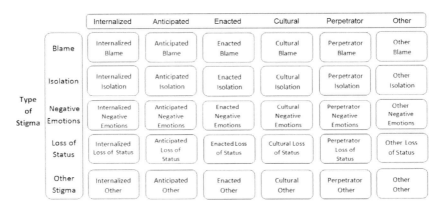

Figure 2.1 The Integrated IPV Stigmatization Model

These components of stigma may result from any of the following sources: internalized stigma (i.e., people's views of themselves), anticipated stigma (i.e., personal beliefs about how one thinks people will respond when others find out they have experienced abuse), enacted stigma (i.e., actual experiences or behaviors directed toward the victims or survivors), cultural stigma (i.e., stigmatizing stereotypes or messages received from the broader cultural and social context), and perpetrator stigma (i.e., stigmatizing words or actions directly resulting from the perpetrator).

Take the following story, for example, and see how stigma impacted a survivor, Nikki, from one of our early interviews.

Nikki's Story

At the time of the interview, Nikki was in her mid-40s. She'd worked in a secretarial position for many years, but she had recently resigned. She was living with her boyfriend, and she described the relationship as "fairly healthy." Her boyfriend struggled with mental illness, so she assumed the role of caretaker to help him manage his medications, go to appointments, and tend to his other needs. Together, they had just started a small business. Finances were tight, and she was applying for disability due to a number of physical health problems. As a child, Nikki's life was very difficult, as she had experienced abuse in her family at the hands of her parent and siblings. Nikki said, "You name it, they abused it. My mother was a doctor, a brilliant but very sick person."

Nikki had been in several abusive relationships. She had been in two prior marriages, which both ended in divorce because of abuse. The relationship she told us about in the most detail was a previous abusive boyfriend. Nikki was drinking heavily during the time of her involvement in that relationship, and she explained that alcohol did not help the situation. He became her everything, and she wanted to marry him. The abuse began slowly. She experienced verbal, physical, and sexual abuse from him. He would bite her, hit her, and pull her hair. He used her financially and became extremely controlling. He kept her isolated from those in his life, and she couldn't understand why that was happening, not realizing that it was part of the abuse. Nikki decided to go to her first Alcoholics Anonymous (AA) meeting around the time when the abuse was at its worst. She somehow managed to go to meetings without her abuser knowing, and she credits the people she met at AA as one of the biggest reasons she was able to end the relationship. She eventually got sober and left the relationship. He tried to reconnect with her, and she refused—she'd found strength through the support group and realized that alcohol had played a huge part in keeping her from coming to terms with the abuse earlier.

When we asked Nikki about the stigmas she faced, she had a lot to say. Isolation occurred because she did not want anything to get out, or slip, so that others would learn about the abuse. In an effort to keep it all secret, she isolated herself from friends, family, and everyone but her abuser. She knew her friends and family would be worried for her if she'd talk to them, and they would know something was wrong, or different. She felt that it was easier to distance herself than run the risk of people getting curious and figuring out what was going on in her relationship.

Nikki experienced a loss of status when she felt powerless in the relationship. Everyone knew her ex-boyfriend, and she felt that there wasn't anyone who knew her at the time, which was also in part because of the isolation since she had lost her network of friends and family, but he had not. She described her ex-boyfriend as having a prominent social status, and she felt completely unknown. Nikki also felt defensive of the relationship in some ways while she was with him. There was a part of her that knew it wasn't right, but she had convinced herself that it would all get better, that he was worth it, and that he would change. She even started to think that her friends and family had a hidden agenda if they expressed any concern or questions. Looking back, she felt ashamed and couldn't believe she had been so manipulated. During the interview, she paused for a moment, shook her head exasperated, and said "What was wrong with me!?" When Nikki finally left the relationship, she was scared that her family and friends wouldn't accept her after she'd been so consumed by the relationship. What if they would not forgive or support her? She used the metaphor of trying to jump out of a frying pan: "Can I leap out of this frying pan, and then am I going to land on the ground, or am I going to land in the fire?"

Nikki also talked with us about how stigma impacted her in the present day. "I don't talk about it much. I have had a lot of harmful and hurtful responses when I have disclosed the abuse." She'd heard blaming responses before, such as the following example she offered: "Women who get hit probably get hit because they deserve it." Nikki stigmatized herself (internalized stigma) in that she felt ashamed that she got herself so deeply involved in an abusive relationship. She described herself as a "loser magnet" and that it was dangerous for her to be in relationships because she becomes "a doormat." She didn't want to talk to her current boyfriend about this either, as she felt afraid that he might think that he could abuse her. Nikki admitted that she doesn't always think clearly about relationships and that there is a part of her that believes that all men are driven to abuse women.

Nikki's story is full of stigma from varying sources and includes multiple components. For example, internalized stigma occurs when victims and survivors start to believe the negative beliefs themselves and stigmatize themselves based largely on the stigmatizing messages that are perpetuated by external influences. Nikki stigmatized herself by thinking she must be a "loser magnet." Anticipated stigma was a part of her experience, since she was afraid that others would react in a stigmatizing way if and when they found out about the abuse. Nikki still didn't like to talk about her past abuse to others, including her current boyfriend, because she was afraid of the reactions that would come. Enacted stigma describes the actual experience of being discriminated against, such as hearing negative comments, being humiliated or stereotyped by others. Nikki faced this enacted stigma when she talked to an acquaintance and shared a little about the abuse, and the woman's response was that "women deserve it." From Nikki's story, we can see that the stigma that victims and survivors of intimate partner violence face can come from many different sources and involve multiple components of the stigma that are depicted in the IPV Stigmatization Model.

Stigma From Professionals

In Chapter 5, we'll look in depth at how stigma may be encountered when victims and survivors reach out to others for help. This is such an important theme that we've found in our research that we also want to introduce it here. Unfortunately, enacted stigma toward victims and survivors of intimate partner violence can originate from those in one's personal life—such as friends and family members—and it also can come from professionals when victims and survivors reach out for help. We know that there are many well-trained, supportive, helpful professionals working to provide support to victims and survivors of intimate partner violence. However, through our research, we have heard countless stories from survivors about negative reactions they encountered from such professionals as medical doctors, law enforcement agents, attorneys, judges, counselors, and even domestic violence shelter staff. Of course, many professionals within these groups do provide positive, non-stigmatizing support to victims and survivors of intimate partner violence, but our research suggests that there are still many people within these professions who lack the knowledge, skills, and/or competence to provide appropriate support. Scholars have studied why stigma occurs from professionals, and there are a few possible explanations for it. First, professionals may lack adequate training for working with a particular issue or population, and this leads to negative attitudes that impair their ability to provide competent support. Second, professionals may feel as though they cannot help in the way that they wish they could, thus leading to feelings of inadequacy or futility. Third, professionals might not receive adequate support or validation from others or each other to help cope with the challenges that come with the difficult work they do. Fourth, in light of the challenges of addressing the crises and trauma involved in abusive relationships, professionals may begin to feel overworked or burned out, and this leads to stigmatizing attitudes. Regardless of the cause, we know that stigma can originate from professionals and that it has damaging effects on survivors when they seek support.

36 Introduction

Our research offers many examples of stigmatizing experiences that survivors had with professionals. Here are a few experiences that participants described that are related to professionals:

- "The local police are a joke. In 10 years I called twice. My first call I had a bloodied lip, and their response was, if he wasn't there, then they could do nothing. My second call was when he yanked me down by my hair with my newborn daughter in my arms. I was told since I had no visible injuries, they couldn't make him leave."
- "They didn't think it was rape because he didn't hold me down or anything. Or at least, he didn't hold me down during the whole time, and I didn't scream or yell."
- "I was told by a judge that if he could have his way and punish me, he would know what to do with me, but since he was to do what was best for the children, he wouldn't go there."
- "My doctor told me I was stupid if I didn't leave."
- "My marital counselor said, 'Make a list of all the sins you committed against him, and ask him for forgiveness.'" And, "He told me I was 'triggering' my ex's controlling behavior and sexual assaults and encouraged me to focus on my own 'contributions' to the problem rather than find[ing] ways to stay safe."
- "One time I went to a counselor because I was having a hard time with my libido (go figure, who wouldn't after experienced such horrors), and the therapist told me to give my ex more blow jobs."
- "I called a domestic violence hotline, in the middle of the night, crying, and the woman hung up on me."
- "The woman assigned to meet with me was mad at the receptionist and told her in front of me that she was done for the day and wasn't pleased that she had to help me."
- "Even DV professionals who think they understand are quick to lump you into the 'weak and helpless' category."

These statements might be difficult for you to read. Trust us; it remains hard for us too! We oftentimes assume that for survivors who seek help—especially given how challenging it is to take the first step by walking through the therapist's door, telling a medical doctor, or calling a shelter for the first time—that the experience will be a positive one. But these quotes suggest that some survivors are met with anything but a positive response. For many survivors, the experience of reaching out for help from professionals becomes re-traumatizing. These stigmatizing responses are especially problematic because they can stunt whatever momentum has been generated to have the strength to disclose abuse, muster up the courage to leave, and begin a new life free from abuse. Going back to Nikki's story, she too faced stigmatizing experiences with professionals. When she sought counseling to help overcome abuse from an ex-husband, her counselor thought she was "unreasonable" and instead supported the husband's abusive behavior. When Nikki called the police during a violent episode with her ex-husband, the police not only failed to respond, but they questioned her loyalty to her husband, asking, "Do you really want to put your husband in jail?" During this time, Nikki was also fired from her job. Her husband had been stalking her at work, showing up unannounced, and bothering her and her coworkers. Her boss "didn't want to deal with it," so she was laid off. Nikki suffered many unfortunate consequences as a result of the abuse. Starting one's life over after abuse is difficult, and Nikki's experiences with professionals added to the challenges. Imagine losing your job as you are preparing to leave an abusive relationship, which takes away your source of economic security for rebuilding a life on your own. Or, imagine the police questioning your choice to have your husband arrested, all during a time when you feel emotionally, mentally, and physically most vulnerable. Sadly, these examples are ones we've heard over and over. Stigma from professionals was an all-too-common experience from survivors who have participated in our research.

Sam's Story

To further illustrate how the stigma surrounding intimate partner violence adds to victims' and survivors' challenges in achieving safety, consider Sam's story. Sam was a female college graduate in her early 30s who worked in the business field. She had been in one abusive relationship, a nearly ten-year relationship with her ex-boyfriend, with whom she had also lived with for part of the relationship. She experienced physical, emotional, verbal, sexual, and financial abuse by this ex-boyfriend. As a result of the abuse, he faced criminal charges and a no-contact order.

The relationship ended over two years before Sam participated in our research study:

> "I left the situation and moved in with family. I was amenable to allowing my former partner to keep and buy the house. It was solely my deed and mortgage. He claimed he would purchase the property, but instead lived off of me for over a year. When I became resigned to the fact I couldn't resolve the situation on my own, I went to the police and sought legal advice. Criminal charges were laid, but this didn't do anything to resolve my 'civil' issue. I was eventually told by the police that if I wanted him out of the house, I needed to figure out when he wouldn't be there and change the locks, and that's what I ended up doing. I tried to resolve things through my lawyer, but my former partner simply played games and cost me thousands in legal bills, and nothing was formally resolved."

Sam experienced multiple forms of stigma related to this abusive relationship. First, she described being blamed for the abuse.

> "I've dealt with blame while attempting to get help, from an attorney stating, 'Be prepared to explain why you stayed in this relationship,' to a friend of my ex's stating that she thought he was suicidal and that I'd be responsible if he acted on this impulse. It's also difficult not to blame myself, such as that I should have been more informed about abusive relationships, and I should have realized the severity of my situation and not chronically minimized my experience."

Sam also faced discrimination:

> "My first lawyer asked me what I thought women's shelters were for. He claimed he had never heard of the police removing a man from the home. The only reason I was able to get help in resolving the issue surrounding my home was because I discovered the police supervisor of the lead investigator assigned to my file was indebted to a lawyer acquaintance. I've had such a terrible time dealing with all of this. Imagine how someone without the level of support I had would manage."

The relationship left Sam feeling isolated.

> "I felt there were few places to turn for assistance. I didn't know where to get help. It's next to impossible for people who haven't experienced it to fully empathize and understand the complexity associated with abuse. I can't fully move past this until it's dealt with by the legal system, and it's been dragging on for years. I can't imagine being at a point where I'd consider dating. I feel exhausted and embarrassed at having to deal with anyone who would associate me with my former partner. It makes me want to retreat."

Loss of power and status was a prominent theme for Sam, too:

> "It's difficult to finally escape a relationship that essentially stripped me of my power, only to be subjected to a justice system that seems to mimic this same dynamic. I feel disillusioned and further disempowered, but that many of the responses must continue to empower my former partner. For example, repeated no-contact breaches on his behalf that result in zero consequences, to the point that I stopped reporting them to the authorities. Also, I worked with/for my former partner. Leaving that relationship wasn't just about leaving him, but about losing my job, my home, and having to withdrawal from my latest degree program."

Sam experienced stereotypes about survivors of IPV in her efforts to seek professional help. She shared the following thoughts on these stereotypes:

> "Even the police officer who was, by far, the most professional and helpful said, 'We don't normally deal with people like you.' Even current anti-violence campaigns seem to perpetuate stereotypes. For instance, most of articles I have read report that 1 in 3 women are 'raped or beaten.' This language is not inclusive. From a legal perspective, I've been sexually assaulted, but I haven't been raped. I've been assaulted, but I wouldn't feel comfortable saying I'd been beaten. I feel it perpetuates stereotypes for both victims and perpetrators. It contributes to the minimizing ideology that, 'My situation isn't that bad.' My former partner once scoffed at my suggestion that certain of his behaviors were abusive, saying he'd 'never kicked or punched' me. For me, a big obstacle to overcome in accepting and escaping abuse was the realization that I didn't have the power to fix or manage the situation. It wasn't about me or my behavior. The violence was inevitable, and all the patience, forgiveness, and empathy, on my part, couldn't stop it."

Professionals, friends, and family members responded to Sam's abuse in stigmatizing ways, as she relates in the following account:

> "The first two attorneys I dealt with were very condescending. I was told by the first lawyer I contacted that the police would do nothing to help me if my injuries weren't serious enough to warrant hospitalization, that I'd waited too long to get help. She said there was nothing preventing me from going back and essentially to go back and wait for him to do it again."

Sam had particularly stigmatizing experiences with law enforcement and court systems. Regarding criminal injuries counseling, the judge questioned her and said, "'Are you sure you need that?'" Sam repeatedly gave potentially incriminating e-mails from her abuser to the police, only to find out, time and again, that they weren't included in her file (when the police assured her they would be). Her attorney also asked her, "'What chance do you really think you stand [in court]?'"

All of these stigmatizing experiences contributed to Sam feeling shame.

> "It's difficult not to feel shame, which I'm trying to contextualize as a product of feeling some responsibility for the IPV, although logically I know it's not a responsibility I should bear. I feel shame that I needed help—that I couldn't resolve it on my own, that I had to make use of the justice system. I feel shame that I spent so many years

in the company of someone like my former partner. I feel shame that I'm not back on my feet financially, that I occasionally need help from my family."

Despite the abuse she experienced, Sam shares inspiration for other survivors by describing the process of overcoming past abuse as

"to truly acknowledge you aren't responsible for what's happened to you; to realize there is a great deal of ignorance surrounding intimate partner violence; to take steps to foster openness, create awareness, and ideally make a change; to attempt to use your experience to benefit yourself and others."

Overcoming stigma is an ongoing journey for Sam. As she said,

"I'm not sure I've necessarily overcome the stigma. I've tried to be open about my experience. I've tried to educate myself. I've been seeing a therapist. I'm trying not to be too hard on myself. I've gotten involved in community efforts."

She offers the following advice to other survivors for how to deal with stigma:

"Do what you can. It's not easy. Talk about it; acknowledge it. Talk to a professional. Make use of risk assessment tools. Unfortunately, realize that leaving is only a first step. Brace yourself to be further abused and re-victimized by a system that you'd hoped would be there to support you. You'll likely have negative experiences, but there will be people who do genuinely care—look to them to help restore your faith in humanity. It's not an easy road, but neither is living, and potentially dying, with an abuser. Don't lose hope."

Added Stigmas

Some victims and survivors of IPV face added layers of stigma that may further complicate their experiences based on unique characteristics about their lives or relationships. As examples, we heard from males who were abused by females, people who experienced abuse in same-sex relationships, and ethnic and racial minorities about how additional layers of stigma impacted them in compounding ways. For these participants, not only did they experience stigma that we described earlier in this chapter, but they also faced stigma related to such factors as their gender, race/ethnicity, immigrant status, and/or sexual orientation. Consider Taylor's story (which follows)—it's an example of how added stigmas can impact those in particular minority groups.

Same-Sex Relationships: Taylor's Story

When she participated in our research, Taylor was a senior in college with just a semester to go before she was set to graduate. She had come from a very small, geographically isolated town in a rural part of Georgia. When we interviewed her, she was living with her current partner, who also was from her hometown. She described a past abusive relationship, which lasted for nearly one year during her senior year of high school. This was a same-sex relationship, which added to the challenges that Taylor faced, especially because she was living in such a small rural area.

That relationship seemed great for the first few months, but it eventually became overrun with mental and emotional abuse, along with some physical abuse at times. In describing the physical abuse, Taylor said that, "For the most part, it was just like grabbing my wrists, or pushing me, or something like that. It was force as opposed to actually hitting me." Taylor said that the emotional abuse was much more challenging to face within the relationship. She said, "Sometimes she would tell me that she was the only person that would put up with me and that I was always being ridiculous, or angry, or crying." As another example of this abuse, Taylor shared,

> "If I would just do something klutzy, like I spilled my drink at a restaurant, she got really, really mad at me. It was like, 'God, I can't take you anywhere. You're so, you're such a klutz. You can't do anything right.' It was less names and more like, 'You can't do anything right.'"

Taylor described her girlfriend as "really jealous" and "controlling." Her girlfriend required her to call her from school before the morning bell rang, "because she didn't want me to talk to my friends," and she also gave Taylor a bedtime. If Taylor missed this bedtime, "She would get really, really mad at me."

Taylor's girlfriend also controlled her choices about what clothes to wear. She started wearing baggy clothes to avoid a fight. "She said she didn't want other people looking at me." She also convinced Taylor that it was because she was so beautiful that she didn't want to share her. Looking back, though, Taylor blamed herself for believing that lie, and still asks herself, "You're so stupid, what were you doing?" Her parents had attempted to ban Taylor from talking to her girlfriend, but that was partly because they weren't comfortable with their daughter being in a same-sex relationship. Despite their discomfort with this, her parents were concerned about the relationship in general, just due to her girlfriend's personality and behavior. They knew that the signs of a dysfunctional relationship were there. Rather than welcome this feedback from her parents, Taylor was defensive, as is typical of many her age. Taylor explained that the fact that this relationship was with another girl "made it harder for me to talk to my parents about, because they didn't know about it. In my very small town, there aren't resources for things like that."

As is common in abusive relationships, the abuse that Taylor experienced progressed over time. First, there were emotional blows, and then the controlling behaviors began to emerge. It would be several months before any physical violence occurred. The frequency grew until Taylor "just got sick of it." Before the final end of the relationship, Taylor tried to leave the relationship a couple times, but "it never stuck." In addition to the messages she received from her parents about the need to end the relationship, several friends also encouraged Taylor to get out of the relationship. Taylor eventually had to decide for herself to end the relationship. With the help of her parents, she stopped answering the phone, had her parents answer the door when her girlfriend started looking for her, and left to stay with a family member in the next state over during a break at school until she felt safe to return home.

We asked Taylor, just as we did the others we interviewed, what prevented her from getting help once she realized she was being abused. Fear kept Taylor in her relationship and from seeking help. She said,

> "The amount of women that either the abuser, nothing happens to them, or they try and do something, and they get killed or something. And, that scared the crap out of me. So, I didn't want to do something to make her really, really mad. A 'good day' for us meant we fought. So, imagine how pissed she'd be if I tried to get her arrested or something. I was afraid I'd be killed."

In the years since Taylor's relationship ended, she faced the lingering effects of the abuse. Remembering all the blame she would face from her ex-girlfriend, in her new relationships, she said, "I still apologize all the time." Even her current partner reminds her to stop unnecessary apologies to which she responds, "I know. I'm sorry." Taylor's past experiences also impact her ability to enjoy her current relationship. She said, "My partner is really nice to me and really does something sweet; it was kind of like, 'What are you doing? This is weird. I can't handle it.' The only time my ex-girlfriend was really nice and really sweet was immediately after she screwed up or hit me."

Taylor also said that, because her ex-girlfriend would restrain her by holding her wrists, "If anyone grabs my wrist, I still like I jerk. Like, I will fight you if you do it." She still has to address the impact on her self-worth as well: "I still have a low self-esteem, but I do know no one should be abused. I deserve better than that. And I'm trying to work on accepting that." Taylor described experiencing stigma in the form of feeling like the black sheep of the family ("I kind of do feel like that sometimes, but it's not because of an abusive relationship. It's because of a thousand other varying factors"), feeling blame and shame, and experiencing a loss of personal power. She noted that the shame she felt made her more susceptible to staying in the relationship: "It kept me from getting out of it. Because I felt like I've always had self-esteem issues. So, I kind of felt like, 'Well, no one else is going to love me. So, if she loves me, I can put up with it.'"

How Multiple Layers of Stigma Impacted Taylor

We highlight Taylor's story because stigma impacted her in a variety of ways. The depth of Taylor's shame is reflected in how she came to view herself through the lens of stereotypes about abuse. She said,

> "I felt like a statistic. My mom would talk to me about a lot of this, because she had been through a lot of bad stuff before. And she was trying to keep me from doing the same thing. And I was always like, my whole young life, I was like, 'It'll never happen to me. I'd never be that stupid. If anyone lays a hand on me, I'll leave right that second.' And I couldn't figure out for the life of me why women didn't just leave. I just could not wrap my head around the idea of someone sticking around. And then, I realized it. At that time, it had been my longest relationship, 11 months. Like, really? Your longest relationship is the abusive one. Good job! I didn't want to be 'that girl,' the one that everyone is whispering about. And, so, I just pretended it wasn't going on. We can't talk about it if it's not happening."

The stereotypes about abusive relationships that are portrayed in the media made it harder for Taylor to understand that what she was experiencing was abuse. She said,

> "With the stuff that the media shows that relates to abusive relationship, I felt like I wasn't in one. Because the, all the stuff that I would see is like women in the hospital, women with black eyes and bruises and stuff. And I never had that. So, I felt like, 'Oh, well, maybe I'm exaggerating about what's going on with me.' I didn't think that there was such a thing as emotional abuse, I guess. Like, they don't really talk about that in the news. So, I felt that I was just in a crappy relationship, not an abusive one. I felt like me complaining about what was going on with me, there were women that were being put in hospitals with broken bones. Like my experience was so much lesser than what others had gone through that it was just me exaggerating . . . I just kind of equated it to not being a big deal. And sort of went with like, 'It's not abuse until I have a bruise.'"

This disconnect was especially pronounced because Taylor was in a same-sex relationship. "The media never talks about same-sex abuse. Like,

I never see it. So, I mean, same-sex relationship abuse and like men being abused by women. Like, those are just things you don't see."

Another aspect of stigma is loss of power. Taylor lost her sense of power in the relationship so subtly that she barely recognized it happening until it was gone. She reflected that,

> "It didn't really register in my head that I essentially lost power until later on, like it had been happening for a few months already . . . I just felt like there wasn't a way out, so I'd just have to stick with it, because it was what I deserved, because it was what I was putting up with. So, obviously, I deserved it."

The process of becoming more isolated, which is also a part of the stigma concept, was drawn out over time for Taylor. In her case, after being in the relationship for a while with an abuser who had slowly and methodically separated her from her support system, she realized that she had lost a lot of the people she would normally go to for support. Thankfully, Taylor did find support around her when she left the relationship for good. She said,

> "I still needed help, and, thankfully, there were still people. Once I expressed the desire to finally be done with it, there were people that were immediately helpful to me, including my parents. When I picked up the phone and called my mom, the first words out of her mouth were, 'Thank God.'"

Negative emotions are a large part of the stigma concept. Types of emotions can vary, but some we have heard about from survivors are shame, guilt, and embarrassment, among others. By the end of the abusive relationship, Taylor had lost virtually any sense of self-worth, especially due to the things her girlfriend would say and do to her. This had a huge impact on her process of leaving the relationship. She explained,

> "It was to a point where she made me feel so awful that I couldn't stand myself anymore. And, in some ways, that would make some people stay, but it was to a point where I was so hidden underneath this rock—I had to crawl out of it. I didn't even know myself anymore. I had no idea what I was doing. I was so mad at myself, and I was so ashamed of what I had been doing, what I had been allowing. It made me, it was like a paradox. Because I thought so little of myself that I knew I was better than that."

Following the end of the abusive relationship, Taylor took several proactive steps to work toward overcoming the abuse. She said that counseling helped "me see how it was affecting my life at the time." Some of the teachers in her high school at the time also helped her to validate her experiences and to understand that the abuse was not acceptable.

Like so many of the survivors we've heard from in our research, Taylor hopes her story will help others. She said,

> "I'm very open about it if somebody wants to talk about it. I don't have any problem with it. That's why I did this interview, because I thought it would be a good idea, because it would be helping, hopefully helping somebody else."

Taylor believes that more open discussions to increase people's knowledge about abuse are essential for ending it. She said,

> "I wish that more people realized how many women are in these situations, and also how different they can be, because they vary from emotional to physical. And it's not even necessarily physically violent. I feel like people don't realize that. I know someone who believes that it's not rape unless you're held down kicking and screaming. Many people believe that if you don't have a black eye and a broken arm, then it's not abuse. I feel like there would be less shame if people understood more. Like, if I felt like I could have gone to somebody without feeling ashamed, and that they wouldn't judge me for being in it, then maybe I would have been more comfortable doing so. There should be more knowledge."

Stigma is hard enough to deal with for anyone. The added layer of a minority status makes it even more complex and challenging. Community-based systems and resources are typically designed to support survivors who are in the majority, and for someone like Taylor who was in a same-sex relationship in a small rural community, her challenges were most likely complicated by her nonmajority status. Taylor felt judged by many before the abuse even started. So once the abuse began, she had already been shunned, judged, and misunderstood. It makes sense then that she became more reluctant to disclose that the abuse was occurring in the relationship. As she pointed out when we interviewed her, the media does not talk about intimate partner violence in same-sex couples. Because abuse within same-sex relationships is not addressed in the media or other public spaces, victims and survivors might not realize that what they are experiencing is indeed abusive. Victim advocates might not know what these signs are either, and they might not be able to intervene, ask the right questions, or provide support. Thus we hope that by reading Taylor's story you are able to understand this notion of multiple layers of stigma and how this impacts some survivors.

Male Victims of Abuse: Joseph's Story

Although the vast majority of participants in our research to date have been women, we also heard from men who were abused by women. These male survivors faced additional levels of stigma, mainly because most people did not believe they were being abused at all. As we mentioned in Chapter 1, it is much more common for women to be the victims of abuse in heterosexual relationships rather than the perpetrators. Many of the male victims in our research were met with disbelief, laughter, and judgment when they reported the abuse. Take Joseph's story, for example. Joseph was a Caucasian, 40-something man with three children: one in the early 20s and two more middle school aged. In our survey, he described a 20-year relationship with his ex-wife, with whom he experienced physical, emotional, and verbal abuse. At the height of the abuse, he took out a protective order against her. However, despite the abuse, he said, "I always thought it would someday get better." Their relationship ended very violently over five years before he participated in our research. He said, "I filed for divorce after she became extremely violent toward me. Two days later, she nearly killed me."

Similar to so many of the survivors we heard from, Joseph said, "I was always blamed when she did something violent. She would say it was my fault for making her mad." Joseph felt an additional level of stigma due to the fact that he was a male being abused by a female. He shared the following thoughts with us:

> "I felt isolated because a man can't tell people that your wife hurts you. Domestic violence is labeled as a man's action. I was hurt in almost every way imaginable over a long period of time, and yet the courts still labeled me as defective. I had no status as a man, parent, or human in my home. I was embarrassed to tell anyone. I constantly felt separated from the rest of the world. I felt ashamed that I wasn't a man and suffered from the horrible things my wife used to say to me, as well as making excuses for all the cuts and bruises."

Joseph felt especially stigmatized as a male victim when he needed help from a variety of sources. When he sought help from an attorney, "I got laughed at many times when I told them my wife physically hurt me." When he sought medical attention, "The only time I told how I got hurt, the response from the nurse was, 'Good for *her* for standing up to you.'" When he sought help from the police, "The police never took it serious. Even they laughed at me. Not all of them, but some of them." Dealing with his kids' school administrators was challenging: "I have custody of my kids, and even after I showed the protection order and custody papers to my kids' school, they still continued to correspond with my estranged wife instead of me." When he sought help from a domestic violence agency, "The victim's abuse advocate outright told me she didn't believe a word of what I was saying. She told me, 'Men commit domestic violence against women, women don't commit it against men.'" All of these experiences were extremely re-traumatizing to Joseph. He said,

> "As a man, I can say it was the worst experience of my life. The experience I had after I decided I'd had enough was more stressful to me than going through the abuse. There are NO agencies available to men. They say they are open for men and women alike, but if you're a man try to reach out to one, they're no help to men."

After the relationship ended, Joseph sought healing through counseling. He said, "I went to counseling for about a year and a half. The experience has changed the way I interact with people. I'm still afraid to get close to another woman." Joseph offered advice to other male victims of IPV. He said,

> "Based on my experience, as a man, I would tell them to document everything. Place audio tapes around the house; hide video recorders. Keep medical records of the injuries. Document the injuries with pictures. Show other people your injuries. Don't be ashamed. Expect ridicule. Prove the abuse happened. If you're a man and you don't do these things, nobody will believe you."

Today, Joseph works to educate others that men can be victims of IPV. He said, "I'm a man. How I deal with it is by letting the world know this isn't a gender problem."

Consequences of Stigma

From research, we have learned about the many consequences of stigma toward survivors. These include hesitancy to seek help and safety; discriminatory practices related to employment, housing, and the criminal justice system; judgment and blame from friends, family members, and professionals; and a loss of status within social organizations, faith communities, and neighborhoods when others learn of the abuse. The various types of stigma have unique negative consequences. For example, remember the term *internalized stigma* that we mentioned earlier in this chapter? This is the self-directed negativity, blame, or label that one feels about oneself. Survivors might question themselves by asking, "Why me? What's wrong with me?" This may result in damaging self-statements such as, "I must have done something to bring this on" or "I will never have a healthy relationship." This is an unfortunate consequence, since victims may begin to believe and internalize negative statements after hearing them so many times from those around them.

Historically, there has been a tendency to blame survivors at societal and individual levels. You might have heard this referred to as victim-blaming. "You could have 'fixed' the relationship by being more caring, or obedient" is only one example of what one might hear. A particularly dangerous consequence of hearing this so many times is that the victim then stays in the abusive relationship rather than believing that a life free of violence can be established. This form of blame also can impact whether or not the perpetrator commits an act of violence, if the victim reports it, and whether a third party responds. Think about this for a moment—these are huge consequences and outcomes! Stigma is important to uncover and end because harmful responses such as these from victims and survivors' families and friends can encourage a return to the abuser or inhibit an attempt to leave at all because of the belief that staying in the relationship is the only option available.

So what is it that impacts others' negative attitudes toward IPV? When we started our research on stigma and negative attitudes, we looked at the literature that existed about the topic of attitudes toward intimate partner violence. The studies we read explained that myths about intimate partner violence impact what people think. For example, people who believe something like, "Any woman who wants to leave her abuser can do so if she really wants," blamed the victim and also minimized the incident significantly.[3] People also tended to blame victims more if the victim returned to her abuser following the abuse. But support for survivors is so important! We know from research[4] that one of the most important factors associated with how women have successfully left abusers was the belief that resources and support from others existed.

Overcoming Stigma Related to IPV

You might be wondering how it is survivors are able to overcome abuse, especially given the stigma that is inherent in the process. You might be feeling disheartened about your own experience, or the experience of someone close to you. Or you might be feeling incredulous about the stories of stigma that we've shared so far from our research. All of this is a lot to comprehend, and at times the barriers seem just too big. However, we believe that stigma related to intimate partner violence *can* be overcome, both at the individual and community levels. In fact, we believe that survivors of intimate partner violence can not only overcome the stigma related to abuse but also become advocates in the fight against stigma. In fact, a theme we heard repeatedly from the survivors who participated in our research was that they desired to use their experiences to help other people and that this desire was one of their biggest motivations for participating in our surveys. We were so inspired and touched, both personally and professionally, by the horrific abuse that many of these survivors faced, but more importantly by their inspirational stories of overcoming abuse. We knew that in order to fully honor the survivors' desire to help inspire others by sharing their stories, we would need to go beyond traditional means of disseminating research results—especially through peer-reviewed scholarly publications—to get the findings of our research into the hands of victims and survivors, their support systems, and professionals who work with them.

We first began our work on the topic of stigma and intimate partner violence in 2010. Fast forward to today when we can say with confidence that we have heard hundreds of stories of triumph, shared countless inspirational quotes from survivors across the United States and internationally, and hopefully inspired victims and survivors in their process of overcoming abuse. We have been working to end the stigma that surrounds intimate partner violence through our See the Triumph social media campaign. Through this social media outreach and advocacy, we've learned even more about how important it is to work toward ending this stigma. So in this section, we'll briefly introduce you to See the Triumph, and we'll revisit the campaign toward the end of the book to offer ways you can connect with us to help join us in our efforts to end this stigma.

See the Triumph (www.seethetriumph.org) began as our social media campaign, with the goal of sharing the stories and examples of survivors triumphing over past abuse and the stigma surrounding it. We launched the campaign on January 1, 2013. Using original words and phrases from participants in our research, we began our goal to eradicate the stigma that surrounds IPV and redevelop views of survivors as triumphant, courageous, and resourceful. The following was our very first infographic posted on our blog:

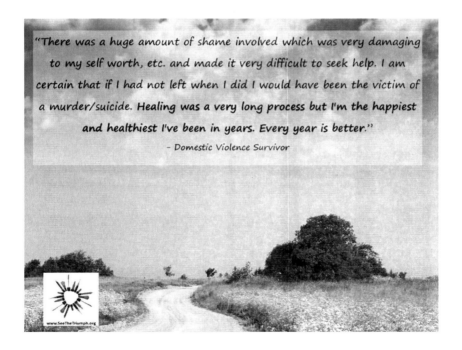

Our goals for See the Triumph are as follows: (a) to share empowering messages that people can overcome their abuse and create positive, nonviolent lives; (b) to describe strategies that have worked for other survivors to help them overcome their abuse and the stigma related to it; and (c) to promote a new view of battering survivors that shows them as triumphant, courageous, and resourceful. Since we began the campaign, See the Triumph has grown exponentially, both in the size of our audience and in the scope of the work we do. Initially beginning primarily as a means of disseminating our research findings, the campaign has launched into a forum for survivors to share their stories (including as guest bloggers and contributors to the campaign), a source of supportive resources for survivors, and a means of sharing strategies to help people advocate for changes in their communities to end the stigma surrounding abuse and support survivors. Readers can connect with See the Triumph on a variety of social media platforms:

- Causes (https://www.causes.com/stopstigma)
- Facebook (https://www.facebook.com/seethetriumph)
- Twitter (https://twitter.com/SeetheTriumph)
- Pinterest (https://www.pinterest.com/seethetriumph/)

We are deeply proud of the innovative, interactive, engaged community we are fostering through the See the Triumph campaign, and we believe the growth of the campaign demonstrates that ending the stigma surrounding intimate partner violence is a cause that resonates with many people. Therefore, we are committed to continuing to grow this campaign for years to come. The lessons we have learned through the See the Triumph campaign, including the input we've received through the campaign from members of our community, will also be incorporated into this book. We encourage you to join our campaign yourself as a survivor, an ally, a friend, a family member of a survivor, or a practitioner or researcher.

Conclusion

Now that we've introduced the concept of stigma as it applies to intimate partner violence, the next chapters will dive deeper into exploring various facets of that stigma. Chapter 3 explores how perpetrators can perpetuate this stigma as a function of the abuse. Then Chapter 4 takes a closer look at internalized stigma. This is followed by a deeper examination of stigma when victims and survivors seek help as presented in Chapter 5 and a discussion of stigma at the societal level in Chapter 6. As you'll see in these chapters, intimate partner violence–related stigma is a pervasive and significant social problem. But we believe that survivors' stories, research, and guidance from leading experts in the field can help us identify meaningful steps that we can take at every level to reduce, and eventually end, this stigma, which you'll find addressed in the final four chapters of the book. Before we can explore these solutions, however, it's important to understand the problem more fully. So let's turn now to exploring stigma in depth, beginning in the next chapter.

Notes

1 Crowe, A., & Murray, C. E. (2015). Stigma from professional helpers toward survivors of intimate partner violence. *Partner Abuse*, 6(2), 157–179.
2 Murray, C. E., Crowe, A., & Overstreet, N. (2015). Sources and components of stigma experienced by survivors of intimate partner violence. *Journal of Interpersonal Violence*, 1–22. DOI: 10.1177/0886260515609565.
3 Yamawaki, N., Ochoa-Shipp, M., Pulsipher, C., Harlos, A., & Swindler, S. (2012). Perceptions of domestic violence: The effects of domestic violence myths, victim's relationship with her abuser, and the decision to return to her abuser. *Journal of Interpersonal Violence*, 27, 195–212. DOI: 10.1177/0886260512441253.
4 We used both of these studies to support this:

- Chang, J. C., Dado, D., Ashton, S., Hawker, L., Cluss, P. A., Buranosky, R., & Scholle, S. H. (2006). Understanding behavior change for women experiencing intimate partner violence: Mapping the ups and downs using the stages of change. *Patient Education and Counseling*, 62, 330–339.
- Flasch, P., Murray, C. E., & Crowe, A. (2015). Overcoming abuse: A phenomenological investigation of the journey to recovery from past intimate partner violence. *Journal of Interpersonal Violence*, 1–29. DOI: 10.1177/0886260515599161.

Part 2
Understanding Stigma

3 Stigma as a Function of the Abuse
How Abusers Perpetuate Stigma

When we began our research to learn about the stigma surrounding intimate partner violence, we believed that victims and survivors would likely face stigma from the people around them—such as their friends, family members, and professionals in their communities—as well as through cultural messages that are conveyed in society, such as through the media. We knew it was possible that the victims and survivors could internalize these stigmatizing experiences and messages as well. However, when we started listening to the stories of the survivors who participated in our research, we learned an important lesson: we were missing a major aspect of the stigma that impacts victims and survivors of abuse. When asked about the stigma that survivors experienced, we heard time and time again that one of the most significant sources of stigma was their perpetrators. Survivors told us that their perpetrators stigmatized them in a variety of ways and that this stigma from their perpetrators reinforced the stigma they encountered from other sources, as we will explore in the following chapters.

In this chapter, we delve into the tactics that perpetrators of abuse use to demean and control their partners. We'll also explore how emotional abuse tactics overlap with stigma and intimate partner violence, as well as how stigma helps perpetrators escape accountability for their abusive behaviors. The chapter concludes with a discussion of the unique challenges that victims and survivors face due to the stigma that perpetrators perpetuate. To set the stage for this chapter, let's begin by looking at five stories of survivors who participated in our research. Each of these stories provides a unique glimpse into the ways that perpetrators can perpetuate stigma through their abusive behaviors and their interactions with the community around them.

Katrina: Katrina was in a long-term marriage that was physically and emotionally abusive. Her ex-husband, Stephan, had manipulated and isolated Katrina, in addition to convincing her that her unhappiness in their marriage was because, as he told her, she was an unhappy person who could not be thankful for what she had in their marriage. Stephan even blamed Katrina for his infidelity and his abusive behaviors. She told us that he would say things like, "Because of you, I committed adultery. Because of you, you provoked me to throw you up against the wall." Stephan also was very skilled at hiding and deceiving so that others in their lives, such as their friends and family, had no idea that the abuse was happening. Beyond their immediate social support network, Stephan would manipulate and lie to various professionals. Katrina said,

> "I've had counselors deceived, because they didn't really see enough of my husband's character to realize what he was doing to them, to manipulate them and their perceptions of me. And then, how he manipulated the conversation. Even with me there, he planted seeds of doubt and speculation. I've seen it with judges. I've seen it with attorneys. I've seen it with police officers when I've had to use police to take their side. It was the 'good old boy' situation, and they'd believe the accusation that my husband made, even when I had plain, hard evidence."

Charlotte: Charlotte is a young, well-educated woman who was married to a man whom she described as unpredictable, irrational, and illogical. Charlotte's ex-husband, Troy, isolated her, controlled her money, constantly blamed her, and would lie and manipulate her. When Charlotte described Troy's abuse, she explained that most, if not all, people in their lives were fooled by him and that nobody really knew who he was except for her. Troy's abuse was extremely demeaning to Charlotte, including one time when he urinated on her.

Kendra: Kendra was in a relationship with Jim, an older man who was viewed by many as an upstanding member of their small community. Their relationship was very emotionally abusive, and Kendra tried to leave Jim many times, but each time he would win her back because he was very manipulative. He also was very controlling and isolating. Kendra shared with us that Jim created a façade in the community. He was well respected in their small town, where "everyone knows everyone," so nobody would ever suspect that he would be abusive. Kendra speculated that people either denied or just didn't want to know what Jim was really like: "As an upstanding member of the community, people just don't want to know." Jim's status in the community complicated her experiences when Kendra left the relationship. She said,

> "If you're the one who gets out of a relationship that's abusive in any way, people look down on you for being in it. They also, at the same time, don't want to know that the person is not an upstanding person, but that the person's actually a scumbag and a crazy jerk. It's just a yucky thing to have been in a bad relationship and have people think that your abusive ex-partner is nice. I don't want to wear a

T-shirt that says, 'He's a jerk,' but at the same time, I would just like a little respect for having been through something that feels as horrific as 'World War Three.' It's crazy. As a society, we fail to support women who have been through anything like this."

Trina: As Trina will tell you, perpetrators can continue to abuse long after the actual relationship ends, especially if one's abuser is intent on using systems to continue to hold control over the survivor. Trina was married to Matt for over a decade, and they had two children together. After the relationship ended, Trina said, "I left and attempted to get protective orders, without success. He is more abusive now than he was during the relationship. He continues to use the family courts to punish and shame me at least once a year." Matt uses the family court processes to manipulate her and control how others perceive her. She said, "Matt has been very public in shaming me, name-calling me, and forcing people—even third-party providers like schools—to choose between us. Because he has more money, he can be seen as being more stable." Trina reported that, immediately after their relationship ended, Matt began to tell people and institutions (their church, for example) that she was crazy and that she hated them in an effort to exclude her from every possible group that they belonged to when they were married. He continues to tell the schools, therapists, and court representatives that Trina is causing the conflict because she is trying to get back at him. All of this public drama surrounding Trina's divorce from Matt has had serious consequences for her. She said, "I have, on several occasions, been turned down for jobs and contracts because of the public nature of my divorce and his shaming of me in public."

Jackie: Jackie was about 20 years old when she began dating Anthony. Jackie had been shy in high school, but she blossomed during college. She said, "It could almost be compared to the image of an ugly duckling and a swan. Boys started noticing me, but I was intrigued by Anthony because, although I knew he was interested in me, he was not aggressive like the others." At least, not at first. Jackie went on to say,

> "We started dating, and he was the perfect gentleman at first, until he had the green light to start mentally re-wiring me and gradually easing into physical abuse. Each time I was abused, he would apologize after and say something along the lines of, 'I'm so sorry. I didn't mean to hurt you. It's just that, when you do X, it really makes me mad, and you should know that by now.' I was blamed for everything and believed it was my fault, that I was so difficult that I could actually push someone to beat me. I no longer had the renewed self-confidence I had built in college. I was not only torn down, but further demolished until I was just a shell. I was a human punching bag with nothing inside."

Anthony also made it harder for Jackie to reach out for the help she so desperately needed.

> "Part of the mental process was isolating me from family and friends, so that when the physical abuse did start, who was I to confide in? The people I had coldly pushed away to spend more time with my new love?"

Abusers' Tactics and Stigma

In reading the stories of how Stephan, Troy, Jim, Matt, and Anthony abused Katrina, Charlotte, Kendra, Trina, and Jackie, did you notice the various ways that their tactics reflected the dynamics of stigma that we discussed in the last chapter? As we discussed in Chapter 2, there are four main components of stigma: blame, isolation, negative emotions, and loss of status. These components played out in different ways for these survivors. For example, consider how Anthony told Jackie he only hurt her because of what she did, or how Stephan blamed Katrina for his abusive behaviors and infidelity. Or, think about how Troy, Jim, and Anthony isolated Charlotte, Kendra, and Trina, and how this led to the women feeling trapped and alone in their relationships. Stephan played upon Katrina's negative emotions by suggesting that any problems she experienced in their relationship were simply because she was unhappy with her life. And loss of status appeared in different ways, from Matt manipulating systems to continue to control Trina long after their relationship ended, to the demeaning act of Troy urinating on Charlotte.

One of the major assumptions that underlie all of our work is that perpetrators are 100% responsible for their own behaviors. Certainly, we need to look to choices that victims and survivors can make to promote their own safety—as is done in the widely used safety planning processes in the context of intimate partner violence.[1] However, we take a clear stance that there simply is nothing that one person can do to provoke or cause another person to abuse or otherwise harm another person. We are not talking about self-defense here—we are referring specifically to violent or abusive behaviors that one person initiates against someone else, especially within the context of the power and control dynamics we discussed in Chapter 1. Therefore, although victim-blaming attitudes are common in society, among perpetrators of abuse, and often even internalized by victims and survivors themselves, we must always place the full responsibility for abuse perpetration squarely on the shoulders of the perpetrator.

In this section, we'll take a closer look at the various ways that perpetrators abuse their partners. Again, a common element that underlies all abusive behaviors is an effort to hold power over and control one's partner. There are many reasons that a perpetrator may seek to have this control, and research on intimate partner violence perpetrators suggests that there are different types of perpetrators with different motivations for their abuse. We explain these next.

There is a growing body of research that demonstrates that there are different categories of intimate partner violence perpetrators. For example, researchers Neil Jacobson and John Gottman[2] identified two main types of battering perpetrators, and they identified some fascinating differences between these two groups. The perpetrators in the first group, which they called the Type 1 group or the *Cobras*—who demonstrated more emotional abuse, anger, and sadness—were more likely to be violent outside of intimate relationships (e.g., they were more likely to engage in violent behaviors across a variety of settings), more likely to have witnessed violence in their families when they were children, and had more characteristics of antisocial personality disorder and higher rates of substance dependence. The perpetrators in the second group, Type 2 or the *Pit Bulls*, were more likely to restrict their use of violence to within intimate relationships, and they also demonstrated lower levels of personality disorder characteristics and substance dependence. One of the most intriguing differences they found between these groups was how they responded to marital conflict: when they were engaged in conflict with their partners, the Pit Bulls responded in the more typical way, in that they were physiologically aroused, such as with a higher heart rate. In contrast, the Cobras actually seemed to calm down physiologically during conflict, which suggests that some perpetrators actually become calm and at ease when they are engaged in aggressive, violent behaviors. It's important to note that there have been mixed findings on this typology since the original research by Jacobson and Gottman was conducted,[3] but their findings overall were instrumental in highlighting that we can't view abuse perpetrators in a "one-size-fits-all" manner.

Another research team, led by Amy Holtzworth-Munroe, a professor of psychology at Indiana University, also has identified different types of battering perpetrators.[4] Research from this group identified three categories of perpetrators based on three main dimensions: how severe the violence is, whether the violence is generalized or used only in the context of intimate relationships, and whether the perpetrator demonstrates characteristics of mental health and/or personality disorders. The first category of perpetrators they identified was labeled the *Generally Violent/Antisocial* group. This group has the highest levels of violence, both within their families and in other settings; they often have a criminal history and abuse substances, and they also demonstrate higher levels of psychopathology and/or antisocial personality disorder. The second category they identified is called the *Dysphoric/Borderline* group. This group, on average, perpetrates violence that is moderately severe and mostly occurs within their relationships, but they may have demonstrated some violence in other settings as well. They also show high levels of mental health distress, including sometimes meeting the criteria for borderline personality disorder. One of their key characteristics is being highly dependent on their partners. The third group was labeled by the researchers as the *Family Only* group, and this group overall is most likely to be violent only in the context of intimate relationships and generally have higher levels of functioning than the other groups. However, they show poor abilities to communicate with their partners and less ability to manage conflict, so conflicts can escalate into violence. Within the research by Holtzworth-Munroe's team, about half of perpetrators were from the Family Only group, and about one-quarter each were from the Generally Violent/Antisocial and the Dysphoric/Borderline groups.

The research we just described is significant for illustrating the potential differences among abuse perpetrators. It is clear that all perpetrators don't look or act the same. Even with these different categories of perpetrators that researchers have identified, it's important to remember that it's much easier to identify differences in large groups of research study samples than it is to pinpoint exactly what type a specific person is. It's common for individual people to have characteristics that could be a mix of different categories. And current practices in the field of batterer intervention have still not fully adapted to these research findings, and often interventions in local communities use the same strategies for all perpetrators. Even still, these research findings call our attention to an important truth about intimate partner violence—perpetration often looks different across different relationships and different people.

This truth has been evident in our research as well. Based on the stories of the survivors in our studies, we've seen that some perpetrators abuse because they are cold, calculating, and manipulative, sometimes even to the point of being sociopathic. Other perpetrators may not consciously seek the control over their partners in a calculating, intentional way, but rather they are driven by their own insecurities and psychological needs that they fail to either recognize or manage in appropriate ways. Some perpetrators engage in abusive behaviors because they've been socialized to believe that it is acceptable to use violent behaviors, such as because they witnessed it in their homes growing up or because they heard messages about the acceptability of violence in their cultural or religious communities. Still others abuse simply because it works for them—they receive benefits from it (e.g., a feeling of power or the submission of their partners to their needs) and experience few punishments or deterrents.

We're certain there are many other reasons why perpetrators choose to engage in abusive behaviors. To some extent, these reasons do matter for the purpose of determining the most effective strategies for deterring abusive behaviors and intervention strategies for holding offenders accountable, as we will discuss in Chapter 7. However, we urge readers, and especially those who are currently involved in an abusive relationship or helping to support someone who is being abused, to not get too caught up in trying to figure out *why* that particular abusive partner is doing what he or she is doing. Rather, it is much more important to focus on the actual abusive behaviors and not the intention behind them, especially as it is occurring. Indeed, we've seen in many survivors' stories that the extensive time they spent trying to understand their perpetrators' behaviors prolonged the time they spent in their abusive relationships, thus further putting their safety and well-being at risk. The bottom line is this: abuse is abuse, regardless of the reason behind it. And perpetrators must be held accountable for their behaviors and held responsible for the abuse that they perpetrate.

To be better equipped to hold offenders accountable, as we'll discuss in Chapter 7, we need to better understand how they operate. Of course, every perpetrator is unique, so we must always remember that abuse can look very different across different relationships. If you're currently trying to figure out if someone you know is being abusive—either to you or someone else—and that person's behaviors don't look exactly like the examples provided in this book, that doesn't necessarily mean that you're not seeing abuse. If you're in this situation, take a step back from the specific behaviors and consider the following questions:

- Does this person's partner seem afraid or fearful?
- Does the suspected perpetrator seem to need to control his or her partner?
- Is the suspected perpetrator extremely jealous or possessive about his or her partner?
- Does the suspected perpetrator limit his or her partner's freedom to make decisions for himself or herself?
- If the suspected perpetrator treats his or her partner in potentially abusive ways (e.g., saying or doing potentially hurtful things), does that person fail to accept full responsibility for those behaviors?

If the answer to any of the these questions is yes, then it is likely that you're dealing with a person who is perpetrating abuse, even if the behaviors you're seeing don't necessarily align with the specific abusive behaviors that are described in this chapter. If you do suspect that you or someone you know are involved in an abusive relationship, we encourage you to seek help, either from a trained professional in your community or a national hotline, so you can further understand the possible safety risks and determine what steps can be taken to promote the safety of everyone involved. In the United States, the National Domestic Violence Hotline can be reached at 1-800-799-7233 or TTY 1-800-787-3224 as well as at their website: www.thehotline.org. The examples we present in this book demonstrate the diversity of forms that abuse can take, but ultimately, any form of abuse serves to hurt and oppress the victim and should be taken seriously.

Perpetrators' Tactics of Abuse

To better understand how perpetrators operate, we'll focus in this section on some of the general tactics that they use to demean and control their partners. In the next section, we'll explore how these tactics intersect with stigma to further add to the challenges and complications that victims and survivors may face. In Chapter 1, we talked about the dynamics of abuse, and in this chapter, we'll take a deeper look to see how abuse is experienced through the words of survivors themselves, especially in how they view their perpetrators' abusive actions.

People who haven't experienced an abusive relationship often ask the question, "Why do people stay in an abusive relationship?" This certainly is a challenging question to answer, but we suggest that this isn't the best question to ask in the first place. In particular, the question of "why people stay" implies that blame for the relationship lasting lies with the victim of abuse. Instead of asking that question, we suggest another question is much more important to consider: "How do perpetrators trap their partners into abusive relationships?" Of course, there are a range of abusive behaviors that can be used for this purpose, and victims can be trapped in abusive relationships both physically—such as if their perpetrators lock them into the house—and psychologically—by instilling fear of the harms that will come to them if they leave. We've heard from the survivors who participated in our research that there are some common tactics that perpetrators use to entrap their partners into staying in their abusive relationships, often long after the victims would want to be in the relationship. These tactics include control tactics, isolation, verbal denigration, and humiliation. Each of these tactics also exacerbates the stigma that victims experience from many sources, especially as abusers add more stigmatizing components to the mix, such as blame and manipulation of others around them. The end result can be the complete instillment of hopelessness, mixed with fear, and leading to a sense of entrapment and having no other options. Let's take a closer look at these tactics.

Control Tactics

We've discussed already how intimate partner violence occurs in the context of underlying power and control dynamics, through which the perpetrator uses the abusive behaviors to gain and maintain control over the victim. And while we know that this is the case, it still can be shocking to see the depths of the extent to which perpetrators often go to achieve total domination over their victims' lives. This control can become so pervasive that victims virtually lose any and all control over their ability to direct their own lives. For example, one survivor who participated in our research said, "To an extent, he controlled everything. He was the

MAN of the household, and I was just the 'woman,' and he treated me like that in front of everyone he invited to the house." Another survivor told us,

> "He controlled everything and did what he wanted to do, no need to discuss it with me. I couldn't do anything without discussing it with him. He made the money, wouldn't allow me to work. I had to ask before I spent anything, while he spent freely. I never won an argument because he would dominate with intimidation. I would always just agree with him because disagreeing would cause abuse. I became subservient."

Perpetrators use a variety of tactics to exert this control. For example, they may limit their victim's access to resources, such as the following quote from a survivor whose former abuser even restricted her access to her own home: "Once, when we were fighting, I left. I came back and he had locked me outside. I had to sleep on the porch." Another survivor spoke of how her former perpetrator limited her access to transportation and took away her possessions: "He took away my car, refused to let me see my family, took away my wedding ring." In recent years, perpetrators have increasingly used technology to monitor and control their victims, as is reflected in the following quotes from our research participants: (1) "I wasn't allowed to keep my phone locked. He told me if I told anyone what he did, he would kill me. He'd take my checks and spend them." (2) "He didn't like me using the computer, especially the Internet." And (3) "He took away a lot of my power by keeping an eye on my phone and on my computer." One of the main reasons perpetrators take control over their victims' technology usage is to limit their contact with their social network as well as their ability to access information that could help them become safe.

Perpetrators can also control their victims' ability to make decisions for themselves. For example, one survivor said, "All my decisions were filtered through what my husband wanted. This left me powerless to do what I wanted or what I thought was best." Another said, "He took my family from me, friends that I had had for years. He said I wasn't allowed to talk to them. I wasn't allowed to do anything he didn't want me to." Still another survivor shared with us that she "was not able to talk to friends or write in a journal. My abuser monitored everything."

Take a moment to reflect upon the depths of control that perpetrators exert over their victims. Virtually all of the survivors in our research live in countries in which they are legally granted personal freedom and have the right to make decisions for their own lives. We are left to wonder how perpetrators come to learn that they have the right to limit the freedom of another person in the way that they limit the freedom of their victims. Furthermore, we are certain that perpetrators would not tolerate if anyone else tried to control them in the way that they control their partners. Nonetheless, by restricting their freedoms, access to resources, and ability to make decisions for themselves, perpetrators further their control over their victims' lives, often rendering it extremely difficult for victims to leave the relationship, even if they wanted to do so.

Isolation

Another form of control is exerted when perpetrators limit their victims' ability to stay connected with others around them. Isolation is a common tactic used by perpetrators of abuse. We heard about this isolation from many of the survivors who have shared their stories with us, and their perpetrators used a variety of strategies to isolate them from others in their lives. For one survivor, this took the form of her perpetrator convincing her that her friends and family members weren't supportive of her:

> "He isolated me from my family and continued to tell me that they were jealous of me and that they want what I have. I lost my friends when he kept telling me that my friends and family were jealous of me."

Another survivor became isolated because the abuse she was experiencing led her to feel disconnected from others: "I did not understand my own feelings or how to deal with what I was experiencing. I was unhappy but couldn't really understand why, which made it difficult to connect with other people."

Some perpetrators isolate their victims by insisting that they are not allowed to socialize with others in the absence of the perpetrator. Consider the following quotes from survivors who participated in our research: (1) "He tried separating me from my friends and family and was possessive and always wanted me to have to be with him. I had to lie to him and tell him I wasn't feeling well in order to hang out with my friends separate from him." (2) "I couldn't go eat with a friend unless it was when he was at work. And that was early in the morning for about 5 hours. He made it difficult for me to do anything without him. I was separated from everyone and to keep things as easy as possible for me, I avoided doing things with others." (3) "I wasn't in his eyes allowed to be just me; it had to be me and him. My friends that didn't like him pushed me away a little because he always was a leech everywhere I went." (4) "He wouldn't trust me to go out with my friends alone (male or female). I started staying inside almost all the time. I would only leave the house to go to work." (5) "I separated myself from my family and friends from fear he would get jealous or they would notice something was wrong. I never was allowed to go out socially with my friends unless it was with him." For these survivors, their former perpetrators virtually did not let them out of their sight in a way that would allow them to have meaningful relationships with other people outside of the relationship.

Beyond requiring victims to only socialize in their presence, some perpetrators exert other restrictions that further isolate the victims within the relationship. Read the following examples of ways that survivors describe the restrictions they faced: (1) "I was not permitted around my friends or family. I wasn't allowed to have friends." (2) "He kept me from my family." (3) "He didn't allow me to have friendships or spend time with family. He kept me at home, except for work or his dysfunctional family parties." (4) "My abuser would not allow me to have friends or close family contact. I was not allowed to talk to them on the phone or go meet them unless he was with me, therefore making it hard to hold on to friends and family." (5) "He would control me by telling me who to be friends with. He hated when I would call my parents, thinking I was telling them about what was going on. But, I never told my mom until recently, and my dad doesn't know." (6) "My ex would not allow me to contact my family and was insanely jealous of any friends I had, so I became very isolated. My parents didn't know about the violence or abuse until my mom came to visit about two years before I left the relationship."

By refusing to allow victims to have contact with the important people in their lives, perpetrators limit the support that victims have, which makes it all that much more difficult for victims to feel that they would have support to seek safety.

It may seem difficult to grasp how perpetrators can "require" isolation and disallow contact with friends and family. After all, presumably both people in the relationship are adults, so it's natural to wonder how perpetrators could make rules and hold such power over their victims. However, perpetrators can be very intentional in their efforts to isolate their victims. For example, some perpetrators literally remove victims' resources for communicating with others, as was the case for one survivor who said, "He would isolate me from friends and family. He used to pull the telephone out of the wall. Or, he would move me away to where I did not know anyone." Similarly, another survivor said,

> "He put a phone in, just to have it turned off after a month. He would not let me check the mail. He would not take me to see his family (my family lived far away). He disconnected my computer so that I could not keep in touch with my family."

Still another said, "He monitored my phone calls." Other perpetrators isolate their victims by limiting their access to transportation or ability to work outside the home, as is reflected in the following quotes: (1) "He kept me isolated by not letting me drive or have a job. We lived away from my family." (2) "He kept me isolated from my family and his family by getting a car with a stick shift that I could not drive. He did not want me to be near his family or his friends or his coworkers." (3) "I was not allowed friends. I had to check in when I went to buy groceries. I was constantly reminded I had no friends and was told to stay home when he took our children out. My car keys were hidden when I was told to stay home."

What is the end effect of perpetrators' efforts to isolate their victims? Ultimately, this can result in victims becoming completely alone within their relationships as well as disconnected from any other social support outside of the relationship. For example, one survivor said,

> "I became separated from everything, just because that was the easiest way to avoid confrontation. If he had a problem with something my parents said, he would force me to confront them even though I agreed with my parents. I avoided contact with everyone."

Another shared with us that "the abuse and control made me not want to do anything with anybody. His control prevented me from doing things without him for the most part." When perpetrators isolate their victims, they increase their own level of influence. When victims are cut off from contact with others, they lack access to other people who could potentially help them recognize how unsafe the abuse they are experiencing is. Thus isolation becomes extremely dangerous for victims, especially when compounded with other strategies that perpetrators use to break down victims' self-esteem, such as verbal denigration and humiliation, which are discussed in the next two sections.

Verbal Denigration

Perpetrators often engage in a pattern of verbal abuse that can eventually tear down any positive sense of self-worth that victims may once have had. When we look at abusive relationships from the outside, it's hard to understand how victims can "allow" perpetrators to speak to them in demeaning ways. But let's look at this abuse tactic in greater depth. First, remember that abusers typically don't show their true colors right away at the start of the relationship. In fact, in the early days of the relationship, perpetrators may be extremely flattering and speak positively toward their partners. Negative comments may start small, and in the beginning, they may be offered under the guise of constructive feedback, which of course is something that occurs in healthy, nonviolent relationships as well. However, when perpetrators of abuse use verbal insults to denigrate their partners, they often play upon their victims' insecurities, or those areas where they are vulnerable and may doubt themselves already. For example, consider the following experiences of one of the survivors in our research:

> "He used my self-consciousness against me in regards to my weight, talent, work ethic, and my intelligence. I have always been a very powerful type of person, in a good way, and have always prided myself on having total control over my own brain and heart, and he broke this down in me to where I felt powerless one of the few times in my life. I was one of the most talented people in my program at college, and he constantly pitted me up against this other person who had just come into the school and purposely compared me to him, saying he was better than I was. He made me feel inferior on purpose."

Another survivor said, "He made me feel shameful about my weight and intelligence while we were together. When we finally split, I felt ashamed that I allowed him to break me down like he did." And yet another survivor said, "I was constantly called a fat loser, a no-hoper, a pathetic mother, a sad excuse for a woman, pathetic in bed, that I have no friends, and then labeled an unsociable bitch." Most people—even people with generally positive self-esteem overall—have some aspects of their lives about which they have some level of insecurity. The difference for victims in abusive relationships is that, rather than support them and help them feel better about themselves, their abusive partners exploit those vulnerabilities to further their control over them.

The verbal denigration tactics that perpetrators use can relate to many aspects of their relationships and their victims' lives. For example, perpetrators may criticize their victims' opinions that differ from their own (e.g., "He would belittle and use violence if I had an opinion on something or if I didn't agree with him."). They also can use verbally abusive behaviors that reflect discrimination based on some characteristics of their victims, such as the following two quotes from participants in our research: "He discriminated against me of my race (we were an interracial couple). He would call me derogatory names. He would embarrass me in public, especially when he was in an alcoholic rage. He always made me cry every birthday." And,

> "He started discriminating against me when he found out that I was bisexual (he found out by reading through my online history). He also would shame, label, and stereotype me because of this. He said that all bisexuals were 'sluts' and 'whores' and could never be satisfied with just one partner. He lost a lot of respect for me, he said."

Finally, perpetrators can use verbal denigration to make their victims doubt their overall value and worth. As one survivor said, "He was always telling me he was the only one who would ever love me and I was worthless." Another said,

> "I felt powerless in the relationship, as he was bigger than me, and I wasn't allowed to work a job for the majority of the marriage. He would make statements like 'You are nothing without me,' and 'You will never survive in this world without me.' I believed him."

Humiliation

Beyond verbal denigration, perpetrators often use a variety of behaviors that devalue their victims, thus rendering them virtual second-class citizens within the relationship. Humiliation is a very powerful control tactic that abuse perpetrators use against their victims. Let's take a look at several examples of this tactic that we heard from survivors in our research:

- "He was emotionally abusive, psychologically abusive, and sexually abusive. With his words and actions, he made me feel worthless. He also took advantage of me sexually. He lied to me about his entire identity and took advantage of my vulnerability. He drained me of everything I once was."
- "I felt I could never do anything right, so I was always getting in trouble."
- "I had to bribe him or have sex with him to go anywhere I wanted to go."
- "I had no status. I was just his maid/caretaker/cook/accountant/housekeeper/nurse, etc. He would not allow me to work, and when other people asked what I did, he would tell them, 'She doesn't do shit.' I did everything that needed to be done but go to work and make money. I was his slave."
- "I was told I was nothing more than a speck of dirt under his shoe. We were military, and he was 'important,' and I wasn't, so everything was kept a secret. I was constantly called horrible names."
- "He constantly called me ugly and fat after I had our daughter and would force me to go on diets and weigh myself in front of him and prove I went to the gym daily. He told me he was going to find someone younger, prettier, and thinner than me. He would make me clean up his mess after he masturbated and said if I wasn't so fat, he would have sex with me, and I wouldn't have to clean up afterwards. He is a powerful professional and always said he would do anything to make sure I got nothing and that he would make everyone believe I was crazy. I could go on for hours."
- "I was bowing down to his demands just to keep the peace and doing what I was told, even when things were against my own morals."

Each of the examples demonstrates how abuse perpetrators can devalue their victims, even to the extent to which some victims come to feel that they are in servitude to their perpetrators. By repeatedly treating their victims as though they are worthless, perpetrators humiliate and belittle their partners until they are left with little sense of self-worth. This form of treatment is especially harmful, because an intimate partner is supposed to be someone who a person can love and trust. In abusive relationships, however, perpetrators exploit this love and trust and use humiliation to solidify their power.

The Overlaps Between Perpetrator Stigma and Emotional Abuse

Together, the aforementioned tactics—control tactics, isolation, verbal denigration, and humiliation—combine to form a powerful force that perpetrators hold over their victims. As we've learned more about these abuse tactics through our research on the stigma surrounding intimate partner violence, we have been struck by the overlaps between the dynamics of emotional abuse and the components of stigma. Although these overlaps somewhat complicate our research in that it becomes very difficult to tease apart all of the various influences on victims' and survivors' experiences, we embrace this complexity because it helps us to better understand how stigma is compounded by the direct effects of the abuse. Stigma and emotional abuse combine to create a bidirectional, synergistic effect that magnifies the challenges that victims and survivors face. First, perpetrators' abusive tactics are so powerful because they are reinforced by the stigma that victims and survivors encounter from other sources, including friends and family members, professionals, and society. Second, the stigma that surrounds intimate partner violence in the larger society plays out between the perpetrator and victim in the microcosm of their relationship. In a sense, the existence of the stigma surrounding intimate partner violence grants the perpetrator permission to act in abusive ways because perpetrators learn that they won't be held accountable for their actions and that victims and survivors are devalued by societal stereotypes about them. We'll look more closely at the accountability of perpetrators in society later in this chapter, but before that, let's turn our attention to three of the ways that perpetrators' abuse tactics intersect with the broader stigma surrounding intimate partner violence: victim-blaming, "crazy-making," and blocking access to potentially helpful resources.

Victim-Blaming

Blaming victims of intimate partner violence for the abuse they experience is one of the major components of stigma, and you'll see throughout this book how that blame can come from many different sources, including friends and family members, cultural messages, professionals, and the media. However, perhaps the most direct source of blame for the abuse comes from perpetrators themselves. As you'll see from the following survivors' quotes, perpetrators can blame victims for virtually any number of hurtful, abusive behaviors:

- "I was always the one blamed for anything that happened. Any fights or arguments always stemmed from something that I did."
- "My abuser always told me that if I had been a better mother, wife, and/or housekeeper, then he would not hurt me, therefore placing the blame on me."
- "He blamed me for hitting me because of my past. I had to maintain everything a secret in fear he would get upset and it would start a fight."
- "He blamed me for everything. It was always my fault."
- "My husband always blamed me. Every time he abused me, he said if I would try harder, if I wouldn't push him, if I would just let him walk away. . . ."
- "My ex would blame me for his behavior."
- "He would blame me for the issues in our lives. He wouldn't care if I was bruised up. He'd say I deserved it."
- "I took the blame for everything he did. It was my fault he cheated because he said I was fat and ugly."
- "It was my fault he didn't achieve his goals. I was a bad influence over him."
- "I was blamed for everything, from something not working right in the house to him having a bad day at work."
- "I blamed myself for being part of a relationship that I recognized as unhealthy and dangerous. It was also frequently communicated by my partner that I would not experience the negative consequences I was experiencing if I were 'more . . .' or if I 'stopped. . . .'"
- "My ex always said it was my fault he got so angry."
- "I was blamed by husband for his abusive behavior and his affairs. He made me believe that if I was 'better' in some way, he would treat me better."
- "He blamed me for cheating and said if I did what I was supposed to do at home, he wouldn't have to cheat on me. But I did EVERYTHING, even kissed his butt to keep him home."

Perpetrators' blaming their victims for abuse is problematic on its own, as it absolves perpetrators from taking any responsibility for their actions and therefore further perpetuates the abuse. However, this blame becomes even more problematic and dangerous for victims when it is compounded by the blame that they experience from other sources. For example, consider victims who have heard repeatedly from their perpetrators that the abuse is their fault, and they deserve it. However, there still is a part of them that knows the abuse is wrong, so they decide to seek help from a friend, family member, or professional. However, upon disclosing the abuse to someone else, they hear more messages that they are somehow responsible for the abuse. When the blame is reinforced from multiple sources, these victims may eventually become resigned to the belief that the abuse must actually be their fault and that they somehow deserve it. Resigned to this belief, they can give up hope that they deserve a safer, better future. Therefore, blame from perpetrators can combine with blame from other sources to magnify the stigma that victims and survivors face.

"Crazy-Making"

The humiliating and devaluing ways that perpetrators treat victims can result in victims coming to feel that they are crazy. Now, it's important to note that victims of abuse are not "crazy" or "unstable," as some common stereotypes in society would suggest. However, perpetrators often manipulate their victims—as well as other people in their lives—into believing this. In some cases, perpetrators play on victims' weaknesses and exaggerate them to make the victims believe that they are deeply imperfect. For example, one survivor said, "He played on my flaws and the fact that my family only knows love in a conditional sense and when it's convenient to them. Also, he made me feel insecure about my religious beliefs, saying I was crazy." Another survivor shared with us that, "He had me convinced there was something wrong with me and it was my fault. Also, his friends never seemed to think anything was wrong, which made me question what I was feeling: Was I just being 'over emotional?'"

This "crazy-making" tactic can move outside of the relationship if the abuser goes beyond just trying to convince the victim that he or she is crazy, to also trying to convince others that this is the case. We heard this from several survivors, including in the following three statements: (1) "I have been stereotyped per his rumors as crazy, manipulative, controlling, a home wrecker, and an evil woman who tried to destroy a charismatic, well-respected community leader. Many people will only hear his version. I have PTSD because of the relationship." (2) "I was labeled as crazy/unstable by my abuser publicly. He made threats to 'take care of' me and my family if I reveal secrets or protest." (3) "I was labeled crazy, a bitch, lazy, an unfit mother. He would have meetings about me with his family and not tell me, and he would do things and make decisions without my knowledge." Similar to what we saw earlier related to victim-blaming, this "crazy-making" strategy involves an intersection of abuse dynamics with stigma—because of their devalued status in society, victims may be more prone to being viewed as "crazy" or unstable by others.

Blocking Access to Potentially Helpful Resources

The intersections of abuse dynamics and stigma also can be seen when perpetrators intentionally work to convince victims that nobody else will help or believe them if they seek help. Earlier in this chapter, we discussed how some perpetrators use abuse only in the context of intimate relationships, and using a positive reputation in the community is one way that perpetrators convince victims that they will not be believed or helped if they tell anyone how the perpetrator is treating them. For example, one survivor told us,

> "I didn't dare tell anyone else the extent of my husband's meanness. He put on a very polite, sophisticated, snobbish persona in public. I didn't think anyone would believe me if I tried to convey what he was like to live with."

Another survivor said,

> "Because of the persona that my ex presented to the outside world (all-around good guy) and the persona he now presents as victim, many people looked at me as if the marital breakdown was all my fault, and the fact that he is having to pay me support as shameful. One 'friend' even said to me when I told her my ex and I were no longer together, 'That's too bad, he was such a nice guy.' That hurt. Victimization doesn't end when a relationship ends. Just like a major earthquake, there are many aftershocks even years after."

Perpetrators can present a very different side of themselves to the outside world, as reflected in the following statement from another survivor: "His personality would also change if family or friends visited."

To carry this dynamic even further, some perpetrators actively work to turn others against their victims. As one survivor said, "My reputation was completely destroyed by his lies." Another survivor stated, "He is so good at making everybody believe that I am the evil, manipulative one." This dynamic may include friends and family, such as in the following three cases: (1) "I was isolated from family and friends. There was a huge fight that preceded every occasion and/or family friend visit, which would be my fault. Because my family loved him, what he did physically, emotionally, or sexually was not true. He was a good Christian man. I must have done something to provoke him." (2) "My husband attempted to separate me from family, or to get family members to take his side against me. All of the lies my husband told worked because he asked people not to share with anyone else what he was saying. He kept people apart from each other. His family is very secretive in part because they are ashamed by the truth of what he is (a freeloading, lying deadbeat), and so they pretend or don't talk about reality." (3) "I faced primarily verbal and mental abuse from my partner, such as making things up that didn't happen to try to make me feel crazy; telling me our friends hated me and my family hated me. He continues to send me verbally abusive emails, calling me names, threatening to take my child, telling me that I am unsuccessful and a bad mother, unable to provide for my child and unable to be stable. This continues because we have a child together, and I am committed to having contact with him because of that (I'm legally bound to), but the abusive contact continues weekly under the guise of contacting me about our child."

By turning others against their victims, perpetrators can cut off potentially helpful resources that could prove useful for promoting their safety. This can become a "he said/she said" type of dynamic, and people who haven't witnessed how perpetrators have treated their victims may be prone to believe the perpetrators, especially if they create convincing lies that turn them against the victims. For example, one survivor shared the following experience with us:

> "I was unaware that my abuser had conducted (and still is conducting) a very large smear campaign. He has blamed me for the kids not speaking to him. Several people have believed him. People have shunned me now because they think I won't let the kids see him."

By manipulating others in this way, perpetrators take advantage of the stigma surrounding abuse, and they extend the control they have established within the relationship to the broader social network surrounding the victim. Furthermore, this tactic makes it more likely that perpetrators will avoid accepting responsibility for their own abusive actions.

Why Perpetrators Often Escape Accountability for Their Abusive Actions

At a societal level, one of the manifestations of the stigma surrounding intimate partner violence is that this issue is not taken seriously or prioritized, and therefore many perpetrators are not held accountable for the abuse they perpetuate. This dynamic plays out at the individual and relational levels in two main ways. First, perpetrators often fail to accept responsibility for themselves. Second, friends, family members, and communities often fail to hold perpetrators accountable. We'll explore each of these dynamics in this section, as they reflect another major intersection between the dynamics of abuse and the stigma that surrounds it.

How Perpetrators Fail to Accept Responsibility for Their Abusive Actions

We discussed earlier how perpetrators often blame their victims for their abuse. This is one of the main ways perpetrators fail to accept responsibility for their abusive words and behaviors. Statements such as the following are commonly expressed by survivors of abuse: "He always said, 'Why do you do these things that make me do this to you?' He always told me it was my fault." In this way, perpetrators make it out to seem as though they were forced to be abusive by some perceived wrong by the victim. Some perpetrators go so far as to fully deny that any abuse even occurred. As one example of this, a survivor who participated in our research said, "We share a child. I have to speak with him on a frequent basis. He does not acknowledge that any abuse occurred." Through deflection and denial, perpetrators are able to avoid placing responsibility where it squarely belongs: on their own shoulders.

It is common for perpetrators to make excuses for their behaviors, and they may force their victims into believing and describing those excuses to others. For example, one survivor shared the following experience with us:

> "Whenever he pushed me, he pushed me hard enough so that I would fall down into things and hurt myself. He always said that was my own fault, and that it wasn't hard enough of a push for anyone to fall over."

This survivor's abuser attempted to manipulate her into believing that her injuries resulted from her own actions rather than on the fact that it was his violence that led her to fall down. In a similar manner, another survivor told us that she "felt ashamed of what he did to me. For example, he punched me in the eye, which left my face and eye swollen and black and he told me to say that I fell over or something ridiculous." By making excuses for the abuse, perpetrators can lead victims to hide from others the abuse they are experiencing.

Another striking finding from our research was that perpetrators may not only blame victims for the abuse, but for a whole host of other problems. For example, one survivor said,

> "I was blamed in every way. I was accused of his drug use, even though I never touch drugs. Accused of his jail term. Accused of taking his kids off him, of ruining our family, for being raped, for him losing his friends, for him losing his business, for everything he did himself."

Another survivor said, "He blamed me for everything when it came to money, the reason why he is losing hair, why we were poor." Yet another survivor said,

> "I was blamed in my relationship every time he got mad. Every time he had a problem with something, which was multiple times a day, the blame would always go to me, somehow. I walked on eggshells every day so as not to upset him. When he abused me, it was my fault, until he calmed down and became sorry."

These survivors' experiences paint the picture of some perpetrators being unable to accept any responsibility or role in any of the negative aspects of their lives. In particular, they deny responsibility for their abusive actions and thereby avoid accepting any level of accountability for changing those behaviors.

How Friends, Family Members, and Communities Can Fail to Hold Perpetrators Accountable

We'll delve more deeply into the issue of stigma when victims and survivors seek help later in this book. In this chapter, we want to highlight briefly how perpetrators can manipulate a variety of social systems to further escape accountability for their abuse and how other people and systems may fail to take action to support people who are being abused and/or how they may protect the perpetrators of the abuse. One of the most powerful ways that people who are aware of an abusive relationship might contribute to the abuse continuing is by remaining silent about it. For example, one survivor shared the following experience with us:

> "Everything was a secret. I had some strange loyalty to him because I feared what he would do if he found out I told someone of his abuse. People saw it but never confronted me about it. I always defended him, even though in my heart I didn't want to and I hated him."

For this survivor, even though other people saw that the abuse was happening, they never spoke up and offered her any support or even acknowledged to her that it was happening.

Being a mutual friend to both partners in a couple in an abusive relationship is undoubtedly a difficult situation, and people may feel uncomfortable choosing sides in that situation. However, when friends in this situation fail to take a stand against the abuse, this further limits the social support available to victims. For example, one survivor said, "Knowing him for over two decades meant that we have many common friends. I had to stay away from them while together with him to protect them from his threats, and after ending things, I stayed away to recover." Some friends in this situation even go so far as to take the side of the perpetrator, especially if that person is using the smear tactics discussed earlier. This dynamic is reflected further in the following statement from a survivor in our research:

> "He had his whole group of friends believing I was a crazy bitch and at fault for everything. He would make fun of me in front of them both to my face and behind my back. He also took a friend of mine with him when he ended our relationship, one of the few I had at the time."

When friends and family members fail to hold perpetrators accountable for their abusive actions, they send a powerful message to the perpetrators that their abuse is acceptable.

This dynamic also can extend to the community level, such as when perpetrators use connections or status in their community to escape responsibility for their actions. One interviewee whose abuser was an attorney said this when she had threatened to tell the police:

> "I did call the police once but then, he was like 'I know all the police,'" and, 'What do you think they're gonna do? Do you think they're gonna come here and believe you? That's the dumbest thing ever.' So the police got there and, you know, I just thought it was a mistake and . . . it was just that once."

When perpetrators believe that their communities will not hold them accountable for their abusive behaviors, they come to feel that, in essence, they have a free pass to act however they want and will not face consequences related to those actions.

Unique Challenges Resulting From Stigma Perpetuated by Perpetrators

In this chapter, we've explored the tactics that perpetrators of intimate partner violence use to control their victims and then how the stigma surrounding intimate partner violence magnifies the end results of these tactics for victims and survivors. To conclude this chapter, we'll share a few examples of the unique challenges that result from this dangerous intersection of abuse and stigma. In particular, we'll focus on the dynamics of fear, the cyclical nature of ongoing stigmatization by abuse perpetrators, and the learned helplessness that may result for victims.

First, there is a critical connection between abuse perpetrators' stigmatizing actions and fear. One of the main reasons why stigma results from the direct actions of perpetrators is that it is interwoven with threats of harm from the abuse, including physical, emotional, and economic harm. It is common for victims of abuse to live in fear of their perpetrators, and this fear is not unfounded. They have experienced the brunt force of their perpetrators' violence and abuse, and they have likely heard threats of harm that may come of them in the future. Two examples from survivors in our research illustrate the compounding influence of fear and stigma. Pay particular attention to the sentences we've italicized. First, one survivor said,

> "His control and abuse created depression in my life. *I was stuck and did not tell anyone about the abuse for fear he would find out and hurt me.* He did not want me to do anything without him, and most

of the time I did not want to do anything with him for various reasons. I stayed isolated because this was the easiest way to keep things running smoothly and to minimize the abuse. I also did not have the energy to do much because daily life was hell."

Second, another survivor shared with us,

"He labeled me as a whore because of my past. *I felt powerless because he threatened to hurt me or take me away from my children.* I felt like I lost my status of who I was because of him. He shamed me for my past and always brought it up when it came to my oldest daughter. I felt like I was the typical stereotype of a woman who lost control and allowed this to continue."

We know that the stigma surrounding intimate partner violence, on its own, has many possible negative impacts on victims of abuse. When compounded with the fear that comes directly from the threats of the perpetrator, the result is an extremely dangerous, isolating experience for victims.

Second, the stigma that perpetrators convey is particularly harmful because it occurs in a repeated, cyclical pattern. Stigmatizing responses from others, such as a friend or professional, may occur on a more short-term, time-limited basis, but abusive dynamics in intimate relationships can occur over a very long period of time. To illustrate this point, we share the following words from a survivor in our research:

"You do not mean anything to the abuser. You may have loved him, but he does not love you. You serve a purpose. You are nothing more than a service provider. You may as well have been their pedicurist, only they'd have treated her better . . . paid and tipped her! These people have a way of creating this huge black chasm between your intellect and your emotions. Your intellect tries in vain to apply logic, rationale, and reason to their abusive, violent, brutal actions and words in order to calm your emotional reaction. You can't find any logic where there isn't any logic, so intellectually and emotionally, you are set up to fail and blame yourself. You are set up to accept responsibility for the guilt, shame, and humiliation, and live in fear of more brutality, degradation, and humiliation to come. You are set up to spend every waking moment trying to be sure everything is 'okay' so this doesn't happen anymore! You are so busy working towards that goal, you don't have time to see anything else. I'm not sure how you learn to overcome those things. I still struggle. Intellectually, I know I did nothing to cause or deserve the abuser's behavior towards me. Intellectually, I know that my reaction to his behavior is what I'd consider normal. I was so hurt and so humiliated, just broken, and I just *knew* if he ever understood how horrible the things he said and did made me feel, he'd be so embarrassed of himself, he'd stop. (You know . . . kind of like a kid who steals a candy bar, and mom makes them go back to the store and suffer the embarrassment of returning it?) He didn't want to know. He didn't care! It took me years to realize this person that you love with every fiber of your being DOESN'T FREAKING CARE ABOUT YOU!!!"

The words of this survivor convey how, over time, the patterns of stigma and abuse can wear down a victim to a point in which she or he becomes a shell of the person she or he once was.

Third, the stigma conveyed by perpetrators is especially challenging to victims because it can lead to a sense of learned helplessness and diminish their hopes for better lives. Many victims feel shame, not just because they may buy into their perpetrators' accusations that they are to blame for the abuse but also because they entered into their relationships in the first place. As examples, consider the following three statements: (1) "I felt self-shame for having entered into a relationship with him at all and for wasting six years that felt like being in a coma/fog." (2) "I was ashamed that I allowed him to abuse me and my children, and I couldn't tell anybody. It was our ugly secret." (3) "My abuser made me ashamed of who I was. He belittled me until I felt ashamed of who I was and what our marriage was. I was also ashamed of the status of our marriage." Sadly, some victims reach such a state of despair that they question whether they want to continue living. The following statement from a survivor reflects this desperation and the further damage that her perpetrator did in response to her misery:

"He always promised he would change; he said sorry after every time he hit me. He called me names, told me I was worthless. I told him I wanted to end my life because I was so miserable. He said, 'I'll give you the knife.' He lied; he didn't let me leave, and he threatened me."

It is a horrible tragedy that anyone would reach such a desperate place, and yet it is understandable when we consider the depth to which victims can feel trapped in their relationships due to the actions of their perpetrators.

Despite the stigma from perpetrators, in addition to the other stigmas and challenges we discuss, there is good news to come later in this book: recovery from abuse, even in the most desperate of situations, is possible, and in fact, it happens every day when victims take steps toward becoming survivors. Even the survivor just quoted, who threatened suicide and was encouraged to end her life by her perpetrator, was able to get out of that relationship and achieve a safe, satisfying life. The details of abusive relationships that were described in this chapter are undoubtedly difficult to read, as they provide a glimpse into the inner workings of abusive relationships and the extent to which perpetrators will go to control and attempt to harm their victims. However, a better understanding of these difficult dynamics helps increase our awareness of the complexity of these relationships, and especially the challenges that victims face at the hands of perpetrators who will go to great lengths to hurt and stigmatize them.

Notes

1 One tool for professionals to assist clients facing intimate partner violence–related safety risks can be found in the *Safety Strategies* resource, which is available for download at www.dvsafetyplanning.org. This resource was created by Christine Murray and her colleagues and presents a format for individualized safety planning.
2 Two resources for learning more about Jacobson and Gottman's work are as follows:
   - Gottman, J.M., Jacobson, N.S., Rushe, R.H., Shortt, J.W., Babcock, J.C., LaTaillade, J.J., & Waltz, J. (1995). The relationship between heart rate reactivity, emotionally aggressive behavior, and general violence in batterers. *Journal of Family Psychology, 9*, 227–248.
   - Jacobson, N., & Gottman, J. (1998). *When men batter women: New insights into ending abusive relationships.* New York: Simon & Schuster.
3 Discussions of these mixed findings can be found in the following sources:
   - Babcock, J.C., Green, C.E., Webb, S.A., & Graham, K.H. (2004). A second failure to replicate the Gottman et al. (1995) typology of men who abuse intimate partners . . . and possible reasons why. *Journal of Family Psychology, 18*, 396–400.
   - Meehan, J.C., & Holtzworth-Munroe, A. (2001). Heart rate reactivity in male batterers: Reply to Gottman (2001) and a second look at the evidence. *Journal of Family Psychology, 15*, 415–424.
   - Meehan, J.C., Holtzworth-Munroe, A., & Herron, K. (2001). Maritally violent men's heart rate reactivity to martial interactions: A failure to replicate the Gottman et al. (1995) typology. *Journal of Family Psychology, 15*, 394–408.
   - Gottman, J.M. (2001). Crime, hostility, wife battering, and the heart: On the Meehan et al. (2001) failure to replicate the Gottman et al. (1995) typology. *Journal of Family Psychology, 15*, 409–414.
4 Citations for Holtzworth-Munroe and colleagues' work include the following:
   - Holtzworth-Munroe, A. (2000). A typology of men who are violent toward their female partners: Making sense of heterogeneity in husband violence. *Current Directions in Psychological Science, 9*, 140–143.
   - Holtzworth-Munroe, A. (2005). Male versus female intimate partner violence: Putting controversial findings into context. *Journal of Marriage and Family, 67*, 1120–1125.
   - Holtzworth-Munroe, A., Bates, L., Smutzler, N., & Sandin, E. (1997). A brief review of the research on husband violence: Part I: Maritally violent versus nonviolent men. *Aggression and Violent Behavior, 2*, 65–99.
   - Holtzworth-Munroe, A., Meehan, J.C., Herron, K., Rehman, U., & Stuart, G.L. (2000). Testing the Holtzworth-Munroe and Stuart (1994) batterer typology. *Journal of Consulting and Clinical Psychology, 68*, 1000–1019.

- Holtzworth-Munroe, A., Meehan, J. C., Herron, K., Rehman, U., & Stuart, G. L. (2003). Do subtypes of martially violent men continue to differ over time? *Journal of Consulting and Clinical Psychology, 4,* 728–740.
- Holtzworth-Munroe, A., Smutzler, N., & Bates, L. (1997). A brief review of the research on husband violence: Part III: Sociodemographic factors, relationship factors, and differing consequences of husband and wife violence. *Aggression and Violent Behavior, 2,* 285–307.
- Holtzworth-Munroe, A., & Stuart, G. L. (1994). Typologies of male batterers: Three subtypes and the differences among them. *Psychological Bulletin, 116,* 476–497.
- Holtzworth-Munroe, A., Smutzler, N., & Sandin, E. (1997). A brief review of the research on husband violence: Part II: The psychological effects of husband violence on battered women and their children. *Aggression and Violent Behavior, 2,* 179–213.

4 Stigma From Within
When Stigma Is Internalized

Shelly is in her mid-20s. A college graduate, she currently works in a job supporting victims of domestic violence, which is especially meaningful work for her since she herself is a survivor of past abusive relationships. Shelly describes the abuse she experienced with an ex-boyfriend as follows:

> "He would make me tell him I loved him. He would start play fighting with me, then hit harder and harder until I begged him to stop. He threw things at me and threatened to push me down stairs if I wouldn't say everything he asked. He had other girlfriends and would flaunt them around me, and if I complained, he would put his hands around my throat and tell me I was his. I was a virgin at the time, and he kept threatening me saying if I didn't 'give it up' he would take it from me."

After that first relationship ended, Shelly had some additional experiences with abusive partners. She said,

> "I was in a relationship where the guy never put his hands on me but would yell all the time and call me a stupid little girl. Sex with him was always rough; he would try to hurt me sometimes or do things I didn't like. He was way bigger than me and would always try to intimidate me with his size. He would insult me if I didn't give him money and bring other women around me a lot. Another guy would always say I wasn't pretty enough and try to dictate what I wore and how I looked. He would hit on other women in front of me and say things like, 'See, if you looked like her or had a butt like hers, I wouldn't hit on her.'"

Shelly's experiences with abuse colored her views about herself in ways that paralleled the stigmatizing responses that she experienced from others. First, she blamed herself for much of the abuse:

> "I felt it was my fault and that for abuse to stop all I had to do was not do things partner didn't like. At the time, I felt if I listened

more that I would get abused less. However, nothing was ever good enough, and abusers would just find new reasons to be angry or put me down."

Second, Shelly felt isolated from friends and family because she kept abuse secret from them and felt she was fighting a war alone. She was afraid to tell people what was going on because she did not want people labeling her as weak or a bad girlfriend. Third, Shelly lost her status as a strong, independent female because she felt that she was allowing a man to talk down to her, hurt her, and make a lot of her decisions for her. Fourth, secrecy was a big factor because she didn't tell anyone until years later. She was afraid of what people would say and how family would react. Fifth, and finally, she felt socially excluded from peers, family, and friends and from herself. "I wasn't even me anymore." Shelly said.

> "I was ashamed of abuse and that it was happening to me. I felt socially excluded because I didn't think anyone understood me. I felt I was the stereotypically 'weak' woman who lets a man beat her and then never fights back."

To Shelly, overcoming the stigma that surrounds abuse involves overcoming this internalized stigma. She said,

> "It means coming to terms with what happened to you and realizing that it was not your fault. You can overcome stigma by realizing that no one can tell you what you should have done because they were not in your shoes."

* * * * * * *

In the last chapter, we focused on how abuse perpetrators convey stigma toward victims and survivors as a function of their abuse. Perpetrator stigma, along with the sources of stigma we will cover in the next two chapters on stigma and help-seeking and societal stigma, results from external forces that are surrounding victims and survivors of abusive relationships. But what happens when that stigma infiltrates a person's inner world? In this chapter, we focus on perhaps one of the most damaging and dangerous types of stigmas—internalized stigma, or the stigma that victims and survivors carry within themselves. Internalized stigma occurs after hearing all of the negative attitudes from others, either overtly or covertly, and then victims or survivors begin to believe it.

We heard so many stories that included internalized stigma from participants in our research. In fact, based on some of the stories we have heard and testimonies about its impacts, we have come to believe that this type of stigma might be the most challenging to overcome. Consider, for example, the following statements that show how abuse can lead to self-directed stigma for victims and survivors:

- "He blamed me, and for a long time I blamed myself to a large extent, both for certain aspects of the abuse and for staying in the relationship for as long as I did."
- "I was completely ashamed to admit what had happened to me, and that I stayed in the relationship. So, I kept it all a secret."
- "I was especially careful to keep secrets from my parents. They were always very supportive, and I believed that my relationship would cause my parents to be disappointed in me, so I maintained a lot of secrecy, and lies with my parents so that they were not aware of the severity of the relationship. I also hid a lot of things from my less accepting friends because I believed that anything I told those friends would be further ammunition for blame."
- "I felt separated from my peers mostly, like I couldn't 'connect' to other married couples."
- "As a person who experienced sexual/emotional/verbal/physical abuse and rape, I feel a sense of separation often. These experiences have changed my sense of self; for a long time, I battled to regain a sense of self at all. I feel a sense of deep connection to others who have experienced any kind of abuse, particularly sexual abuse, but feel a sense of being 'separate' from others, particularly those who have normal, healthy sex lives, married couples with healthy, mutually respectful relationships."
- "I think shame was probably the most difficult of the experiences. I was profoundly ashamed of myself because I was working on my education in psychology, and through the course of the relationship, I learned about the cycle of abuse, but didn't seem to be able to extricate myself from the relationship. I think that the shame was based in my academic self while the more empathetic part of me recognized that I was part of a pattern that is normal. I think the final aspect of shame was related to my perception of myself as strong and independent. It was, and has been hard to stop feeling shame because my perception of myself and the realities of my behavior did not seem to fit together in any way I could make sense of."
- "I have overcome an enormous amount of shame; I hesitantly state I no longer feel a sense of shame, but there are times I still experience it, primarily in response to situations in which someone infers 'they should just leave, I would never put up with that' and in response to media portrayals of rape or any references to rape."
- "I isolated myself because my friends judged me for my willingness to remain in an abusive relationship. I also found that it was difficult to talk to friends because I didn't feel well understood by my friends. My partner also worked to isolate me from my support group; as a

consequence I found that my support group shrank dramatically during the abuse."
- "I labeled and judged myself for being willing to accept and 'put up with' the abuse despite my education level and my understanding of the process of abuse." "I sometimes feel labeled, like people have expectations about me once they find out about the abuse. Like I am weak or stupid because of it."
- "I felt to blame because I couldn't be the woman he wanted me to be. I was shamed because I had let the same thing happen to me."
- "I spent a great deal of time assuming I was the reason for the abuse. I allowed myself to be removed from things I loved. I gave up social opportunities, had no friends, and felt completely isolated."
- "I have lots of shame because of who I allowed in my life."
- "I was completely ashamed to admit what had happened to me."
- "I felt powerless in much of my personal life; I was distanced from my friends and family, and my primary support person hurt me more than he supported me. I felt like my life was completely out of control with the exception of my academic life. I was able to regain some sense of power in my life through positive academic performance."
- "I felt a huge loss of power while in the relationship, and as I realized just how far I had fallen through the lies I had believed about myself; it was devastating. For a long time, I felt completely paranoid and unable to trust myself, much less anyone else. I still struggle with those feelings sometimes, and on feeling like things happen to me instead of seeing myself as a strong person who makes things happen."

These statements reflect how deeply experiences of intimate partner violence and stigma can impact how victims and survivors see themselves. As introduced in Chapter 2, the Integrated IPV Stigmatization Model that we developed with Nicole Overstreet includes internalized stigma as one of the core sources of stigma that victims and survivors can experience. We weren't the first researchers to examine internalized stigma. In fact, in the prior research literature on stigma, researchers had identified how internalized stigma affected such groups of people as those who had serious mental illness as well as described how internalized stigma develops over time.

In a model of internalized stigma developed by Amy Drapalski, a research psychologist at the Veterans Affairs Capitol Healthcare Network,[1] and her colleagues, multiple pathways exist through which stigma and discrimination lead to a variety of negative outcomes for people with mental illness. For example, stigmatizing experiences can negatively impact one's self-esteem and self-efficacy. They also can lead to isolation and withdrawal. Together, these negative outcomes can exacerbate mental health symptoms, such as anxiety and depression. In this way, stigmatizing experiences can become part of a vicious cycle in which the initial challenge—in the case of Drapalski's model, mental illness—is compounded by the additional challenges of the associated stigma, which can then in turn exacerbate the original symptoms. This certainly parallels the experiences of stigma for people experiencing intimate partner violence, since we know that the stigma surrounding the abuse can exacerbate the traumatic effects of the abuse.

Before we began working with her, our colleague, Nicole Overstreet and her collaborator, worked to develop an earlier conceptualization of intimate partner violence–related stigma.[2] Their original IPV Stigmatization Model addressed internalized stigma as one of three main types of stigma, along with enacted and cultural stigma. An important takeaway from their discussion of internalized stigma is that internalized stigma can have negative outcomes for victims and survivors of abusive relationships. For example, shame and embarrassment from physical and psychological abuse can lower self-efficacy in seeking help as well as lower one's sense of self-worth. Internalized stigma can also lead to self-blame, guilt, shame, and low self-esteem, all of which can become barriers to leaving the abuse and accessing services. Negative self-talk (or the negative things we say to ourselves) can also become a part of the internalized stigma experience. This negative self-talk exacerbates feelings of worthlessness and shame. Self-doubt and low self-esteem contribute to feelings that others should not help and that the survivor does not deserve help to leave. Take a moment and consider the complexity of internalized stigma. There are many factors that combine, become internalized, and lead to a host of potential added challenges that victims and survivors may face.

Overstreet and her colleague also discussed that when a survivor reaches out for support and is met with a stigmatizing response from someone in his or her support network (whether this is family, friends, or professionals), this can reactivate the process of internalized stigma and impede future decisions to seek help. This makes sense when you think about it. If you finally muster up the strength to get help and you feel somewhat strong enough (but are probably still on shaky ground) and then are met with a negative reaction, this response will likely trigger reminders of any sort of negative messages that might be lying dormant in you, such as the stigmatizing messages you've been hearing from your abuser throughout your relationship.

The Stigma Internalization Process

Just how does stigma become internalized? Based on the prior research discussed earlier and our own research on stigma and intimate partner violence, we propose that stigma becomes internalized through a developmental process that follows from the direct and indirect outcomes of the abuse and stigmatizing messages and experiences from external sources. We depict this process in Figure 4.1, the Stigma Internalization Process.

86 *Understanding Stigma*

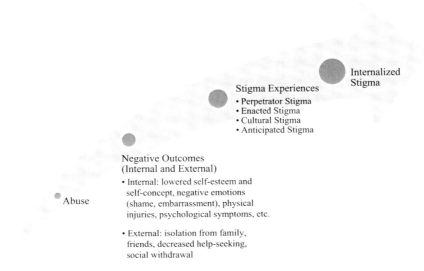

Figure 4.1 The Stigma Internalization Process

Essentially, the Stigma Internalization Process, as pictured in Figure 4.1, begins with the experience of being abused. Abuse, as we all know, leads to a variety of direct and indirect negative outcomes. These can be internal outcomes, such as lowered self-esteem, feelings of shame, and embarrassment. It also can lead to physical injuries or mental health symptoms, to name a few. External negative outcomes also occur because of intimate partner violence. These might include isolation from the victim's family or support network and social withdrawal, either because the perpetrator controls the victim's behavior, or because the victim no longer wishes to socialize with others who might be suspicious, or because doing so might put the victim at risk for a physical attack from his or her abuser. The victim might also not believe that he or she is deserving of support or help, or might be putting his or her safety at risk by seeking help for the abuse.

These negative outcomes can then lead to stigmatizing experiences. For example, if victims have lowered self-esteem, they may then anticipate that they will be met with stigma if they were to try and seek help or support from someone. When we don't feel good about ourselves or our ability to do something successfully, we begin to doubt that good things can come, that we can be successful at something, or that we will be met with a supportive, helpful response if we reach out for support. The victim then internalizes this stigmatizing experience so that he or she believes the negative messages from others in a deeper way. This model conveys one of the most significant ways that we believe internalized stigma develops over time. Most likely, there are other processes that can take place that result in the stigma becoming internalized. For example, some victims and survivors may enter into an abusive relationship already feeling internalized stigma from other experiences or some marginalized social identity, and then the abuse and stigma surrounding it can reinforce the preexisting internalized stigma. However, based on what we have heard from survivors in our study, and what we have read from others in the professional literature on internalized stigma, we believe that the Stigma Internalization Process is a common experience and reflects the vicious cycle that can occur as stigmatizing experiences from external sources come to influence how victims and survivors view themselves. One of the major influences on internalized stigma are the messages that victims and survivors receive from external sources, so it's important to consider how victims and survivors may come to believe in these messages, even if they recognize how negative, harmful, and untrue they are.

There are many reasons victims and survivors begin to believe the negative messages that they receive from external sources, such as their perpetrators, other people in their lives, and the broader society, including the media. One of the major culprits that we have heard about from many survivors is victim-blaming. Victim-blaming occurs in the general population, in the media, from those who are in a victim's personal life, and even from professionals. Public victim-blaming messages are all too common and suggest that victims somehow are to blame for being abused—that it is somehow the victim's fault or responsibility. Think about how often you see messages in our society that are directed at the perpetrators of abuse. These types of messages would be something like "Stop abusing your intimate partner!" or "Don't attack someone who is walking alone at night!" Instead, most public messages are directed to victims. These include messages such as "Don't walk alone at night" or "Get support from a friend." Subtle or not, the messages assume that it's victims who need to hear how to prevent abuse rather than perpetrators, and that victims are able to take action to prevent all abuse and violence. This contributes to cultural beliefs about who is to blame, who is responsible, and who is supposed to get help in the context of intimate partner violence. Victim-blaming is common enough that we can point to many common messages that are often found in the general population. Some of these common negative perceptions include the following: victims must like the abuse, victims are not strong enough to end the abuse, victims must have done something to cause the abuse, victims could have or should have left a long time ago, or it's easy to leave abuse. We could list more, but you get the idea!

When a victim hears these negative messages enough and from such a variety of people and sources, he or she can begin to believe it. Some might wonder why a victim can't just brush these messages off, look the other way, or feel strong enough in his or her convictions to know that these messages are not accurate. As a response to this question, we challenge you to imagine yourself in an already compromised position.

You are the victim of abuse, and you are being controlled, manipulated, harmed, and threatened, as well as told some of these harmful messages by your abuser. Abuse of any kind compromises you, whatever strengths and supports you had before the abuse are lessened, and you are whittled away into someone who is a shell of a person, not the normal you who might be able to overcome this. Normally, you would able to decipher right from wrong or ignore a comment or negative that might be hurtful from others. But not now. Not when you are in this state. In this state, it's more difficult to ignore others' hurtful messages. It's more challenging to remember that you are better than this, that you don't deserve this, and that it is the abuser, not you, who is at fault.

Additionally, the supports you once had are likely to be gone once you are deeply involved in an abusive relationship. In an abusive relationship, the perpetrator often isolates you from those who used to be in your life. Many survivors have told us that, after being in an abusive relationship for a while, it's easier to isolate themselves rather than having to lie and cover up the abuse that is occurring. So, normally, if you were having a problem and weren't involved in an abusive relationship, you might call a friend or family member, or maybe you would reach out to talk to a professional in order to get support. But in the context of an abusive relationship, you are likely cut off from sources of support that would help you to challenge any negative, stigmatizing messages you are receiving from the outside world and your abusive partner.

And so, as victims become more deeply involved in an abusive relationship, their protective resources—both internal and external—become whittled away. In this vulnerable state, negative, stigmatizing messages are harder to fend off, and it becomes more natural to internalize them. Hearing anything enough eventually becomes your truth—for better or for worse—and in this case, victims turn these messages inward and begin to believe them.

A Closer Look at the Impact of Internalized Stigma

Now that we've considered how internalized stigma develops over time, let's take a closer look at the various facets of this source of stigma and how it impacts victims and survivors. In our Integrated IPV Stigmatization Model, as discussed in Chapter 2, we identified four major components of stigma (i.e., blame, isolation, negative emotions, and loss of status) as well as four main sources of stigma (i.e., perpetrator, internalized, enacted, and cultural). Focusing in on internalized stigma, we heard examples of each of the components of stigma as the survivors who participated in our research internalized them. An example of internalized blame was as follows: "I accepted the blame for everything that went wrong" and "I have often felt responsible for letting it get as far as it did by not reporting him." A quote that illustrates internalized isolation is as follows: "I tend to isolate myself at times from the world. It's more peaceful and easier," and "I felt isolated because I did not want to tell people." Reflecting an internalized loss of status, one participant said, "I felt powerless for a long time," and "I keep my feelings to myself so I can come off as not damaged goods." As an illustration of internalized negative emotions, one participant had the following to say, "I am ashamed that I have put my family, daughter, through this; I have ruined my husband's life by leaving him and turned his world upside down! The guilt is terrible. I feel that I have burdened my family!"

The theme of internalized stigma was prominent among the stories we heard in our research. In fact, in one of our studies,[3] we quantified how common the various sources and components of stigma were among a set of statements made by survivors in one of our surveys. One of the major findings of this study was that the type of stigma that was most common was internalized stigma. This was an important finding, because so often, when people talk about stigma, they are referring to stigma that is received from external sources. However, this finding demonstrates that stigma from within is just as important—if not more important—to address than stigma from external sources.

To further understand internalized stigma, in that same study, we examined which components of stigma were most commonly experienced from each source. In this analysis, we learned that negative emotions were the most frequently experienced component of internalized stigma experienced by our sample of survivors. So this means when stigma is internalized, it is the shame, embarrassment, or other negative emotions that really impact victims and survivors. We heard repeatedly that these participants felt a great deal of shame and negative emotions toward themselves for feeling like they had "let this abuse happen" to them.

Internalized stigma is thus a complex, multifaceted concept that has a profound impact on victims and survivors of intimate partner violence. It is a powerful phenomenon that we believe is critical to understand in order for us all to work together to eliminate it from the experiences of victims and survivors. It is harmful enough that stigma experiences happen with others, so we must make sure that survivors are not turning any of these messages inward and adding to the challenges that are a part of overcoming abuse.

To give a more in-depth illustration of internalized stigma, we turn now to Cassie's story. Cassie took our survey and had a lot to share about how stigma impacted her while she was in her abusive relationship, as she was thinking about leaving, and well after the abuse ended. Internalized stigma was very much a part of her journey, which is why we chose to highlight her experience in this chapter.

Cassie's Story

When she participated in our study, Cassie was in her early 20s. She worked as a journalist and had been out of her abusive relationship for two years. The relationship lasted about five years and was physically, sexually, emotionally, and verbally abusive. Her boyfriend had mental health concerns, and Cassie attributes some of the abuse to this. He struggled with anxiety, depression, and substance abuse. When the abuse would happen, he would apologize afterward and promise to get help for his mental health struggles. He said he couldn't control himself. Cassie stayed in the relationship because she thought that if he could get the right help, he would change. Instead, the abuse only got worse. His controlling behaviors grew more and more severe. Soon he controlled every single aspect of her life, and the cycle of abuse and violence would occur daily. The control would manifest in several different ways. First, he isolated her. Eventually, she became completely isolated from all close friends and family—literally only spending time with him and his family and friends. Even at work or school, she stopped communicating with others. Cassie felt ashamed of what was going on and ashamed of herself for staying. She stopped wanting to talk to other people.

Eventually, Cassie was completely separated from her support network.

> "He would tell me I didn't love him when I didn't spend time with him, or if I wanted to hang out with a friend, or a family member. After a while, it was much easier to just keep him happy then to suffer the consequences when I didn't."

Soon, even small decisions were made by Cassie's abuser: what to wear, what to eat, and when to do things. He said he needed to feel comfortable with these small decisions, so he made them for her. He blamed Cassie for the abuse, and this eventually led to her internalizing the blame. "The abuse was my fault, and something was wrong with me, or what I was doing to make him not trust me. I blamed myself for this and for staying with him." Blame eventually led to shame, and this is something Cassie still struggles with, even though she is no longer in the relationship.

> "I was very ashamed of what happened and still struggle with that. Even though I know I never asked to be abused, I wonder why I entered and stayed in the relationship, ignoring signs of abuse. This makes me feel like I can't let anyone know because they will judge me."

We don't know too many details about how Cassie's relationship ended, other than the fact that her abuser broke up with her, and Cassie moved out of the house they shared. They have not seen each other since then. He ended it because, as she described, "The anxiety which caused him to be abusive became too much, and he finally saw the way to end it was to end the relationship." He said that he was never happy with the way he treated her, yet he could not control it, so he felt that the only way to stop it was to end the relationship. He had taken such control of Cassie by that point that the only way she had imagined the relationship ending was by dying. She describes it as a miracle that he ended the relationship.

When Cassie started her life over after the abuse, everything was extremely difficult. The effects of isolation, in particular, lingered long after the relationship ended. She had been cut off from friends and family for so long that when the relationship ended, Cassie struggled to reconnect with friends. She didn't know how to explain herself or what had happened in the years since she'd drifted away. Cassie has continued to struggle with knowing whom she can trust with disclosing the details of her past relationship. She said,

> "As far as job and education, my employer does not know I am a survivor of domestic violence . . . I didn't seek help from counseling when it ended, probably because I know there would be stigma associated with it. I often want to attend a support group, but don't. Due to my job, I talk myself out of it by saying people wouldn't be comfortable with me there. I know this is just an excuse. There was stigma from family and friends, knowing what I went through but not knowing how to talk to me about it, instead talking about me and labeling me."

Cassie continues to work to overcome the internalized blame she carries from the relationship. She said, "I say all the time, 'No one asks to be abused,' but then wonder how I asked for it." Because she hasn't told too many other people about the abuse, she says,

> "I honestly haven't had many problems with outside stigma, because I have continued to keep the situation so private, but this really means that I haven't overcome the stigma. I'm still too afraid to talk openly about it. I'm ashamed of the role I feel I played by staying and worried people won't understand the magnitude or believe me."

Even still, Cassie encourages others to reach out for the types of support she still hasn't yet felt comfortable reaching out to for herself. She offered these words of encouragement to those who are still experiencing abuse,

> "Reach out to someone you know and trust for help and then take their help. Don't worry about them judging you, and if they do judge you, it's still better than continuing the current situation. When you are out of the relationship, you will be amazed at the knowledge that you survived, that you in fact still exist, and that others love you."

Cassie ended her participation in our research by reflecting on how internalized stigma is her worst enemy and that it far exceeds the stigma she felt from others.

> "While I felt stigma from family and friends, I did not feel the judgment I thought I would feel. When my relationship ended and I came home to my parents, my dad hugged me and said he was proud of

me. That's all I needed to know he knew I had been through something hard and had the courage to let it end. No one said, 'Why did you stay?' Rather, that's a question I continue to ask myself. The majority of stigma comes from me."

As you see from reading Cassie's story, internalized stigma is a very present phenomenon and something she is still working to overcome. Unfortunately, Cassie is not alone in her struggle to fight against internalized stigma. We heard about internalized stigma from hundreds of women and men who participated in our research. Internalized stigma is damaging enough when a victim or survivor is already in a compromised position and is trying to overcome abuse. But what about when this internalized stigma is reinforced by others?

To some extent, Cassie was fortunate in that she wasn't met by many stigmatizing responses from people close to her. Unfortunately, for many other survivors, internalized stigma can be reinforced when a victim goes to seek assistance from others and is met with negative attitudes. If victims and survivors encounter stigmatizing reactions in their social support systems, or among professionals and institutions they encounter, then it is likely to grow bigger. If someone is already thinking, "Maybe I did something to bring this on," and then has a negative experience with someone from whom they are seeking support, this experience only adds to the messages that might already be internalized, or it plants the seed for that being a thought that a survivor has. For example, consider a woman who is already feeling like she is to blame for staying in an abusive relationship or that she is at fault for the way her partner treated her during the most recent abusive incident. If this woman is then told by her medical doctor that she is "stupid" if she doesn't leave the relationship (this was an actual experience from a woman in one of our studies), this negative belief is reinforced, and the woman walks away feeling that the doctor has validated whatever negative beliefs were already there.

The Added Challenges of Internalized Stigma

Internalized stigma adds to the inherent challenges that victims and survivors already face during and after an abusive relationship. One of the major added challenges of internalized stigma that was noted by Overstreet and Quinn[4] was the way that internalized stigma impacts victims' and survivors' willingness to seek help. Through the internalized stigma, many victims and survivors begin to believe that they do not deserve to get help from others, that they will be judged by the person they reach out to for help, or that no one will be able to help. Formal help-seeking is defined as planned, problem-focused interaction with a health-care professional.[5] Help-seeking can also involve informal support, such as from friends and family members. As part of their literature review, Overstreet and Quinn focused on how stigma affects each stage of the help-seeking process for victims and survivors of intimate partner violence and how centrality and salience (to be defined next) of the person's identity in relation to the abuse also influences this process. Here are the definitions of these two terms:

- Centrality–the extent to which a person believes an identity is an important part of how they define themselves.
- Salience–the extent to which the identity is prominent for the person.

We include these definitions because they are important points to consider as we look at the process of internalized stigma and how this adds to the challenges to those experiencing intimate partner violence. According to Overstreet and Quinn, the most significant internalized stigma-related barriers to help-seeking included shame, guilt, self-blame, and embarrassment, and these served as barriers to seeking help from both formal and informal support networks. When women who had a desire to leave abuse, but who were not sure that they could, were asked what challenges they encountered—guilt and self-blame were among the top-five challenges.

Duke University researchers[6] have examined health needs and barriers to health care for women who have experienced IPV. Their study included both in-depth interviews and survey research in order to examine the needs as well as factors that inhibited their obtaining assistance for physical and mental health needs. Results from their study revealed a variety of factors that served as barriers, such as cost and control by the abuser, as well as low self-esteem and self-efficacy. Some women in their research described a sense of shame and embarrassment about the abuse. These feelings prevented them from seeking help, especially when it might have been related to a physical injury caused from the abuser. The women feared judgment from health-care professionals who might not understand why they did not leave the relationship. Also, shame and hopelessness, even when the person might have had financial means to seek help, led many women in their study to decide to not seek services.

Williams and Mickelson (2008)[7] researched what happens when an individual believes she or he will be stigmatized for IPV (in our research we call this experience *anticipated stigma*, but these authors call it *perceived stigma*). The authors conducted two studies—in Study 1 they researched the stigma related to poverty and in Study 2, the stigma related to IPV in a sample of women. We focus here on Study 2, which was the portion of the research related to IPV stigma. What the authors found was that anticipated stigma was related to indirect help-seeking. Indirect help-seeking is defined as help-seeking strategies that allow one with a stigmatized identity to seek help while keeping one's identity hidden. For example, a victim of intimate partner violence might seek counseling for depression, but not reveal to her or his counselor that she or he is experiencing abuse. Or he or she might disclose to a friend that there is something going on that is causing sadness, but not disclose what the root of the sadness is (abuse). Now, you might be reading this and thinking that indirect support seeking is better than no help-seeking at all. Well, that's actually not entirely true. In Williams and Mickelson's research, they found that indirect support seeking was related to *un*supportive responses from informal networks (e.g., friends, family). So, in other words, friends and family were not supportive when IPV victims tried to hint that something was going on that was upsetting. So when someone anticipates that stigma might occur because of the abuse, this person might use indirect help-seeking strategies. But these strategies result in unhelpful responses from friends and family so that the person who is hinting at the issue is not met with the support and services that they need and deserve. And remember from the Stigma Internalization Process that we described earlier in this chapter that this stigmatizing event with a professional, family member, or friend then leads to stigma that is internalized by the person being abused. To us, this further underscores how impactful stigma from others is and how it leads to that stigma being internalized.

Even further, Overstreet and Quinn also cited previous research showing that internalized stigma are related to self-doubt and low self-esteem, which were both major contributors to the belief that the victim was undeserving of resources and support. We know that, in order for victims or survivors to believe that they are worthy of receiving help from supportive resources, a shift has to be made from thinking, "I must have done something to deserve this/I don't deserve help," to, "My abuser is to blame/I do not deserve this." This change in thinking is a critical shift and one that very often needs to happen in order for someone to feel ready to seek assistance. Once the person has this shift in beliefs, he or she becomes more likely to pursue helpful resources. When victims readily disclose abuse or seek formal help for intimate partner violence and are then met with stigmatizing responses from others (either professionals or those in their personal lives), as we'll discuss further in the next chapter, it can reactivate stigma that was internalized and negatively impact future decisions to seek help. Together, all of these findings demonstrate that internalized stigma impedes decisions to seeking help when individuals are considering leaving an abusive relationship. So it is clear how impactful internalized stigma can be.

Take, for example, Janet's story. Janet was one of the original 12 women we interviewed about the concept of stigma and intimate partner violence. Janet had been free from abuse for well over 30 years, but she still could relate to the stigma questions we asked her. Much of what we discussed that day during her interview was related to the stigma she internalized as the abuse occurred and the internalized stigma that she still feels now. She talked a lot about self-esteem and how much the abuse decreased this for her. When she was in the abusive relationship, she suffered so much from the emotional and psychological abuse that she was suicidal at a few points in time. Much of this was due to feeling as though she didn't deserve help. Read the following quote from Janet that describes her abuse, one of her low emotional points, and how abuse impacted her:

> "I thought I was going to kill myself because he verbally, mentally, and physically abused me so much. More verbally and mentally than he did physically. He only did things like pour milk over my head, and throw food at me, and push me down on the floor, and I got a black eye from that. You know, stuff like that was not as awful as, I mean, it was pretty awful at the time. But the mental and verbal abuse was . . . I had no self-esteem, none."

Still today, 30 years free of abuse, Janet's self-esteem remains diminished because of the relationship. "I feel inadequate, because that's the way that he made me feel all the time. He would call me terrible, horrible names." During the interview, we talked about how she felt stigmatized by professionals and those in her personal life. She said that her "rock bottom" was when she called the police for help and very quickly got the impression that she would not be getting help from them that night:

> "Hardly anyone knew of the abuse, except for me. I called the police a couple times. Well, one time, I could see that I wasn't going to get any help from them. And, that's when I was sitting with a shotgun in my hand, thinking, maybe I should really kill myself because I'm no good to anyone. But, I'm pretty level-headed, so I, I got rid of that idea pretty quickly. It was a pretty bad night. I just figured there was no, no reason to live any longer. 'Cause I was just no good to anyone. That's the way he made me feel."

Janet also explained that she turned to her mother to get support and that her mother did not believe her when she told her she was being abused.

> "Well, the fact that my mother, or really no one else, believed me. They thought I was doing something wrong. It was my fault. And, that just really got me. I felt isolated because I felt no one was there to help me, no one, I had no support, from anyone."

Still today, Janet struggles with self-blame and low self-esteem.

> "Self-esteem, inadequacy, and blaming myself for doing some of the things, or being the way I was at the time, that perhaps I could have handled it differently. But I know consciously that I couldn't have.

I know consciously there was nothing that I could have done. But I still feel that there was something that I should have been able to do. If I had done this, instead of this . . ."

It's clear that these types of internalized stigmatizing beliefs still haunt Janet and have made it more difficult to recover fully from the abuse.

Understanding Internalized Stigma to Support Victims and Survivors

Given that it is such a powerful force, support for overcoming internalized stigma is especially important. As we conclude this chapter, we share further examples from survivors who participated in our research that demonstrate why understanding internalized stigma is so important for being able to provide appropriate support to victims and survivors of intimate partner violence. Perhaps one of the largest tasks we can accomplish to assist victims and survivors in overcoming internalized stigma is to understand it first. We must understand how it gets in the way of people overcoming abuse, what exactly it is, and what survivors might need in the way of assistance to overcome it. We must be able to recognize it in victims and survivors, ask about it as a friend or professional, and address it in the context of the complex process of seeking lives free from abuse. If we can understand the experience of living with internalized stigma, know what it looks like in survivors, and know the signs that someone may be facing internalized stigma (e.g., isolation, withdrawal, feelings of depression, and decreased self-esteem), then we can better assist those who are struggling. For example, if you are a friend of someone who confides in you that he or she is being abused, this person might not have the ability to believe that he or she could leave the relationship, could live without the person, or is deserving of a life free from abuse. It will be important for you to take a stance that these beliefs are false, but also withhold judgment or blaming responses that could further stigmatize the person. This is so important because internalized stigma is so complex. Take the following quote, for example. It's a response from a survivor who took our survey about stigma, and it shows just how complicated one's thinking can be in the context of abuse.

> "I felt like I know that I'm better than this, and I know that it's a bad situation. But, then, again, I don't feel like I'm better than this. I feel like if I'm willing to put up with it, then, obviously, I deserve it. Which sounds ludicrous, but made sense at the time."

This survivor obviously had many, many thoughts about how she deserved better, but these positive thoughts would wax and wane with the negative feelings she had about herself. In addition, she convinced herself that if she was so willing to put up with abuse, she must be deserving of the abuse. This quote highlights the complexity of messages that one internalizes and how this impedes the ability to free them from abuse. As someone who might need to support a victim or survivor in the process of recovery, the more you can understand and empathize, the more the person will feel understood, empowered, and perhaps ready to leave. Survivors who are out of the abuse still struggle, so we also encourage family, friends, and professionals to continue to offer support well after the person has left. Think about Janet who we spoke about earlier—it was 30 years later, and internalized stigma was still something she was fighting against. Many survivors still feel "different" for some time, even after successfully leaving and overcoming abuse.

The shift from seeing oneself as a victim to seeing oneself as a survivor is a very difficult hurdle to overcome. One participant explained how this is something she deals with:

> "I have a hard time seeing myself as a survivor instead of a victim. I have a hard time feeling normal and acceptable. That leads into social exclusion, which I feel in spite of having friends and family who truly love me. Because I have been abused and they were not, sometimes I feel like we speak a different language or see the world in different colors. Things that they find funny, like balloons popping or a silly joke, leave me shaking, hyperventilating, and on the verge of tears. It's hard to feel 'normal' and included when you are so obviously different. When you feel broken, it's hard to feel like you fit in with all the bright, shiny, whole people around you."

As the quote suggests, even though she is indeed a "survivor," having overcome abuse and moved on to a life free from it, she still feels different, even though she also feels healthy and happy.

One metaphor related to always feeling different from others that we heard from many survivors was the notion that they feel as though they had a "scarlet letter" on their chests, even after being free from abuse for some time, referring to Nathaniel Hawthorne's story of Hester Prynne who was forced to wear a scarlet letter A on her dress, which referred to adultery. This seemed to describe the notion that, despite the years free of abuse, or even after creating new lives for themselves, they still feel that there is a mark of disgrace that they wear and that scarlet letter might be in part due to never feeling quite normal, despite what others say or what the survivor does to create a new life.

Another participant from our research said something similar when we asked about internalized stigma. She said that, most of the time she does not feel ashamed, but that there are times when something that someone says can still trigger negative emotions. The following quote explains this:

> "I hesitantly state I no longer feel a sense of shame, but there are times I still experience it, primarily in response to situations in which someone infers, 'They should just leave; I would never put up with that.'"

Even though she has resolved herself from most of the shame she once felt, there are times when these feelings get drummed up by others.

When victims and survivors are supported by those around them, they can more realistically assess their circumstances, make decisions related to safety and well-being, begin to feel strong enough to challenge some of the negative beliefs and self-talk they might have internalized, and begin to become more objective as they take steps to overcome their abuse, such as make decisions that change the courses of their lives, enter new relationships, apply for new jobs, or work toward recovery as they build lives free from abuse. Victims also can begin to see that they are not alone in the ways that they feel about themselves and relationships. Finding a community of others, for example, can be hugely powerful for someone who is just beginning to make plans to leave an abusive relationship. Seeing that others might feel blamed, understanding what internalized stigma is, knowing that abusers use this as a way to manipulate, and learning how the negative impacts can impede the process of overcoming abuse can be extremely useful. Helpful, supportive responses might be exactly what are needed to change course so that survivors can make the shift from understanding themselves as victims to survivors.

Internalized stigma is a dangerous phenomenon in the lives of those who are impacted by IPV. We hope that this chapter helped with understanding the concept so that you can feel empowered to fight against this form of stigma yourself, or assist with doing this with someone you know. As we will discuss in more detail later in the book, internalized stigma is most certainly something survivors can overcome, especially through intentional efforts to build internal strength and support, as well as resources and information from others.

Notes

1 Drapalski, A.L., Lucksted, A., Perrin, P.B., & Boyd, J. (2013). A model of internalized stigma and its effects on people with mental illness. *Psychiatric Services, 64*, 264–269.
2 Overstreet, N.M., & Quinn, D.M. (2013). The intimate partner violence stigmatization model and barriers to help seeking. *Basic and Applied Social Psychology, 35*, 109–122.
3 Murray, C.E., Crowe, A., & Overstreet, N. (2015). Sources and components of stigma experienced by survivors of intimate partner violence. *Journal of Interpersonal Violence*, 1–22. DOI: 10.1177/0886260515609565.

4 Overstreet, N. M., & Quinn, D. M. (2013). The intimate partner violence stigmatization model and barriers to help seeking. *Basic and Applied Social Psychology, 35*, 109–122.
5 Cornally, N., & McCarthy, G. (2011). Help-seeking behaviour: A concept analysis. *International Journal of Nursing Practice, 17*, 280–288.
6 Wilson, K. S., Silberberg, M. R., Brown, A. J., & Yaggy, S. D. (2007). Health needs and barriers to healthcare of women who have experienced intimate partner violence. *Journal of Women's Health, 16*, 1485–1498.
7 Williams, S. L., & Mickelson, K. D. (2008). A paradox of support seeking and rejection among the stigmatized. *Personal Relationships, 15*, 493–509.

5 How Stigma Impacts Victims and Survivors When They Seek Help

Beatrice was a professional woman who worked in social services. When we interviewed her, she had been out of her abusive relationship for about a decade. She described her abusive relationship as a rebound relationship that she entered into quickly. Before she began dating her abuser, her 20-year marriage had ended in a dysfunctional and hurtful way. One of the first things that Beatrice noted about her past abuser was that "we weren't a good fit" professionally, as she had a graduate degree, and he saw work as a "job" rather than a profession or career. When we asked how long they were together, Beatrice said it was on and off for about five years.

Beatrice's relationship was unique in that there were no signs of abuse during the relationship, but, "When I went to permanently end the relationship, he began stalking me." The stalking began subtly. As Beatrice said, "At first, it was just coming around, 'Oh please, let's go back out to dinner.' And then, over time, this really ugly, frightening stuff started happening." The stalking continued for over a year, during which time he would do things such as deflate her tires, show up unexpectedly at her job, and tell lies about her at her workplace. He stole one of her pets, stole money from her, followed her when she went out on dates, and turned off the electricity at her house.

The psychological toll of this kind of stalking was profound. Imagine for a moment living under that level of fear and uncertainty about where and how your stalker might next appear. Beatrice described the uncertainty and fear "as it kept escalating . . . I was always wondering what would be the next thing?" Beatrice noted that she struggled to get help from the police during the time when she was being stalked. She said, "Even the police, when you call them, it takes them a long time to believe that it's happening. So, it took six or eight months to get them to really be on board with it." However, she was persistent, and she reported, "He did eventually get prosecuted and put in jail" for about eight months. At the time of the interview, however, he had been released from jail and had attempted to make contact with Beatrice via social media. This was horrifying because, while he was incarcerated, Beatrice had moved to another town as a measure of protecting herself. It was very upsetting that he had managed to make contact again, despite her attempts at protecting and distancing herself.

One of the biggest challenges that Beatrice faced when seeking help was simply being believed. She described the following experience when reporting the stalking to police one time: "I kept telling the officer, you know, I kept saying, 'This is, this man is following me. This man is doing this stuff to me.' And she wasn't believing me." She went on to say,

> "For the most part, they were dismissive. Like, for example, when I would call 911, and I would be standing in my house, lights off, and you know, this was like the ninth time this had happened, and the 911 operator is going, 'But, why are we coming.'. . . Some of the male officers made unsavory comments, and I guess there really wasn't anybody who got what the trauma and terror I was in to kind of like pick me up and carry me along."

These struggles continued as the stalking case was heard through the prosecution process. As Beatrice described,

> "The criminal justice system is not supportive of folks who have been through this . . . I was pretty shaky, and the people who worked for the criminal justice system for the most part were anywhere from matter-of-fact, which was OK, to just downright harsh. If I hadn't had the ability to advocate pretty strongly for myself, I'm not sure that I could have made it through all that."

Beyond this challenge to get others to believe her, Beatrice struggled with feeling isolated and ashamed. This was especially pronounced in her workplace, in which her employer had implemented some safety measures after learning about the stalking. Even though these measures were necessary for her safety at the time, Beatrice felt a sense of vulnerability because her coworkers knew about the abuse. She said,

> "I would say that there was some shame with the work situation. I mean, even though, intellectually you can say, 'Gee, I know this isn't my fault,' there is still like a part of you that thinks, 'Huh, you know, here I am sitting with all of my colleagues, and they are knowing all of my private business.' And who knows what they thought, or didn't think."

Even years after the stalking had ended and her ex-boyfriend had been put in jail, Beatrice continued to feel the effects of the stalking. For example, she said, "I did a lot of work dealing with the PTSD. I think I'm more jumpy than I used to be." In addition, although she would prefer to be living in her former hometown, she didn't feel she would be safe there. Another area in which Beatrice continues to face struggles is in new intimate relationships. She said, "I feel very uncertain of my ability to make good judgment around choosing a partner. I don't trust my ability to be able to choose."

One positive by-product of her abusive experiences was that Beatrice turned them around to become motivation to help others in similar situations. She said,

> "I think that I can be more helpful to survivors and victims than a lot of other folks. Having been through it and studied it so much, I think I can understand the dynamic more. I think I can offer a lot of really valuable suggestions . . . So, that's what I try to do."

Beatrice also noted that the media fails to bring much-needed attention to the dangers of stalking, in particular.

We ended each of our original interviews with survivors by asking them what they believe is needed to end the stigma related to IPV. Beatrice responded to this question by saying, "Believe these people when somebody tells you this is happening." She also believes we need to educate the community about intimate partner violence and signs that abuse might be occurring: "When you have somebody who's isolating, or who has bruises that aren't explained, what you can do is to provide them information." We also asked participants to say in their own words what victims need to know and how they can be better supported. "Victims need to know their options, so that they can make choices when they are ready to." When it comes to supporting victims, Beatrice said, "I think that teaching specific skills on how to be able to manage their life and to be proactive is really the most empowering thing that you can do."

※　※　※　※　※　※

Beatrice's safety was placed at a significant risk in light of the abuse and stalking she was experiencing. When a victim of intimate partner violence is being stalked, reaching out for help can be especially dangerous. Their abuser could be tracking their every move, such as by monitoring their phone calls and electronic communications and by physically following them from place to place. Therefore, Beatrice was extremely courageous to reach out for help, and we can only begin to imagine how much time and consideration she must have given to making the choice to reach out for help. Unfortunately, when she did seek help, she was met with a variety of negative responses, such as being disbelieved and dismissed, as well as having insensitive comments directed her way.

Stigma, as we have discussed, is a damaging phenomenon to those who have experienced intimate partner violence. There are so many consequences of stigma, and we know that when it occurs, it can lead to a host of negative consequences for the person experiencing it. In Chapter 4, we spoke of the stigma that survivors turn inward and begin to believe. The focus of this chapter is the stigma that survivors experience when they seek help. We will talk about stigmatizing responses that both informal (e.g., friends and family) and formal (e.g., professionals) sources of support can convey when victims and survivors of intimate partner violence reach out for help. To some extent, the stigma surrounding abusive relationships is a pervasive, daily experience for people who have experienced victimization. Any stigma can be harmful, but consider especially how potentially harmful stigma can be when a victim or survivor finally musters up the courage to speak out and reach out for help about the abuse they are experiencing only to be met with stigmatizing responses, just as Beatrice experienced. These stigmatizing responses can be especially risky—they may make it even less likely that victims and survivors will reach out for additional help in the future if they fear they will experience similar responses if they seek help again.

To begin this chapter, we will consider how informal sources of support can stigmatize victims and survivors when they learn about experiences of abuse. The rest of the chapter will consider what happens when professionals are the ones who convey stigma to victims and survivors of abusive relationships. Before we delve into these topics, however, we want to restate that we know that there are many people—both professionals and members of the general population—who do offer helpful support and non-stigmatizing responses to victims and survivors of abuse. In addition, although this chapter will explore stigmatizing responses from within certain professional groups, we also do not believe that there is any professional group that is wholly stigmatizing of victims and survivors of abusive relationships. Rather, we believe that there are *individuals* within various professional groups and communities who have responded to victims and survivors in a stigmatizing way. Certainly, there are organizational policies and professional practices that could contribute to group-level stigmatizing responses, but we believe it is critical to remember that there are also people within every professional group and every community who offer helpful support to victims and survivors in ways that do not further add to the stigma they face.

Many of the survivors who have shared their stories with us have been able to identify people in their lives who responded with this kind of support as well as those whose responses were stigmatizing. Therefore, we must keep in mind that each individual victim and survivor is likely to face a vast array of responses when they disclose abuse and reach out for help. For this reason, it is important to consider each unique person's experiences of stigma in relation to their abuse. As examples of the variations that may occur, consider the following three hypothetical examples:

1 Joe faced abuse by his partner, Marcus. When he told his immediate family members, who were not supportive of him being in a same-sex

relationship, they judged him and told him that they knew the relationship wasn't going to be any good for him and that they thought it was what he deserved. However, when the violence escalated to the point that he called the police during a particularly violent episode, they were extremely helpful to him. The police officers who responded to the call connected him with a local domestic violence agency, which offered him advocacy services and helped to connect him with a safe place to live while he worked toward ending the relationship.

2   Tania was being abused by her husband, Paul. After Paul had broken her left arm by throwing her to the ground, she went to the emergency room at the local hospital. When she told them that Paul had injured her, the attending physician's initial response was to ask Tania why she stayed in the relationship with Paul. Later that day, Tania called her best friend to tell her what happened, and her friend told Tania that she didn't deserve to be treated that way by either Paul or the physician.

3   Monique regularly attends church with her husband, Lamar, with whom she has two young children. Lamar has been extremely emotionally abusive since their marriage began, and recently he has begun to use some physical violence toward her as well. Monique sought the counsel of her pastor as to whether she should leave the relationship, and her pastor told her that divorce was not acceptable within their religion, so she should just work on becoming the best wife she can be to Lamar to help improve the marriage. Monique had also confided about the abuse to her mother, who encouraged her to reach out to the local domestic violence agency, but Monique decided that she should listen to the pastor's advice first, because she was afraid that the staff at the domestic violence agency would just tell her to leave the relationship.

What did you notice about Joe, Tania, and Monique's stories? Each person received some level of support from some of the people in their lives, although others were not helpful and even conveyed stigmatizing responses. Through the stories of the survivors who participated in our research, we have learned that this type of variation is extremely common. Sometimes support comes from places where people might not expect it, such as if they're afraid to call the police, but once they do, they find that the officers are helpful and informed about the dynamics of abusive relationships. On the other hand, sometimes stigmatizing responses also come from unexpected places. We could also consider a law enforcement agency in which the officers are not trained to understand intimate partner violence, and so when victims reach out for help, they are stigmatized, judged, and unsupported. The same could be said for virtually any group of people—such as friends, family members, neighbors, counselors, medical professionals, even professionals who work in agencies that are specifically designed to help people affected by intimate partner violence. Within each group, there are people who are ready and able to help, and there are likely people who, for a variety of reasons, are unable or unwilling to respond in non-stigmatizing ways. Therefore, as we move forward throughout this chapter, we urge readers to consider the various factors that might lead people from all walks of life to respond in either helpful or unhelpful ways when a victim or survivor reaches out to them for help and support.

Stigma From Friends, Family Members, and Other Sources of Informal Support

> "My mother made it clear that she thought that I was in the wrong for leaving my ex, even after I told her that he had raped me. She kept talking about how much he must miss me, how much pain I was causing him, etc. She also believed that it was my responsibility to rehabilitate him so that he wouldn't rape anyone else. She and my stepfather tried to talk me out of taking any safety precautions when I had to deal with my abuser to get my things from our apartment, and encouraged me to stay in touch with him. They also indicated that they thought that my emotional responses to the rape and abuse were excessive and overdramatic."
> ~ *Anonymous Survivor*

Similar to the survivor quoted here, many victims and survivors of intimate partner violence will disclose their abuse experiences to friends and family members long before they reach out to professionals. There are many reasons for this. First, people may simply feel more comfortable sharing their experiences with someone close to them. Second, they may feel that their friends and family members already have an idea that the abuse is occurring, or they may even have experienced abuse in front of their friends or family members, and so the conversation may occur naturally after that happens. Third, help from friends and family members may be viewed as more accessible, as no appointment is likely to be needed, and the cost is likely free. Fourth, and finally, there can be a stigma attached to seeking help from professionals, especially since intimate partner violence is often viewed as a private family matter.

On the other hand, many people in the general population are not fully equipped to know how to help a friend or family member who has been abused in an intimate relationship. Through our work and in our own personal social networks, we often are asked for our advice on how someone we know can help a friend or family member who is in an abusive relationship. In fact, this topic comes up so often for us that we've developed a whole collection of resources through our See the Triumph campaign on the topic of "How to Help a Friend."[1] The main suggestions we offer—including remaining nonjudgmental, asking victims or survivors what kind of help they need, and telling them that they deserve to be treated with dignity and respect—seem relatively simple. And yet, many people feel overwhelmed and confused if they are close to someone who is being abused. It's one thing to understand the importance of remaining nonjudgmental—it's another thing entirely to withhold judgment when you fear for the safety of your loved one, but you don't think he or she is making the best or safest choices for him or herself!

In general, we believe that most friends and family members who respond to victims and survivors of abusive relationships in stigmatizing ways do not do so because they want to hurt their loved ones. Rather, we believe that most of these stigmatizing responses result from friends and family members not understanding fully the dynamics of abusive relationships as well as from a genuine desire to help, although their views on how to help may not align directly with what the victim or survivor actually needs. As a result of feeling overwhelmed and confused, in combination with not understanding the complexity of abusive relationships, many people close to victims and survivors respond in ways that are unhelpful and even stigmatizing.

Regardless of the reasons—and even possibly the good intentions—behind friends' and family members' stigmatizing responses to victims and survivors disclosing abuse and reaching out for help, these stigmatizing responses can have a profound impact on the person's future willingness to reach out for help as well as for how they come to view themselves, as we discussed in Chapter 4 on internalized stigma. A closer look at the experiences of some of the participants in our research will illustrate the challenges of stigmatizing responses from friends and family members.

First, we heard from many survivors that friends and family members reacted in stigmatizing ways because they believed that the survivor waited too long to disclose that the abuse was occurring. Survivors told us that friends and family members felt as though they should have disclosed sooner, or that they felt betrayed that the survivor did not trust them enough to disclose that the abuse was occurring, because the friends and family members claimed that they could have or would have helped the survivor leave the abuse. One survivor from our study said,

> "My family members and friends could not understand why I did not come to them for help first while I was in the relationship. My father was the one person who affected me the most during this time. He actually blamed me for the situation by telling me that I asked for it since I stayed in the relationship and didn't ask him for help. Eventually he apologized, but it has still caused a wedge between us to this day and is still a topic that I will not discuss with him."

This reaction of a survivor somehow "asking for it" since he or she didn't disclose the abuse has lasting effects. As you can see from this example, this participant still feels distant from her father even after he apologized for his reaction. Thus stigmatizing responses when one expects to be met with support, validation, or encouragement can be especially painful to a survivor.

Stigmatizing responses also can occur after an abusive relationship has ended, when survivors reach out to others in their personal lives to disclose the abuse, ask for support, or seek information. In these instances, survivors are still stigmatized, even though the abuse is not currently taking place. Stigma at this point in time also can be damaging. Even though the survivor may have overcome the abuse, he or she might still be recovering and learning to trust him or herself and others and therefore still feeling vulnerable. Rather than getting a listening ear, emotional support, or resources, when stigmatizing responses occur in this context, survivors might feel disheartened by the responses or doubtful of others' capacity to understand or empathize, which may lead to further feelings of isolation. A participant from our research offered one example of this when she explained her experiences of overcoming abuse, reaching out to others after she'd left the relationship, and starting to tell others about the abuse:

> "I experienced blame after the relationship ended because some people, including family members, blamed me for what happened simply because I stayed in the relationship longer than what is expected. Some people even went as far as to ask me what I did to provoke him to do those things, because he never seemed violent to them. I was labeled as a victim and weak, which are two adjectives that I will never use to describe myself. They completely overlooked the courage it took for me to get out of that dangerous situation."

Rather than hearing that she had overcome abuse, and seeing her as courageous, triumphant, and resourceful for having left, people in her support network questioned why this survivor didn't leave sooner, questioned whether the perpetrator was in fact abusive, and blamed her for staying with him, implying that she somehow deserved to be abused.

Some survivors experience stigmatizing responses long after the abuse has ended. This might occur as they discuss their process of leaving, steps they have taken since leaving, or the services or support they have sought. In these moments, friends or family sometimes react in a negative way about what they believe would have been helpful or what still might be helpful to the person. Unsolicited advice giving or judgment about what the survivor has or has not done as far as formal support services might be conveyed by the survivor's friends and family members. For example, consider the following quote from a participant who explained that she still feels judged by many people in her life: "Because even when I was trying to heal from it, even now, the things that I do. They say, 'Well, why don't you do this? Why do you have to go to mental health? Why are you taking medication?'" This survivor's friends and family members were missing an important opportunity to validate the choices that she was making, perhaps because they were too focused on their own views about what she needed to do.

Again, many friends and family members respond in stigmatizing ways due to a lack of awareness about the dynamics of abuse. Many do not understand the complexities and nuances of abusive environments, such as perpetrators, the dangers involved when thinking about leaving the abuser, the notion that decisions about safety of the whole family have to be considered, and that the manipulation and control from the abuser might make it impossible to leave. These responses highlight an ongoing need for more community awareness about intimate partner violence and the needs and experiences of survivors so that any member of the community can be prepared when they learn someone in their lives needs support related to a past or current abusive relationship. We'll revisit this issue in Chapters 9 and 10 of this book. But before we leave the topic of how stigma impacts victims and survivors when they seek help, we turn our attention to another important source of potential support—community-based professionals who are on the "frontlines" of response systems for people impacted by intimate partner violence. Unfortunately, sometimes these professionals also miss opportunities to provide support and rather respond in ways that further add to the stigma that victims and survivors of abusive relationships face.

Stigma From Professionals

One of the first studies we conducted on intimate partner violence and stigma involved examining what happens when victims and survivors reach out to professionals for help.[2] In this study, we examined the stigma that survivors experienced when reaching out to various types of professionals for help. To set the stage for our discussion on how professionals may stigmatize victims and survivors of intimate partner violence, consider the following quotes from participants in this study. These quotes capture the variety of stigma experiences that survivors may have as they try to ask for help from professionals, before and during an abusive relationship:

- "After separating from my husband, he hurt my arm; I felt a sense of secrecy and shame about this because I told my primary doctor and my physical therapist what caused it so I would have a medical record, but neither wrote it down or wanted to discuss it. Their avoidance of my situation really surprised me."
- "My parents told me, 'You made your bed, now you must lie in it.'"
- "My marriage counselor said, 'Make a list of all the sins you committed against him, and ask him for forgiveness.'"

- "The police who responded to my call for help said, 'You need to stop provoking him.'"
- "My pastor said, 'You need to submit yourself to God and become a better wife.'"

In these examples, professionals responded to the survivors with subtle (e.g., not recording on a medical record or discussing the abuse in the doctor's visit) or blatant (e.g., "You made your bed, now lie in it.") stigmatizing responses. After hearing the vast array of statements along the lines of the ones listed earlier, we were interested in looking for some commonalities among the survivors' stories. As a result of our analyses of these stories, we identified seven specific types of stigmatizing responses that survivors received from professionals from whom they sought help, which are as follows:

1. **Blame:** Professionals may stigmatize victims and survivors when they place responsibility for the abuse on them, not on the perpetrators.
2. **Discrimination:** Professionals may display prejudiced attitudes, actions, or treatment of victims and survivors based on labeling and stereotyping, oversimplifications, or uncritical judgment.
3. **Loss of status:** Professionals may act in such a way that conveys that victims and survivors have lost standing or power as a result of their experiences with abuse, such as in their communities, workplaces, and other social systems.
4. **Isolation:** Professionals may treat victims and survivors as separated from and different than themselves, thus contributing to victims and survivors being disconnected from social support resources and networks.
5. **Shame:** Professionals may treat victims and survivors in ways that invoke shame and secrecy, which describes a painful emotion felt about oneself caused by consciousness of guilt, shortcoming, self-blame, or impropriety.
6. **Dismissed/denied:** Professionals may disbelieve victims or survivors, such as by "looking the other way," implying that they do not qualify for help and support, failing to take any action to provide support, or empathizing with survivors' perpetrators.
7. **Blatant unprofessionalism:** Some professionals act toward victims and survivors in ways that are blatantly unprofessional or unethical, such as through name-calling, breaches of confidentiality, or the blurring of professional boundaries.

Victims and survivors of intimate partner violence deserve nothing less than positive, helpful experiences when they go to access services and seek help from professionals. Therefore, it is essential to understand how negative attitudes and behaviors can exist among professionals in order to identify ways to prevent this from occurring. Negative attitudes from professionals toward victims of abuse are a long-standing problem.

For example, early research from the 1970s documented that various professionals, including law enforcement officers and crisis professionals, may hold negative attitudes toward women impacted by violence.[3] Unfortunately, more recent research—including our own—demonstrates that these attitudes persist among some professionals, even today. Two professional groups that have gained the attention of researchers recently are law enforcement officers and medical doctors.

Let's focus for a moment on the relationship between victims of intimate partner violence and law enforcement. In recent years, many law enforcement agencies have devoted significant time, resources, and attention to improving their responsiveness to victims of intimate partner violence as well as to training officers to understand the dynamics of abusive relationships. Even still, we know that many victims do not report incidents of abuse for fear that law enforcement agencies will be unwilling and unable to act on their behalf. We also know that officers report frustration when assisting victims during intimate partner violence incidents. Attitudes and beliefs about intimate partner violence inevitably shape how law enforcement officers respond to incidents. An exploration[4] of police officers' perceptions of intimate partner violence demonstrated both positive and negative attitudes from the 309 officers who responded to the survey. Most of the officers (84%) felt that intimate partner violence calls took up too much of their time and effort, and the vast majority (93%) also reported a high level of frustration with repeat calls from the same address. This same percentage (93%) of officers also believed that too many calls were received for only verbal arguments. Other key findings from this study revealed that only 24% of officers believed that more training on intimate partner violence would help them assess abuse scenes. Male officers and older officers were more likely to describe intimate partner violence calls as problematic. Positive responses included that 87% of officers indicated that they did not agree that intimate partner violence is a private matter, and 64% of the officers agreed that offenders need to be arrested, even when the other party involved in the violence does not want the person to be arrested. One of the largest implications from the study was the need for continued training for police officers, even if it is viewed from the officers as unnecessary.

Another important professional group in the lives of victims and survivors of intimate partner violence are medical doctors. Physicians play a vital role in screening for intimate partner violence, since approximately one-quarter of a million hospital visits occur as a result of IPV annually.[5] In 1999, a group of researchers[6] asked how many medical professionals screened for intimate partner violence, and they found that only one in ten physicians said they did. When physicians were asked about the barriers that get in the way of asking about intimate partner violence, responses ranged from practicalities—such as lack of time, training, and resources—to fears of offending the patient, feeling unable to "fix" the problem, doubt that the patient will change, and a fear of opening "Pandora's box." In January 2013, the U.S. Preventive Services Task Force recommended IPV screening as a routine preventive service to be administered by physicians.[7] This initiative represented a major cultural shift for the medical profession, and thus it has become increasingly important that physicians and other medical personnel receive adequate training to ensure that they can respond competently to patients who have been impacted by abusive relationships.

Earlier in this section, we referenced our study that looked at stigmatizing responses that participants in our study faced from professionals. In that study,[8] we surveyed 231 survivors of past abuse about any experiences with stigma from various professionals that participants might have had. The professionals included mental health professionals, attorneys and judges, health-care professionals, law enforcement, professionals in survivors' workplaces or educational systems, and parenting-related professionals. The results of this study revealed that our participants did, in fact, encounter stigma from these professionals. The most common types of professionals that survivors felt stigmatized by were professionals in the court system and law enforcement officers, and the most common aspects of stigma they experienced from these professionals were feeling dismissed and denied and feeling blamed by them. To provide additional information about the types of stigmatizing experiences that survivors shared with us, the following summary includes quotes describing messages survivors received and their experiences with various professional groups.

Law Enforcement

Law enforcement agents in our study had a number of stigmatizing responses toward our survivors. When one woman called law enforcement to report a violent episode that was occurring in her home with her abusive husband, the agent responded, "You need to stop provoking him." Another participant in our study described an event that occurred in a parking lot in her town. She called the law enforcement agent when she felt as though her husband was threatening her safety. She said the following about the agent who responded to the call, "Long story short the officer told me 'you married him' and was very perturbed about having to tell a man to leave a parking lot." Another participant in our study described the law enforcement in her town as a joke. Her experience involved two separate calls that both involved serious physical injuries related to abuse. She was told they could not assist her. Here is what she said about their response:

> "The local police are a joke. In 10 years I called twice. My first call I had a bloodied lip and their response was if he wasn't there then they could do nothing. My second call was when he yanked me down by my hair with my newborn daughter in my arms. I was told since I had no visible injuries they couldn't make him leave."

Yet another law enforcement agent told one of the survivors in our study that because her abuser was part owner of their home, he could not be asked to leave the property.

Court System

We also asked participants in our study about stigma they faced when dealing with the court system. Survivors told us about experiences they'd had with attorneys, judges, and other professionals that were stigmatizing as they attempted to navigate through the legal system and get assistance for the abuse. One participant told us about a judge who said the following, "She often asked me why I hadn't done anything earlier and if I was telling the truth she would assume I would have done something about the abuse earlier." Another survivor talked about how she was told that it was her fault:

> "The statement that I 'got myself into' it was one I heard from many— My lawyer, my brother and sister-in-law, and a couple of the very few friends I had left by the time the marriage ended (my husband was very good at isolating me from any support). And I was too wounded and weak at that point to argue. I had heard so often that it was 'my fault' from my husband, heard 'you brought this on yourself' so many times that hearing it from them was not much different."

Another example we heard was about a judge who actually told a survivor that he'd like to punish her. "I was told by a judge that if he could have his way and punish me he would know what to do with me, but since he was to do what was best for the children he wouldn't go there." Less blatant stigma was also found related to court experiences that our survivors experienced. One survivor talked about how her abuser was able to "fool" the courtroom by showing up to court dates in military uniform and that this seemed to excuse his behavior. "My ex was military. He would just show up to court in his military dress and nothing would ever happen to him."

Medical Professionals

We also asked participants to tell us about any stigmatizing experience they had had with those in the medical professions. We heard many examples related to this. Two different participants were called or made to feel "stupid" as they re-told stories of stigma while seeking medical help. "I was made to feel stupid for being in such a relationship." and "My doctor told me I was stupid if I didn't leave." Another participant explained that when she revealed her past abuse she'd experienced in childhood, she felt labeled and stigmatized as "destined" to be abused as an adult: "Because I was abused as a child without receiving help I was destined to be abused as an adult." Yet another survivor in our study was told that her medical doctor "didn't want to get involved in domestic violence injuries."

Mental Health Professionals

When survivors in our study sought assistance from a mental health professional (e.g., counselor, psychologist, marriage and family therapist), they were met with stigmatizing responses. Some responses were blaming and suggested that the survivor had done something wrong and needed to fix this. For example, one marriage and family therapist said the following to the survivor: "Make a list of all the sins you committed against him, and ask him for forgiveness." Another survivor was blamed in the following way:

> "The therapist I was seeing during the abusive relationship didn't identify what was happening as abusive. He told me I was 'triggering' my ex's controlling behavior and sexual assaults, and encouraged me to focus on my own 'contributions' to the problem rather than find ways to stay safe. He also referred the two of us for couple's counseling, which also reinforced the idea that I was partially responsible for my ex's abusive behavior."

Another mental health professional was blatantly unprofessional to a survivor who had sought support for having a low libido. "One time I went to a counselor because I was having a hard time with my libido (go figure, who wouldn't after experienced such horrors), and the therapist told me to give my ex more blow jobs." Yet another survivor in our study spoke of two different experiences with mental health professionals: one who did not believe her when she disclosed that she had been raped and another counselor who learned of the rape but then never brought it up after the survivor disclosed it in session. Here is how the survivor described her experiences:

> "My counselor did not believe me in the most recent rape/sexual assault, so that was very shaming. Because she 'latched' onto this, instead of helping me with my presenting issues, I did not return. Instead I suffered in fear that he [abuser] would find out I went to a counselor. The other counselor I saw was more accepting, but never really addressed it with me. I wanted to hide from it, and she let me."

Domestic Violence Agencies

Participants in our research experienced stigma when they sought help at domestic violence agencies as well. One type of response that participants described was that of blame. Take the following quote, for example: "An employee blamed me for not leaving with my son. She smugly told me I should have called their agency or the police all the while acting like I should have known better." Similarly, another survivor felt judged for the timing of her decision to file a protective order. "During our meeting, she asked me why I was just now trying to put a protective order on my ex-husband." Other participants gave us examples of blatant unprofessionalism from DV staff members, "The woman assigned to meet with me was mad at the receptionist and told her in front of me that she was done for the day and wasn't pleased that she had to help me." For this survivor who had mustered up the courage to seek assistance, it was very upsetting to be met with this sort of unprofessional response.

Religious Organizations

Many survivors in our study shared examples of stigma while seeking assistance from religious leaders in their places of worship. For many survivors, they assumed that this would be a safe and supportive place to get support and resources related to the abuse, but they were instead met with judgment, blame, and other stigmatizing responses. For one participant, her pastor said the following when she disclosed about the abuse she was experiencing: "You need to submit yourself to God and become a better wife." Another person was told, "God hates divorce." Yet another survivor was asked, "Why don't you let him come back?" Survivors were also told that they might be punished by God for not allowing an abusive partner back into the house. These were the specific quotes that our participants told us: "You need to let your husband come home. You know, God's gonna do so-and-so to you." Others within the church excused abuse or tried to normalize it: "If domestic violence were grounds for annulment, everyone would be divorced!" Still other survivors felt as though their places of worship turned their backs on them, as the organizations believed that divorce was ugly: "I was shunned by a few churches who were not willing to have a single/divorced woman staining their perfect aisles."

Employment and Education

When we asked survivors to tell us about their stigmatizing experiences, we also were curious to know if those affiliated with employment (e.g., bosses, coworkers) and education (e.g., teachers) stigmatized survivors when the abuse was revealed. For some survivors, stigma occurred from administrators or colleagues at work. One survivor was told that she lost her job because she was "a high risk for calling in." For survivors who experienced any sort of episode with an abuser at their place of work, they suffered the consequences (rather than the perpetrator) for the incident. One survivor was stigmatized "because he attacked me in the parking lot," while another person we heard from was asked to resign from her job because of her husband's stalking her at her place of employment. Other participants lost their jobs because of missing too many days as a result of the abuse, while we heard from other participants about the discomfort and negative experiences that ensued when coworkers knew what was happening but did not want to acknowledge that it was occurring: "They knew what was happening and didn't want to deal with it." One last quote related to workplace stigma highlights an example of a time that a survivor felt stigmatized by a supervisor who knew of the abuse but did not respond in a supportive way:

> "She looked at me as if she felt disgusted by me and proceeded to tell me that if I was in a bad situation I needed to be smart enough to get out. She also sent me home because I looked awful."

These statements from professionals are difficult to read. When we imagine victims and survivors reaching out to get services, we assume that the professional will be just that—professional. For victims and survivors who are in a vulnerable place when seeking help, it is that much more important for them to be met with support and encouragement, as well as a warm demeanor and a nonjudgmental environment. This is not to say that *all* professionals who assist victims and survivors are stigmatizing in their responses. We know that there are many outstanding professionals in a variety of fields who do incredible work every day and put in tireless efforts to support victims and survivors.

At the same time, though, it is important that we work to ensure that no professionals, in any context, convey stigmatizing attitudes and behaviors because they are particularly damaging to people who are trying to leave and recover from the abuse. Many participants in our research have called these experiences with professionals re-traumatizing, and this is easy to believe. When someone hears these sorts of messages from a professional in a position of power, it is all too easy for those stigmatizing messages to become internalized. For many victims and survivors seeking help, if they encounter stigmatizing messages, they will be similar messages to the ones they've received from their abusers, which means that they can have a reinforcing effect. Such messages can become deeply internalized and affect victims' and survivors' beliefs about how likely they can receive the help and support they need.

Just as we mentioned earlier in the context of friends and family members responding in stigmatizing ways to victims and survivors of abuse, we also feel certain that many professionals who convey stigmatizing responses are not acting intentionally to harm them. In many cases, some professionals might not even be aware that they are stigmatizing victims and survivors as they convey certain messages. Many believe that their responses are valid, and helpful, even. Alice Sebold's book *Lucky*[9] affirms this notion. In her story, she tells of her experience of being brutally raped as a college freshman at Syracuse University. In her interaction with a law enforcement officer, he told her she should consider herself "lucky" to have lived through it and that another young woman had been murdered in the same area where the rape had occurred. As we think about the police officer in the interaction, a first response might be one of shock, or disbelief, or anger. Why would anyone think that a rape victim would find solace or comfort in hearing that he or she is *lucky*? How could anyone ever consider being raped as lucky? And why would this sort of statement cross the officer's mind as a helpful response? Although we can't speak for the officer in the situation, we might assume that he was in fact not aware that his statement would have a profound and lasting effect on Sebold and that she would title her memoir about the event after his words. He may truly have been trying to help her look at her situation from a positive view in that she could have been murdered after the rape, so in his mind, he may have though he was helping her look at her situation in a more positive light. Nonetheless, the remark stayed with her and left a profound impact on her life. Even with the best of intentions, we believe that there are some professionals out there who do not realize that what they say is not helpful and in fact hurtful.

Factors That Can Contribute to Stigmatizing Responses Among Professionals

In light of the earlier discussion, let's assume that most professionals do want to provide help, support, and non-stigmatizing responses to victims and survivors of abuse. (We acknowledge that there may be some professionals who do not hold such a vision of their work, but we believe that this is likely a very small percentage of professionals, especially since professionals with especially damaging attitudes and practices are likely to be "weeded out" of their professions through organizational policies, training programs, and professional supervision.) All of this leads us to an important question: how is it that there are so many well-meaning professionals who end up responding to victims and survivors in unhelpful, stigmatizing ways? So where do these attitudes originate in professionals? For those who especially are in a helping profession, we assume that attitudes would be positive in nature and helpful to those seeking services. We believe that there are three main factors that can contribute to these responses: a lack of training; a lack of resources, support, or validation; and personal biases, assumptions, and struggles.

Lack of Training

Far too many professionals lack sufficient training and knowledge to work with survivors and victims of intimate partner violence. In many professional fields in which people work with clients impacted by intimate partner violence, standardized training to understand and address intimate partner violence is lacking. For example, a survey[10] of mental health professionals found that just over half of the providers surveyed had received training on intimate partner violence, with this training typically occurring in continuing education courses. The content and format of continuing education courses can vary widely, and these could offer anywhere from a very short (e.g., 1 hour) to lengthy (e.g., 40 hours) duration of trainings. A more recent survey[11] confirmed that many mental health professionals still lack extensive training on the topic of intimate partner violence and that mental health professionals without such training are less likely to use assessment and intervention practices that address intimate partner violence in ways that reflect best practices for promoting safety. Given this information, it appears that many mental health professionals lack awareness of the dynamics of abusive relationships, and services may not be in place to address these issues. Beyond mental health professionals, training may be lacking in a variety of other key professional groups, including law enforcement agencies, court personnel, medical professionals, and educational professionals who work with children impacted by parental intimate partner violence.

To illustrate further how a lack of training can lead to stigmatizing responses, we will offer an example from our own field of counseling. Generally speaking, training in family violence and intimate partner violence is not required for all trainees in professional counseling programs. Therefore, a student could graduate from a graduate program in counseling with minimal or even no training in this topic. Without this basic training, counselors may not know the signs of an abusive relationship, which could lead them to fail to recognize when clients they serve are involved in an abusive relationship. Therefore, they may stigmatize clients by failing to ask about experiences of abuse at all, or by failing to ask about it in ways that will make it more comfortable and safe for victims to disclose abuse. Furthermore, it is considered best practice in the field of couples counseling for couples to not be seen together for conjoint counseling if violence is present.[12] Seeing partners together in couples counseling when violence is present could pose safety risks for victims, and it also implies a stigmatizing message that both partners share responsibility for the abuse, thus suggesting that victims are at least partially to blame. A counselor who is not aware of this best practice because he or she has never been trained in it may be inclined to offer couples counseling for couples in which abuse is occurring, even believing that this treatment modality could help them improve their relationship. Thus without sufficient training to address intimate partner violence, professionals can inadvertently engage in stigmatizing responses, which can also increase safety risks for victims.

Lack of Resources, Support, or Validation

One of the other culprits for professionals' stigmatizing responses is a lack of resources, support, or validation. When professionals do not feel supported in their work, we begin to feel resentful, burned out, or emotionally depleted. If a professional does not have resources to offer someone seeking services, this too might manifest into negative attitudes. In many cases, the organizations through which professionals who serve victims and survivors of intimate partner violence work are sorely under-resourced, especially because many rely on public, governmental funding or are nonprofit organizations. In addition to tangible and financial resources, moral support from colleagues or supervisors might promote helpful, non-stigmatizing responses, but in fields that are challenging and stressful, coworkers often struggle to take the time to do this for one another. In many agencies that serve victims and services—including law enforcement agencies, mental health and health-care settings, and domestic violence agencies—the numbers of clients seeking services continue to rise, while at the same time, budgetary resources have dwindled. Thus many professionals are seeing more and more clients but have less and less time to do things, such as consult with each other about a client, take a restful break during the workday, or engage in non-work-related conversations as a way to support and validate the difficult work that is inherent in fields such as mental health or social services. Ongoing feelings of isolation and a lack of support can begin to wear on professionals who might then begin to exhibit negative responses toward clients.

Personal Biases, Assumptions, and Struggles

Unexamined personal biases might be another source of stigmatizing responses from professionals. Personal attitudes impact behaviors. Thus if a professional holds unchecked biases or assumptions toward victims and survivors of abusive relationships, these might translate into stigmatizing responses. For example, if a medical doctor holds an assumption that all people should be able to get out of a physically abusive relationship, for physical health reasons and to protect themselves from physical harm, then that medical doctor might fail to understand the nuances in a victim's reasons for staying in an abusive relationship, despite the physical safety threats. The doctor might then attempt to push his or her patients toward leaving and ask questions in a way that implies that they are foolish for staying in abusive relationships.

Professionals are in a prime position to be able to help and support victims and survivors of abuse. And yet the safety risks involved in abusive relationships are highly complex, and each person's situation is unique. Therefore, professionals may face situations in which they feel hopeless and helpless—they may be at a loss as to the best way to help someone they are serving. Even when professionals are highly trained, no professional can be expected to have all the answers, and even highly skilled and knowledgeable professionals will face situations that push them to the limits of their knowledge. These situations can take a significant emotional toll on professionals, which can lead to stress, burnout, emotional exhaustion, mental health challenges, and impaired well-being. When professionals are impaired in these ways, their ability to serve victims and survivors effectively can become compromised. Therefore, it remains critically important for professionals working in these fields to ensure that they engage in positive self-care so that they can remain consistently able to respond compassionately and supportively to victims and survivors who seek their help.

The Harmful Nature of Stigmatizing Responses From Professionals

Stigmatizing responses from professionals are harmful for at least three reasons, which we will explore in this section. First, stigmatizing responses from professionals can stunt emotional healing that might have taken place post-abuse. Stigmatizing responses from professionals can be re-traumatizing. A survivor or victim is already dealing with trauma from the abuse. When these sorts of responses occur, it can send that person back into feelings that were starting to recover and heal, and this can serve as a major setback in their progress toward overcoming abuse. Second, stigmatizing responses from professionals are harmful because these responses can exacerbate internalized stigma. Stigmatizing responses from a professional from whom the victim or survivor sought help can become internalized if the person goes on to believe that maybe what the person said was, in fact, true.

Third, stigmatizing responses from professionals are harmful because of the power imbalance between professionals and the clients they serve. Professionals naturally hold a position of power in relation to clients who seek their help. When a professional responds in a harmful way, these negative responses can lead victims and survivors to experience feelings of helplessness, especially if they view the professional as an "expert" or one who holds a significant amount of knowledge or power. Consider Table 5.1 that we have created, which compares the power that a professional might have when compared to a client. This table conveys some of the potential sources of this power imbalance, especially when the professional also holds a majority status and the client holds a minority status in a particular domain. We acknowledge that not all professionals have all the sources of power listed and that not all clients have all of the sources of vulnerability. However, even if just a few of the sources of power and a few vulnerability sources are present, the scales are tipped rather than balanced, and this can have a significant impact on the relationship. When a significant power differential is present, professionals must use extra caution, care, and concern in how they interact with clients in a vulnerable position. If they do not, even very subtle responses that convey stigma can have a powerful, negative effect.

In this chapter, we have explored the stigma that occurs when victims and survivors seek help from others, including informal and formal sources of support. Many friends and family members—even if they are well intentioned—respond to victims and survivors in ways that add to the stigma that they face from within and/or from their perpetrators. In addition, it is clear that there is a need for more education and training for the various types of professionals who come into contact with those impacted by intimate partner violence so that stigmatizing experiences no longer occur. Survivors are triumphant, resourceful, and courageous people, and they deserve supportive networks of both informal and formal resources to help them achieve safety and overcome abuse. However, as one survivor who participated in our research stated,

> "There are just times that I cannot deal with the outside world. There are days I simply don't want to deal with reality or with ignorant people who don't understand or who say stupid things. PTSD sometimes makes me want to stay safely within the bubble of my home, where my triggers are few to non-existent."

We believe that no one should have to retreat in their own safe bubble as a way to avoid negative experiences. Rather, victims and survivors should

Table 5.1 Sources of Power and Vulnerability

	Source of Power	*Source of Vulnerability*
Role	Professional	Client
Age	Adult	Youth/adult/elderly
Gender	Male	Female, transgender
Sexual Orientation	Heterosexual	LGBTQ
Race	Caucasian	Any person of color
Physical Resources	Ability, large physical size, physical strength	Disability, small size, physical "weakness"
Economic Resources	Wealth, job skills, credentials	Poverty, lack of job skills, lack of credentials
Intellectual Resources	Information and knowledge, access to information	Lack of these
Psychological Resources	Breadth of life experience, stability	Inexperience, lack of coping skills
Social Resources	Support, community, contacts	Isolation
Life Circumstances	Security, well-being	Need, crisis

be able to rest assured that, if they reach out for help, they will be met with responsive services and resources, as well as the offer of support, validation, and encouragement.

Notes

1. http://www.seethetriumph.org/blog/category/how-to-help-a-friend.
2. Crowe, A., & Murray, C. E. (2015). Stigma from professional helpers toward survivors of intimate partner violence. *Partner Abuse*, 6(2), 157–179.
3. Field, H. S. (1978). Attitudes toward rape: A comparative analysis of police, rapists, crisis counselors, and citizens. *Journal of Personality and Social Psychology*, 36, 156–179.
4. Gover, A. R., Paul, D. P., & Dodge, M. (2011). Law enforcement officers' attitudes about domestic violence. *Violence Against Women*, 17, 619–636. DOI: 10.1177/1077801211407477.
5. National Center for Injury Prevention and Control. (2003). *Costs of intimate partner violence against women in the United States*. Atlanta, GA: Centers for Disease Control and Prevention. Retrieved August 17, 2016, from http://www.cdc.gov/violenceprevention/pdf/IPVBook-a.pdf.
6. Gerbert, B., Caspers, N., Bronstone, A., Moe, J., & Abercrombie P. (1999). A qualitative analysis of how physicians with expertise in domestic violence approach the identification of victims. *Annals of Internal Medicine*, 131, 578–84.
7. http://www.uspreventiveservicestaskforce.org/.
8. Crowe, A., & Murray, C. E. (2015). Stigma from professional helpers toward survivors of intimate partner violence. *Partner Abuse*, 6(2), 157–179.
9. Sebold, A. (1999). *Lucky*. New York: Scribner.
10. Campbell, R., Raja, S., & Grining, P. L. (1999). Training mental health professionals on violence against women. *Journal of Interpersonal Violence*, 14(10), 1003–1013. DOI:10.1177/088626099014010001.
11. Murray, C. E., Davis, J., Rudolph, L., Graves, K. N., Colbert, R., Fryer, M., Mason, A., & Thigpen, B. (in press). Domestic violence training experiences and needs among mental health professionals: Implications from a statewide survey.
12. Murray, C. E., & Graves, K. N. (2012). *Responding to family violence*. New York: Routledge.

6 Stigma in Society
Stereotypes of Abuse and Victims at the Societal Level

> "Society chooses to believe certain things about abused women: They are weak; they could have done something about it; they did something to cause it; they should have been a better wife. They never say it to your face, but it is the questions they ask. Why didn't you do this? How could you do that? Why did you let that happen?"
> ~ *Domestic Violence Survivor*

So far in this book, we have looked at the stigma surrounding intimate partner violence primarily at the individual and relational levels, focusing on how perpetrators convey stigma, how victims and survivors internalize it, and how friends, family members, and professionals respond to victims and survivors in stigmatizing ways. We can't ignore the fact that all of these aspects of stigma occur within societal contexts, and in this chapter, we turn our attention to the ways that the stigma surrounding intimate partner violence is perpetuated at a societal level. At the current time, it isn't possible to tease apart fully the complex interplays among society, relationships, and individuals with regard to the stigma surrounding intimate partner violence. It may never be possible to tease apart fully how societal stigma influences individuals as well as how stigma at the individual and relationship levels influences societal stigma. Most likely, these influences go both directions: stigma at the societal level impacts individuals, and stigmatizing beliefs that individuals hold contribute to the perpetuation of stigma in society.

What we do know is that many victims and survivors of abusive relationships feel the stigma from society in a variety of ways, and this stigma presents a number of challenges both during and after the relationship. In this chapter, we'll explore some of the most significant ways that societal stigma occurs, including common social stereotypes about intimate partner violence and the people who experience it, stigma that occurs within cultural groups, and stigmatizing messages about intimate partner violence in various forms of media. Before we delve into those topics, let's take a closer look at how societal stigma can impact individual victims and survivors through the story of one of the survivors who participated in our research.

Naomi's Story

Naomi is a multiracial woman in her mid-20s who has a graduate degree and was a full-time student at the time she participated in our study. Naomi is a survivor of two past abusive relationships. In the first relationship, Naomi's partner was

> "emotionally abusive, psychologically abusive, [and] sexually abusive. With his words and actions, he made me feel worthless. He also took advantage of me sexually. He lied to me about his entire identity and took advantage of my vulnerability. He drained me of everything I once was."

After that relationship ended, Naomi became involved in another abusive relationship, which ended over five years before she shared her story with us. That relationship was a two-year, committed dating relationship in which she experienced physical, verbal, emotional, sexual, and financial abuse. After Naomi realized that this boyfriend was abusive, she said, "I had started to try and keep my distance from him." One particularly violent incident led to the end of their relationship. This incident occurred out in public, and Naomi said,

> "If it wasn't for a bystander who noticed and threatened to call the police, I think he would have killed me. In that moment, I realized that if I were to stay in that relationship, I wouldn't make it out alive. So, as soon as it was safe, I ran as far as I could, called the police, and pressed charges. He knew it was over then because I had broken the golden rule of 'snitching' to the police."

Naomi pursued criminal charges against her abuser after that incident, but, "because of a loophole, charges were dropped."

Naomi says that her past experiences with abuse have had a long-term negative impact on her life. She said,

> "You can never be the same after such horrific things happen to you. Years later, I still don't know how to cope with the pain or make peace with what happened. I am still struggling with the effects of the abuse. My self-confidence has been shattered, and I no longer believe that I am worthy of love and understanding. I still suffer daily. I had issues with addiction as a result of not being able to cope with the things he did to me. I also tried to commit suicide. I feel very alone and stigmatized by society. It was the biggest tragedy in my life."

Naomi shared with us that she has been especially impacted by the societal stigma that surrounds intimate partner violence. She said,

> "My experience was horrible. The aftermath and the stigma were unbelievable. He managed to hurt me long after leaving him. To this day, people still don't get it—violence against women is so serious, yet people judge and blame victims, fail to empathize with the effects of abuse, and condone violence against women."

Naomi further shared that she simply cannot understand the extent to which survivors of abusive relationships are stigmatized in society. She said,

> "I hate society and how it condones violence against women. Why is it socially acceptable to degrade women? To belittle them, call them names, threaten them, neglect them, beat them? Seriously. What is it about the disrespect of women that is so socially acceptable? This kind of mindset is so deeply ingrained."

Despite her long journey of recovery, Naomi shared the ways she is working toward overcoming her past abuse. She said this involves "understanding why it happened to you (how vulnerable I was, how he took advantage of that), forgiving yourself, better understanding the dynamics of abuse, trauma-specific therapy; group therapy (sharing stories), speaking out, not being ashamed to share my story." Some of the specific steps that Naomi has taken toward this overcoming process are "educating myself; refusing to silence myself, sharing stories with other survivors, working on my broken self-confidence, and wanting to create a change because people and the justice system did me so wrong." Even in the face of her own challenges related to the abuse, Naomi offered hope and encouragement to other survivors, saying, "There is hope. There is a life outside of the terror you are living. And you deserve so much better."

Common Stereotypes About Intimate Partner Violence and the People Who Experience It

Naomi described her past abuse and the societal stigma that surrounded it as "the biggest tragedy in my life." Unfortunately, this tragedy is one that is experienced by far too many victims and survivors of abusive relationships. In addition to the trauma that results directly from their abuse, many victims and survivors are re-traumatized by the stigma they face in society. One of the biggest sources of societal stigma are the common misconceived stereotypes about abuse and people who experience it that are held by many people in society. In Naomi's words, people are often quick to judge and blame victims, which serves to condone violence at a societal level. In this section, we'll present some of the common stereotypes that victims and survivors face, in their own words.

Stereotypes About Who Does, and Who Does Not, Experience Intimate Partner Violence

Many people in society hold beliefs that there are only certain types of people who experience abusive relationships. Often, this means that people believe that abuse only happens to people other than themselves, and other stereotypes hold that abuse may only happen to people who are of a lower income or educational attainment level. Rigid views in society about who experiences abuse and in what types of relationships it occurs can have a negative impact on victims and survivors, especially if they affect their ability to get the resources they need or if they cause them not to be believed when they tell others about their experiences.

One version of this stereotype is that abuse only occurs with male perpetrators against female victims. Indeed, as we've discussed elsewhere in this book, women are more likely to be victims of severe intimate partner violence perpetrated by men.[1] However, this stereotype doesn't hold true for other gender configurations in abusive relationships, and it is important to remember that violence does occur in other types of relationships. As one survivor of a same-sex relationship that was abusive said, "People didn't think abuse could happen between two women." Male victims also may be especially likely to face challenges in seeking help. Consider the following statement by a male survivor who was abused by a female perpetrator:

> "Being male, when she went for a restraining order, it was like I was fighting a losing battle. Being female, everything was there to help her. Being male, you feel isolated, as there is no help. Victim advocates are female-oriented, and police don't help as you're male. Being male, there is huge shame in being abused by a female, both physically and mentally. We're told to just 'walk away.' Regarding stereotypes: I'm male, and it doesn't happen to males, right?"

Another common version of this stereotype is that abuse survivors can't be strong, educated people. For example, one participant said,

> "Many individuals I meet do not believe emotionally strong, feminist women can end up in an abusive relationship. Intimate partner violence happens to all types. That's why I'm so glad that Meredith Vieira just revealed her own experience with abuse.[2] As an esteemed anchorwoman, she's the least likely in many eyes."

Another survivor shared with us that

> "I feel like others often see my/view my experiences as an anomaly. I am seen as a well-educated, independent, smart, strong woman, so the, 'You're not the typical victim, though,' is a frequent challenge from those who are not well-versed in domestic violence dynamics. I feel the stereotype of the 'typical' victim/survivor is so entrenched that I am provided a different set of standards, at times dismissed as not facing the same challenges, as if the experiences should in some way not affect me as deeply. It's difficult for me to put this into words. I also get the sense that, when hearing about my experiences, the experiences of other women who do not have the same protective factors I had are dismissed as well, as if it's more their fault somehow, or as if they 'put up with it' because 'that's all they've known.'"

Still another survivor said, "They pity you, and we don't need to be pitied. We need people to recognize that it is a serious situation, and it happens in all types of lives, all classes, all races, all professions. It doesn't discriminate. It affects us all." All of these survivors' experiences demonstrate that stereotypes about who in society experiences abuse can be harmful to victims and survivors on many levels, especially as they seek help and as they strive to have their stories heard and validated by others.

Stereotypes That It Is Easy to Leave an Abusive Relationship and That Victims Are Somehow to Blame for the Abuse They Experienced

Another category of societal stereotypes about intimate partner violence involves victim-blaming attitudes that attribute culpability for the abuse to victims because they stay in the relationships. Inherent in this stereotype is the assumption that it is easy to leave the relationship. Victims and survivors may encounter this stereotype in many ways, both during and after the relationship. We heard many examples of how this stereotype impacted the survivors who participated in our research. Consider, for example, the following quotes:

- "When the O. J. Simpson trial was going on after my ex left me, I was in the elevator with some woman who commented that Nicole must have done something to set O. J. off, and why did she not just leave, and if her husband EVER laid a hand on her, that she would leave that instant. I told her that she does not know what she would do until that moment happens, and that I hoped she never ever had to go through something like that, but until you go through it yourself, you do not know what you would do, or what you could do. I hate stereotypes and judgmental people!"

- "Everyone asks what YOU did to cause it. For example, when I didn't leave my abusive fiancé after he started abusing me, people said, "Well, if it was so bad, why didn't you leave?," thus making me feel like it was MY fault."
- "I faced some blame for the abuse by others. 'Why didn't you just leave?' type of stuff."
- "I feel that society tells women in abusive relationships that it is their fault for not leaving."
- "'Why does she stay with him?!' is quite often the phrase when a news item comes on where a woman in an abusive relationship has been murdered or something."
- "Being labeled is a big one. I was actually called stupid for staying with my boyfriend. The stereotypes were mostly that I did something to deserve the abuse or that I must not have minded it because I stayed."
- "I experienced blame by others stating that staying was my fault or that my not 'fighting back' somehow made me responsible."

Victim-blaming is a particularly harmful societal stereotype about intimate partner violence because it releases perpetrators from accepting full responsibility for their abuse, and it also minimizes the dangers that may arise when victims attempt to leave abusive relationships.

Stereotypes That Victims and Survivors Are Not as Valuable as Other People

Some societal stereotypes about intimate partner violence hold that victims and survivors are devalued members of society. These stereotypes fail to acknowledge victims' and survivors' strength, resilience, and resourcefulness required for the day-to-day survival within an abusive relationship. Rather, they imply that victims and survivors must have some inherent flaws that led them to become involved in the abusive relationships. This inaccurate view can be extremely hurtful to victims and survivors, especially when they encounter these devaluing societal messages directly. The following quotes from survivors who participated in our research demonstrate the powerful negative impact of this stereotype:

- "I am somewhat looked down upon in our community and put in the same category as him. I am labeled a victim in this town and not a survivor. I'm not seen as a person that is of any importance, and therefore am not considered valuable to this community because I am a single mother and they think women need a man where I live."
- "If you come out about your experience, you suddenly become either a victim or a whore. Everyone has an opinion, and you're suddenly put on trial. You're ostracized from a group. You're an outcast."

- "I feel like assumptions are made about me as a survivor of intimate partner violence. I feel like I have been degraded and broken by his actions, in the eyes of others."
- "People discriminate, and they label you as a weak, troubled person who must have an alcohol or drug problem."
- "I feel that each time I disclose that I am an IPV survivor I am labeled in some way, either as a victim, a survivor, stupid, etc."
- "I feel once you disclose, people feel they now know who you are or what you are about. I also feel that people assume things about your ability to be in a healthy relationship, that you now can't function in a healthy relationship."

Stereotypes That Victims and Survivors Are Impaired in Their Work and Parenting Abilities

Beyond the more general devaluing stereotypes we just discussed, victims and survivors may face stereotypes about their abilities in specific areas in their lives. Two examples we heard in our research involved their ability to be good employees and their parenting abilities. For example, one survivor told us, "I experienced most discrimination and labeling and stereotyping when looking for work afterwards. As a result of this, I became very secretive about my past." Employers may deem victims and survivors as too risky or as a liability if they view them as unreliable, nonassertive, or weak. However, this overlooks the potential skills and assets that these individuals may bring to a place of employment. Stereotypes of victims and survivors as having impaired parenting abilities can appear in a variety of social systems, including family courts and schools. Consider the experiences of the following survivor:

> "Unfortunately, we have shared legal and he has full physical custody for over ten years now. My son was very little when we divorced. My ex had control of all of our money, so he was able to pay for the best attorney in town, while I was a broke student stuck with an inexperienced attorney right out of law school. My ex engaged in parental alienation, even after winning custody, and continues to do so despite being divorced for so long. I was victimized first by my ex, by the courts, by law enforcement failing to protect me, and by society for blaming me—'She didn't get full custody, so surely she must be lying or have a drug problem.' Neither of these was ever true. The victim, especially the mother, not receiving custody happens much more than what people realize. Society re-victimizes us by making assumptions such as those I mentioned."

These stereotypes about victims' and survivors' abilities to work and parent their children can compound the other challenges they face in seeking safety and recovering from abuse, as they may negatively impact their economic independence or force them to stay in unsafe relationships to remain connected with their children. Therefore, stereotypes about victims' and survivors' capabilities related to work and parenting are an especially negative aspect of the societal stigma surrounding intimate partner violence.

Stereotypes That Abuse Should Not Be Discussed Openly and Publicly

The stereotype about intimate partner violence that perhaps does the most harm toward the ultimate goal of ending intimate partner violence in society is that abuse should not be discussed openly and publicly. This stereotype is manifested in the silence that surrounds the issue and keeps many in society from acknowledging it as a significant problem. For victims and survivors, this often means that they feel pressured to keep their experiences a secret and to not discuss openly and publicly the abuse they have survived. For example, one survivor told us, "Secrecy means having to keep secrets from family, friends, colleagues, those in the medical profession, etc., because this kind of thing still isn't really talked about in the general world." Another said, "The less they know, the better. In most of my cases, someone finding out would only mean more shame and punishment." Intimate partner violence and other forms of abuse are indeed difficult subjects for many people in society to acknowledge and discuss. However, the silence that surrounds them allows them to continue to thrive, because it is harder for a society to take action against social ills that its members do not acknowledge.

Stigma That Occurs Within Cultural Groups

Now that we've examined some of the general stereotypes about intimate partner violence that perpetuate stigma at the societal level, we'll turn our attention to the ways that societal stigma occurs within specific cultural groups. As harmful as broader societal stereotypes about intimate partner violence can be, we believe that victims and survivors can be impacted even more powerfully by the messages they receive from the unique cultural groups and community contexts to which they are most closely connected. It is not our goal in this section to single out any particular cultural group or religion, as we have heard stories from many different cultures and religions that either helped to provide support and/or added stigma to those experiences based on cultural norms. We believe that any cultural group's norms could be used as either a positive or negative factor related to stigma and intimate partner violence. Therefore, in this section, we have removed the details about the specific religion or cultural group to which survivors were referring so that we can keep the focus more broadly on how cultural norms in general can perpetuate the stigma surrounding abusive relationships.

Two of the major contexts we'll examine in this section include cultural and religious groups. To set the stage for this discussion, consider the story of Nina, a survivor who participated in our research. Nina is an immigrant to the United States, and she started out as friends with Michael, an immigrant from a different country. Nina described the start of their relationship as follows:

> "We don't really date in my culture, so this started off as a really close friendship, and I had never been in a relationship prior. He gradually started taking advantage of our friendship, such as starting to molest me, in addition to emotional and verbal abuse. The relationship was never really labeled, but I think that's part of the way he works, so that he can have an easy out and/or get with multiple women at a time."

Nina described intimate partner violence as a serious problem in her cultural community. When we asked her if she felt that her cultural background impacted her experiences with abuse, she answered,

> "Yes. I think even though I was in my late 20s, developmentally, when it comes to relationships, I was very naive and this allowed the person to take advantage of me. We don't talk about relationships or dating in our culture, and with immigrant parents, they have their own set of stressors and adjustments to deal with, so they tend to be out of touch with those of us who have grown up here primarily and the struggles we face. I also think a more candid discussion of relationships either culturally or in our religious community would be so helpful to other girls as well. It is just not talked about!"

Nina's experiences illustrate how both cultural norms and religious influences (in the form of silence around the issue of intimate partner violence) can impact the experiences of victims and survivors of abusive relationships. In this section, we take a closer look at various contextual influences, and then we'll conclude by discussing how multiple levels of stigma can create an especially challenging climate for some victims and survivors of abuse.

Cultural-Group Norms

The norms and values of one's cultural group impact a person's individual values and what they view as acceptable and unacceptable. In the case of intimate partner violence, this can play out on many levels, but perhaps most powerfully in determining (a) how abusive behaviors are defined and (b) whether it is acceptable to end a relationship in which abuse is occurring. As an example of the former, one survivor told us, "He was not a U.S. citizen and from a country with no domestic violence laws." This is an extreme example, but it illustrates that intimate partner violence is defined differently in different countries and cultures, and in fact, there are some countries in which it is not viewed as illegal. Even in cultures in which certain aspects of abuse are defined as illegal, there still can be variation in how cultural groups determine what types of abuse are considered acceptable or unacceptable. Consider such forms of abuse as emotional/psychological abuse (which typically is not illegal), marital rape (which only became illegal in all 50 states in the United States in 1993[3]), and honor killings (which continue to occur throughout the world and in the United States even today[4]). In some cultural groups, various forms of intimate partner violence may be justified and condoned through either overt approval or through a lack of disapproval of these forms of abuse.

Cultural norms also can impact whether people view it as acceptable to end a relationship—especially a marriage—on the basis of abuse. For example, one survivor told us,

> "In my culture, 'divorce' is a bad word. When I tried to share with my mother the bad things that were happening, she said, 'You must do your best to make this relationship work. He is a good man, and he needs and loves you. Sometimes you are stubborn and conceited, so you need to change that. I don't want to know what people will say if you are divorced!' "

Another survivor said,

> "In my culture, divorce is not a good thing. When it happens, family and parents are worried about family members' and relatives' opinions. And whatever happens is your fault, so you should try no matter what to keep your marriage."

In these cases, victims and survivors may be shunned or bring disgrace to themselves and/or their families if they choose to leave their spouses, even when their safety is at risk if they stay in the relationship.

Cultural-group norms also can contribute to a lack of support that group members provide to victims and survivors, which may result in others looking the other way and failing to help when victims and survivors reach out for support. As one survivor said,

> "My ex was from a very patriarchal culture, which tended to look the other way when it came to domestic violence. His family knew what was going on, and they refused to intervene. I felt cut off from my friends and family and had little support. I called the cops on him once, and they never showed up."

Another shared,

> "I had to face shame of stigma. The friends in my cultural group who were our common friends avoided me and cut my phone, never returned my phone call and would listen to me pretending they are my friends and then try to take advantage of my situation."

When a cultural group's norms directly or implicitly condone intimate partner violence, the end result can be a lack of support for victims and survivors.

Religious-Group Norms

Religion and spirituality can serve as a powerful source of healing and coping for many victims and survivors of abuse. Religion and spirituality can provide a sense of hope, faith in a higher power, a self-affirming belief system, and positive social support, and so we do not want to underestimate the potential supports that many victims and survivors can draw from these resources both during and after an abusive relationship. However, the relationship between intimate partner violence and religion can also be a complicated one for many victims and survivors. In some cases, religious-group norms may serve the function of perpetuating abuse, and this can put victims and survivors in grave danger and limit their access to potentially supportive resources. In this section, we examine some of the ways that religious-group norms can contribute to the stigma surrounding abusive relationships.

Perpetuating Blame

One way that religious norms can contribute to stigma is if religious beliefs contribute to victim-blaming attitudes, either as internalized by victims and survivors or held by other people. Consider, for example, the following statement from a survivor who participated in our research:

> "I am frightened of being singled out if told many people, especially in the conservative faith community in which I grew up. I still haven't told my parents that it happened because I'm ashamed and feel that I'll be judged heavily for 'engaging in premarital sex,' even though it wasn't my choice to begin with. I worry that people will think I'm a slut, that I'm passive, that I 'asked for it.' The truth was, it wasn't what I was wearing, what I said, or how I walked. There was no alcohol involved. I had a manipulative partner who wanted to put me down and wanted sex and he wouldn't take no for an answer."

This survivor feared that others in her faith community would view her experiences of abuse as some form of punishment for 'engaging in premarital sex,' even though she describes her sexual experiences as being forced. In this way, it appears that she feared that her religious community would view the abuse as somehow justified because she did something to deserve it.

Using Religious Beliefs to Justify Abuse

We heard from survivors who told us that members of their religious communities justified the abuse they were experiencing on the basis of their interpretations of religious teachings or beliefs. For example, one survivor said, "My mother told me once that it was my job to 'make it right,' that 'God says divorce is bad.' This was shame I carried with me for a long time." Another survivor told us, "The abusiveness was encouraged by a religious cult whose membership we were part of during our courtship, and most of the marriage. Controlling and treating the female partner as less than were integral to the cult's teachings." Two other examples of this dynamic are reflected in the following survivors' quotes:

> "I talked to a religious leader, insisting I feared for my safety, and was told that this was happening to me because I did not have enough faith and did not want to have a child with him. If I had a child, he said, all this would go away." And, "Getting a divorce was a sin. Staying married would have been martyrdom. In fact, I was told by a preacher that I had to go home and ask my husband for forgiveness for filing a divorce. If I were to die, I would die a martyr for Jesus. I did stay, and in a short time after that, he attacked me and raped me."

Perpetrators Using Leadership Positions to Cover for Their Abuse

As we've already discussed throughout this book, perpetrators often are not abusive outside of the context of their intimate relationships. In cases in which perpetrators are in leadership positions in religious institutions and hold other reputable positions in the community, they can trick community members into believing that they would not be capable of the abusive behaviors in which they engage. As one example, a survivor who participated in our research said,

> "My ex-husband is and was a minster in our church, and no one believes to this day a minster could do such things to his wife or children. He is still trying to get me back after all this time just to make himself look good in the eyes of the public."

It is natural and normal for people to view their religious leaders as moral and ethical leaders and role models. However, when abuse perpetrators hold these positions, they are able to use their positional authority to help convince others that they are not abusive, thereby further controlling and diminishing their victims' power and options for seeking safety.

Creating a Context for Spiritual Abuse to Occur

Spiritual abuse occurs when an abuse perpetrator engages in controlling behaviors that diminish the victim's spiritual well-being and limit the victim's ability to make spiritual decisions for her or himself. When religious norms condone intimate partner violence, or when they are silent on the issue of abuse all together, this creates a context in which perpetrators have more opportunities to engage in spiritual abuse. The following example from a survivor in our research illustrates this dynamic:

> "My abuser isolated me by moving me away from all family and friends and using religious texts to shame me into compliance. This is highly isolating, as you will be further victimized by telling a church leader, who in my case was always male and had the misogynistic attitudes that my abuser did. If I said anything he would counter that relaying of information with a story about my 'not being submitted.' Most male pastors in fundamentalist churches do not tell women to leave for safety if the husband counters her claims. You learn through unwritten rules and the 'no talk law' in the spiritually abusive churches to stay isolated from others. Many women I know are stuck in the cycle of abuse because of the community of faith, which is mostly very abusive and feeds the stereotypes and shame. In a fundamentalist faith community you will lose your status as a good wife and mother. It is akin to 'shunning' that goes on, without the formalized disciplinary measures. This is also why you simply keep a secret of what is happening. Others even observed his harshness and kept silent. I think various faith cultures do more to shame women and stigmatize them into staying in abuse than help them! After I left my seriously abusive partner, I was a victim of the severest social exclusion and had a stereotype of being a failure because *I* could not make my marriage work. That is what chained me into my second abusive relationship. The deep shame of divorcing twice kept me in it for many years after I realized how dysfunctional the marriage was. Finally, I had to totally break free of the spiritual abusiveness to leave my second husband. He used to mock me and say to me, 'You will never leave me. You were ashamed to ever be divorced, and the people in church will never understand your divorcing twice.'"

Spiritual abuse can be an especially challenging aspect of intimate partner violence, particularly because of the powerful benefits that victims and survivors can experience from a positive connection to spirituality and religion. Religious-group norms that contribute to the stigma surrounding intimate partner violence can be very impactful to victims and survivors for whom religious and spiritual beliefs play a central role in their lives. They can lead to a great deal of confusion, especially as victims and survivors try to determine from a religious or spiritual standpoint how they should respond to the abuse they are experiencing. Therefore, societal stigma that is perpetuated by religious-group norms exerts a potentially powerful force through the process of surviving and recovering from an abusive intimate relationship.

Multiple Levels of Stigma

Thinking beyond intimate partner violence, certain other groups of people may experience stigma in society based on a specific set of characteristics they may share. For example, people with mental illness, people who are HIV-positive, immigrants, and people who are members of the lesbian/gay/bisexual/transgender/intersex (LGBTI) population may experience stigma in modern society because their experiences are not well understood by many people who are not members of those populations. Disclosing abuse is difficult for virtually any victim or survivor of abuse, but it can be especially difficult for those who are members of otherwise stigmatized populations, particularly if disclosure of the abuse requires also disclosing another stigmatized identity at the same time.

To consider how multiple levels of societal stigma can intersect, let's look closer at the issue of same-sex intimate partner violence. As we've discussed earlier in this book, existing research suggests that intimate partner violence occurs in same-sex relationships at about the same rate as in heterosexual relationships.[5] However, same-sex intimate partner violence has been referred to as a "second closet" because victims face both the stigma of being abused and the stigma of being a member of a sexual minority population.[6] Even as same-sex marriage has become legal throughout the United States, members of the LGBTI population still may not be fully open about their sexual orientation or gender identity, either with some or all of the people in their lives. If someone in an abusive same-sex relationship hasn't yet disclosed that they are gay or lesbian, then seeking help for the relationship may also mean that they need to reveal their sexual orientation. Even when people have come out about their sexual orientation, the stigma surrounding their sexual orientation can hinder their willingness or ability to receive adequate support. Consider, as examples, the following two stories from survivors in our research:

- "The abuse wasn't taken seriously. It was seen as some sort of 'byproduct' for my being gay and 'choosing a gay lifestyle.' I was only 18 when we met. I had little experience in the outside world due to a strict religious upbringing that shielded me from society as a whole and discouraged any sort of involvement with the rest of the world. I think he relied on the inherent discrimination in society at the time and in our community to control what I did. My family still doesn't know the degree to which is got abusive and, for that matter, has never expressed any desire to find out despite knowing some of what went on in those 5 1/2 years."

- "Secrecy is the biggest. Being in a lesbian relationship makes IPV even more secret. I didn't want anyone to know about it because I felt like it would give people more power to illegitimize our relationship or same-sex relationships. I didn't want anyone to know that it truly was a bad relationship. I know that relationships can be good or bad, no matter the sex of each partner, but I didn't want to give homophobic people ammunition to say that all same-sex relationships were bad."

Experiences of people who are abused in same-sex relationships illustrate how multiple levels of societal stigma can intersect to compound the challenges that victims of intimate partner violence face. Other stigmatized and marginalized groups, in addition to the LGBTI population, can face similar challenges. In addition to the stereotypes about intimate partner violence in general, they may face stereotypes about their other stigmatized identities. In addition, laws and supportive resources designed to protect victims from abuse may not fully capture the nuances of their experiences. And because they face compounded stigma based on multiple identities, they may be more likely to be blamed and devalued for their abuse. Overall, societal stigma can be compounded by cultural-group norms that perpetuate abuse, and this is especially true when multiple levels of stigma are compounded for victims and survivors who are part of marginalized groups.

Stigma in the Media

Another powerful force that contributes to the societal stigma surrounding intimate partner violence is found in the media. Representations of intimate partner violence in various forms of media—including news, music, television shows and movies, and social media—can contribute to the stigma surrounding abusive relationships. Media is a powerful force in shaping the public's views toward intimate partner violence,[7] especially for people who may not have direct, personal experience with abusive relationships. In fact, except for people who grow up in violent homes or who witness abuse in their neighborhoods, forms of media are likely the first ways that many people are exposed to the topic of abusive relationships, whether that is through a story from a local or national news outlet, in the plotline of a movie or television show, or through a popular song or music video.

The media can be a positive force for raising awareness about intimate partner violence, such as when news stories are done that educate readers or viewers about the dynamics of abuse and resources that are available in communities to help support people who are being abused. The media can also illustrate the dynamics of abusive relationships, for example, through a documentary that tells the story of survivors and their experiences with seeking help. Because the media is so pervasive in today's society, the potential reach of these awareness-raising tools is vast, and many advocacy agencies work closely with media partners to help bring attention to the important issue of intimate partner violence in society.

On the other hand, there are many ways that the media can also perpetuate societal stigma surrounding intimate partner violence. Consider the following three examples:

- Social media platforms, most notably Facebook, have come under criticism for failing to remove content that glorifies violence against women and treats intimate partner violence as a topic of humor.[8]
- Two major popular music hits in recent years—*Blurred Lines* from Robin Thicke[9] and *Animals* by Maroon 5[10]—faced major criticism for music video images and lyrics that promote sexual assault and/or stalking, and yet both songs received frequent airplay on radio stations and earned the musicians large sums of money.
- In September 2014, video footage taken from an elevator showed professional football player Ray Rice punching his wife in the face. Although the incident had occurred several months earlier, it was not until the video emerged that much of the general public knew about the incident. The National Football League came under fire for having only punished Rice with a two-game suspension for the violence, and eventually the NFL handed down a much steeper punishment.[11] A flurry of news coverage surrounded the Rice case, although stigmatizing messages were conveyed through some of this coverage, such as news show hosts making jokes about the violence and commentary that had themes of blaming victims for their abuse.[12]

All three of these examples have brought greater awareness to the public about intimate partner violence and other forms of abuse. However, this type of awareness can be a double-edged sword for advocates for ending the stigma surrounding abuse. A lingering effect of ongoing news coverage of these and other current events surrounding interpersonal violence is that more people start talking about these issues when they are kept at the forefront of our attention through the media. On the other hand, each of these examples demonstrates that there remains a conflict between stigmatizing and non-stigmatizing messages about intimate partner violence in the media. For the controversies related to social media, we see that content glorifying violence exists, and in many cases, there is little that advocates can do to remove it. Regarding the two popular music songs, both songs caused an uproar about the messages they conveyed about promoting violence, and yet they remained popular and received a lot of airtime and visibility in the digital realm, as well. Videos of both songs can still, as of this writing, be easily found through an Internet search. The Ray Rice case brought immense attention to the issue of domestic violence, and several other professional athletes have faced similar media scrutiny for violence since that case emerged. However, the fact that it took a video of a woman being punched in the face to bring this case to light demonstrated the unfortunate truth that it often takes very extreme circumstances for the issue of intimate partner violence to be recognized in the media.

Problematic Practices of Reporting Violence in the Media

The Ray Rice case demonstrates the importance of considering *when* and *how* intimate partner violence is covered in the media and by news outlets in particular. Several years ago, one of us (Christine Murray) began having conversations with colleagues about the selective nature of coverage of intimate partner violence in the news.[13] These conversations began during the month of October, and we were discussing how October is both Breast Cancer Awareness Month and Domestic Violence Awareness Month. Of course, breast cancer is a major and important public health issue. And yet, we were struck by the fact that the news media is saturated with stories and advertisements about breast cancer during October, making it nearly impossible for anyone not to be aware of all the pink (the breast cancer awareness color) around them. On the other hand, where was the similar attention to domestic violence? Purple—the domestic violence awareness color—was much more scarcely seen than its pink counterpart. This attention was lacking to such a significant effect that we felt certain that, at the time, many members of the general public probably had no idea that October was also Domestic Violence Awareness Month.

To take a deeper look at the issues we discussed, we embarked on a study of media coverage in our local newspaper about domestic violence.[14] Of the 26 stories in our local newspaper that we examined that discussed specific cases of intimate partner violence, 85% reported on homicides, meaning that domestic violence cases that didn't result in fatalities were rarely reported. This trend for domestic violence cases to receive minimal attention in the news media has also been shown in other research studies examining coverage in other geographic locations.[15] In fact, domestic violence cases also may be less likely to be covered in the news media than other forms of violence,[16] and abusive relationships that encompass only emotional abuse are very rarely acknowledged in news media stories.[17] In our study, we also observed many other problematic patterns of reporting intimate partner violence in the news during the time period in which we reviewed news stories. Beyond merely looking at *when* news outlets choose to cover stories on the topic, we must also consider *how* this type of violence is reported and described.

We recall one news story we saw in which the newspaper reported that a man had beaten his female partner because she didn't cook the steak the way he liked it.[18] When reporters say that abuse occurs because a victim doesn't cook the perpetrators steak the way he likes, they miss the mark completely. As you learned in Chapter 1, abuse has nothing to do with the way she cooked his steak and everything to do with power and control. The reporting of this story about the steak is far from an isolated incident. We've seen other stories in which abuse was attributed to such factors as an argument over leftover fried chicken, a wife requesting to stop driving to use the bathroom, how a perpetrator's girlfriend cooked pizza, and a man's girlfriend waking him up from sleeping.

It's natural for people to want to try and explain why violence occurs. And reporters have a responsibility to state the known facts of the stories they report. However, reporting overly simplistic reasons for abuse is problematic for at least two important reasons. First, by trying to identify these situational causes of domestic violence incidents, reporters trivialize the violence and inadvertently misinform readers about the dynamics of abusive relationships. By confusing the real reason that abuse occurs—because one partner is trying to control the other—the wrong message gets sent to the community and perpetuates the stereotype that intimate partner violence occurs as a result of a unique fight or one person's inability to manage his or her anger. Second, by reporting on victims' actions before a violent incident occurred, media stories imply that the victim may somehow have been to blame for the violence they experienced. These stories suggest that, had the victims just cooked the steak properly, not asked to use the bathroom on a long car ride, or not eaten the fried chicken leftovers, the violence would not have occurred. Professionals who work to address intimate partner violence know, however, that the violence almost certainly still would have occurred; there just would have been a different triggering incident that set it off. Again, abuse is not about the content of a "fight," rather it is about power and control. Of course, we need ongoing media coverage about the issue of intimate partner violence to continue to raise awareness in the community and to demonstrate the scope of the problem. However, responsible reporting practices are essential for educating the public about the issue and accurately depicting the dynamics of abusive relationships.

Conclusion

Societal stigma surrounding intimate partner violence can be considered a container for the stigma that is present at other levels—within individual victims and perpetrators, among friends and family members close to the individuals involved in the relationship, and within professionals who work with individuals impacted by abuse. Societal stigma provides the climate in which stigma at the other levels continues to grow and permeate individuals' attitudes and cultural groups' norms related to intimate partner violence. As individual victims and survivors are embedded within the broader social context, they can encounter societal stigma both while they are involved in the abusive relationship and during their process of recovery after it ends. Societal stigma compounds the challenges they face already from the direct effects of the trauma of abuse, such as when they encounter negative stereotypes, cultural-group norms that perpetuate abuse, and harmful representations of intimate partner violence in the media.

Throughout the first part of this book, we've taken an in-depth look at the stigma surrounding intimate partner violence—including stigma from perpetrators, internalized stigma within victims and survivors, stigma that is experienced from others (e.g., friends, family members, and professionals), and societal stigma. We've heard the stories and words of many survivors of past abuse that demonstrate the various ways that victims and survivors are deeply impacted by this stigma. Indeed, stigma is a powerful force at work in the lives of victims and survivors, and we've seen many ways that the stigma adds to the challenges of working toward fully ending abuse in our society once and for all.

The stigma surrounding intimate partner violence is not, however, insurmountable. We believe that this stigma can be overcome—by individuals, families, communities, and society at large. As we shift into Part 3 of this book, "Overcoming Stigma," we encourage readers to hold on to this belief that abuse, and the stigma that surrounds it, can be overcome. The stories you will read in the next section will provide proof that this is possible. We have seen that survivors of abuse can overcome seemingly insurmountable odds to rebuild their lives and create positive, non-stigmatizing environments. Let's turn our attention now to how we can build upon, and learn from, their successes and overcome abuse and stigma at all levels.

Notes

1 For example, consider the following statistics quoted by the National Domestic Violence Hotline, based on data from the U.S. Centers for Disease Control and Prevention and the U.S. Bureau of Justice Statistics (http://www.thehotline.org/resources/statistics/):

- "Females ages 18 to 24 and 25 to 34 generally experienced the highest rates of intimate partner violence."
- "Nearly 3 in 10 women (29%) and 1 in 10 men (10%) in the US have experienced rape, physical violence and/or stalking by a partner and report a related impact on their functioning."

- Nearly, 15% of women (14.8%) and 4% of men have been injured as a result of IPV that included rape, physical violence and/or stalking by an intimate partner in their lifetime."

2. To read more about Meredith Vieira's disclosure of a history of a past abusive relationship, please see http://www.usatoday.com/story/life/people/2014/09/17/meredith-vieira-reveals-history-of-domestic-violence-explains-why-she-stayed/15762049/.
3. Bergen, R. K., & Barnhill, E. (n.d.) *Marital rape: New research and directions.* Retrieved January 7, 2016, from http://www.vawnet.org/applied-research-papers/print-document.php?doc_id=248.
4. For more information about Honor Killings, please see http://hbv-awareness.com/faq/ and http://www.theatlantic.com/politics/archive/2015/04/honor-killings-in-america/391760/.
5. Murray, C. E., Mobley, A. K., Buford, A. P., & Seaman-DeJohn, M. M. (2006/2007). Same-sex intimate partner violence: Dynamics, social context, and counseling implications. *The Journal of GLBT Issues in Counseling, 1*(4), 7–30.
6. West, C. M. (1998). Leaving a second closet: Outing partner violence in same-sex couples. In J. L. Jasinski & L. M. Williams (Eds.), *Partner violence: A comprehensive review of 20 years of research* (pp. 163–183). Thousand Oaks, CA: Sage Publications.
7. Palazzolo, K. E., & Roberto, A. J. (2011). Media representations of intimate partner violence and punishment preferences: Exploring the role of attributions and emotions. *Journal of Applied Communication Research, 39*(1), 1–18. DOI:10.1080/00909882.2010.536843.
8. See, for example, Romano, A. (2013). What will it take for Facebook to care about violence against women? *The Daily Dot*, May 28, 2013. http://www.dailydot.com/business/wam-fbrape-violence-against-women-facebook/.
9. For a commentary on the Blurred Lines video, please see http://www.theguardian.com/music/2013/nov/13/blurred-lines-most-controversial-song-decade.
10. For a commentary on the Animals video, please see http://national.deseretnews.com/article/2514/maroon-5s-new-music-video-sparks-outrage-among-advocates-against-sexual-violence.html.
11. For a complete time line of the events surrounding the Ray Rice domestic violence case, please see http://www.sbnation.com/nfl/2014/5/23/5744964/ray-rice-arrest-assault-statement-apology-ravens.
12. For more on this topic, please see the following See the Triumph blog post: http://www.seethetriumph.org/blog/intimate-partner-violence-stigma-the-media-series-introduction.
13. Portions of this section were published previously in a See the Triumph blog post, which can be found in its entirety here: http://www.seethetriumph.org/blog/intimate-partner-violence-stigma-and-the-media-part-one.
14. Brown, B., Murray, C. E., & Smith, P. H. (2013). Domestic violence representation in media: A toolkit for advocacy professionals. Poster presented at the UNCG Public Health Education internship poster session.
15. Studies on this topic include the following:
    - Berkeley Media Studies Group. (2003). Distracted by drama: How California newspapers portray intimate partner violence. Retrieved September 11, 2012, from http://www.bmsg.org/pub-issues.php#issue13.
    - Carlyle, K., Slater, M., & Chakroff, J. (2008). Newspaper coverage of intimate partner violence: Skewing representations of risk. *Journal of Communication, 58*, 168–186.

16 Berkeley Media Studies Group. (2003). Distracted by drama: How California newspapers portray intimate partner violence. Retrieved September 11, 2012, from http://www.bmsg.org/pub-issues.php#issue13.
17 Sims, C. (2008). Invisible wounds, invisible abuse: The exclusion of emotional abuse in newspaper articles. *Journal of Emotional Abuse, 8,* 375–402.
18 Portions of this section were originally written in a blog post for See the Triumph, which can be found in its entirety here: http://www.seethetriumph.org/blog/its-not-about-the-steak-how-news-reports-miss-the-mark-when-they-report-the-reasons-for-domestic-violence-incidents.

Part 3
Overcoming Stigma

7 Holding Perpetrators Accountable for Their Abuse and the Stigma They Perpetuate

> "Overcoming the stigma means waking society up and throwing harsher consequences on abusers and repercussions, embarrassing ones, and educating society that it's not a victim's fault. There is some education out there, but we still allow for victims to struggle in order to get out. Society still wants to avoid the confrontation, wants to avoid talking about it, facing it, avoid the pain involved, the long-term negative effects on children. There is so much about the stigma, mainly the lack of society concern, yet it's a huge concern on taxpayers if you look at the cost to get the victim out and on her/his feet again. The abuser should pay for it all, especially if it's like mine who has a secure job and gets away with it."
>
> ~ *Domestic Violence Survivor*

Every day, in the United States and around the world, countless perpetrators are getting away with horrific abuse against people they are supposed to love and care for. Think about it for a moment: every time perpetrators speak an abusive word or commit an act of violence and face no negative consequences for that abuse, they are free from taking any responsibility for the harm they are doing to their victims, children, and others. It is true that there are laws against many forms of abuse, and therefore perpetrators may face consequences if their abuse is brought to the attention of the criminal justice system. However, even when cases of abuse actually make it to the criminal justice system, there are many loopholes in the system that can have the end effect of perpetrators escaping accountability for their abusive actions. To this day, far too many perpetrators of abuse fail to receive any meaningful consequences for their abuse.

In this chapter, we take a closer look at how perpetrators escape accountability, and then we turn our attention to possible solutions to building systems in communities that ensure that offenders are held accountable. This chapter begins Part 3 of this book. Thus far, we have explored the complexity and dynamics of the stigma surrounding intimate partner violence. In the remaining chapters, we turn our attention to strategies for ending and overcoming this stigma at multiple levels. Holding perpetrators accountable for their abuse is an important first step toward ending the stigma surrounding abuse. Of course, we can't focus solely on holding offenders accountable, as we must also address other important goals—such as providing support for victims and survivors, building non-stigmatizing organizations and communities, and preventing future violence—at the same time until abuse is completely eradicated. Ultimately, however, the responsibility for abuse falls squarely on the people who perpetrate it. Thus, as an important step toward completely ending violence in our society, we must determine effective approaches for holding perpetrators accountable so that all people will know that abusive behaviors will not be tolerated in our society.

How Perpetrators Escape Accountability

In Chapter 3, we took an in-depth look at how perpetrators themselves fail to accept responsibility for their abusive behaviors. Many survivors have told us how their perpetrators denied that they were responsible for their own abusive behaviors, and often perpetrators even blame their victims for the violence. This dynamic of abusive relationships is reinforced by the stigma surrounding intimate partner violence, of which perpetrators are among the strongest reinforcements of the stigmatizing messages that victims and survivors receive. But perpetrators of abuse are often not alone in refusing to accept responsibility for their abuse. In far too many cases, abuse perpetrators are also not held accountable by the communities around them. This can play out in extended family relationships, workplaces, neighborhoods, religious and cultural groups, the criminal justice and court systems, and in public policies and laws. People and organizations in each of these settings have opportunities to hold abuse offenders accountable. And yet it is all too common that the very systems and resources that are potentially available to hold offenders accountable fail to do so. We've heard this point from many survivors in our research as well as from many professionals we've met who work with victims and survivors of abuse daily. To illustrate how various systems surrounding an abusive relationship can fail to hold perpetrators accountable, consider the following four ways that we heard that perpetrators were not held responsible by various potential resources from survivors who participated in our research.

1. People Become Too Afraid to Help

First, in some cases, the perpetrator is so frightening to others around the victim and relationship that they become afraid to step in and help. For example, one survivor told us, "No one wants to help. Everyone is scared of my former partner." Some perpetrators hide their abusive behaviors from others, and nobody but their victims knows about the violence they are capable of committing. But in other cases, perpetrators can be so threatening and scary to others that they feel fearful of providing help and support to victims. A common stereotype about intimate partner violence is that it is a "private family matter" in which others shouldn't become involved. And while much intimate partner violence does remain contained in the context of the couple's relationship, there is a growing recognition of the threat that perpetrators may cause to their entire communities. For example, a recent analysis of mass shootings by the national advocacy group, Everytown for Gun Safety,[1] found that, of a total of 133 mass shootings that occurred in the United States between January 2009 and July 2015, nearly 60% of the shootings involved shooters killing current or former intimate partners or other family members. This finding highlights the fact that, although intimate partner violence often occurs behind the closed doors of private homes, it can also spill out into the community. Indeed, intimate partner violence perpetrators can pose a serious threat to the safety of their victims as well as to the community surrounding them. Perpetrators also may make direct threats toward friends, family members, and/or coworkers of victims, and this can further prevent others from stepping forward to support victims and take action toward holding perpetrators accountable.

2. *Professionals Failing to Take Action*

A second way that perpetrators can avoid being held accountable for the violence they perpetrate is when professionals fail to take action, even when they become aware of the extent to which a perpetrator is engaging in abuse. This can occur with professionals in any field who are in a position to take steps to hold perpetrators accountable. Some of the specific examples we have heard from survivors related to doctors, legal professionals, and law enforcement officers. Regarding doctors, one survivor said,

> "The doctors would not talk to me when he was admitted. They all told me that it was not my concern. They never asked me what was going on with him and they let him tell them he was fine even after he flew off the handle in a rage a few hours before. The police were not going to take him to jail until I told them he had fired a gun in the house. They made him go to the hospital, but no further action was pursued. It was like what happened was my fault. He had been violent and threatening on many occasions, but I was made to feel like it was my fault in some way."

Other survivors shared with us how lawyers they encountered took either no action, or were very slow to help activate potential legal protections that may have helped them end the relationships or become safe. One survivor said,

> "The lawyers here take advantage of situations like mine. It took almost a year to get a child support order and two years for divorce. The attorneys have lunch and drag your case out so they can soak you for more money; they are all friends. Domestic violence is viewed as, 'It was your fault,' in our area."

Another said, "One attorney actually turned down my case because he found narcissists exhausting; he believed that my ex would just keep bringing me back to court, wasting everybody's time." Still another survivor told us

> "the domestic violence agency told me they would not stand behind me when I wanted to report the Prosecutor to the Governor for dropping the charges on my ex without my knowledge. The Prosecutor's office told me they could not protect me and my children."

Some survivors encountered professionals who failed to take action when they reached out for help. This occurred for many when they needed assistance from law enforcement. As examples, consider the following quotes from participants in our research: (1) "The police officers in my experience were completely unhelpful. I would call and ask someone to remove him from the parking lot across from where I worked. He was just sitting there watching me, and a protective order was in force. Long story short, the officer told me, 'You married him,' and was very perturbed about having to tell a man to leave a parking lot. I also had to involve them when he threatened to kill himself; they couldn't understand why I wouldn't talk to him myself." (2) "Both the attorney and police did not pursue charges, saying that he was not there when they arrived at the scene so they had no proof it was him who did it, even though my daughter was present and heard the entire fight." (3) "When law enforcement seemed very indifferent, it almost like they didn't care or take domestic violence seriously." (4) "I called 911. One of the two police officers responding stated, 'It's his house (even though we were separated, and the house was mine). He can punch a hole in the door if he wants to.'" (5) "The arresting officer actually stated, 'Don't make us come here again.' If I had continued this relationship, I would have been hesitant about seeking assistance from the police if I needed it again." We know that there are many professionals in all of the aforementioned fields who *do* take intimate partner violence seriously. However, far too many victims and survivors have encountered responses of inaction from professionals who could have taken action to hold offenders accountable and responsible for their abusive actions.

3. Minimal Legal Consequences

Even if the professionals from whom victims initially seek help do take action toward holding offenders accountable, the ultimate consequences that perpetrators face through the criminal justice system are often far below what would be fitting for the nature of the crimes they commit. The laws that govern legal consequences for intimate partner violence vary from state to state, but in this section, we'll share examples of the consequences that perpetrators faced—or avoided facing. First, one survivor told us the following:

> "Police and court was the worst of the lot, and I don't know why I even bothered sometimes. For example, he strangled me until I gave up trying to breathe. I was left with bruises around my neck. I did a video statement. The court date was brought forward without my knowledge, and he got off with a $2,000 fine."

In this case, the perpetrator strangled the survivor to the point at which she almost stopped breathing, and his only legal consequence was a $2,000 fine. This was not for lack of evidence, as she had actual bruises around her neck, and she also testified in the video statement. Although $2,000 certainly is a lot of money for many people, it is clearly not commensurate with a life-threatening act of violence such as strangulation.

Similarly, consider the extent of violence experienced by the following survivor:

> "The police came to my home after I was yanked across my kitchen, resulting in an instant bruise. I had to jump out my window to escape, as he cornered me, in bare feet. It was raining, and my kids were in the house. The police showed up, but he called them before I did, so they made me stand outside in the rain in bare feet while they spoke to him. Once inside, they told me the bruise was old looking, as the abuser said I was lying and didn't know what I was talking about. The police let him leave with my child. They did not record the visit. I tried to press charges later and was told there was no call to the house on that day. I had to press a complaint against the police department. Later in time, the abuser sliced my car tire when I was out. I then called to press charges, as the police do not come out to tire slashing calls. Finally I was able to press charges, but the charges are still pending on the abuser."

Keep in mind that this survivor had been out of her abusive relationship for at least two years, as that length of time was the minimum requirement for participating in our studies. This means that, at least two years after these acts of violence, this survivor was still waiting to see if her perpetrator would face any legal consequences for his actions.

Another survivor shared the following experiences with us:

> "When seeking help from the police department I felt like I was wasting their time. A cop that my abuser knew pulled up next to him at a red light and said, 'I have some papers at the station I need you to come fill out *when you have the time.*' When my ex violated the restraining order by coming to my family member's house and knocking on all the windows, I was told that because he didn't directly talk to me it wasn't technically a violation. When my ex told me he would kill me if I didn't drop the charges against him, I was forced to tell a judge in court that I wanted to drop the charges. I had to do this in front of my ex. If I had been able to speak with the judge privately, I might have had the courage to tell him about the threat. Instead, I was told that I was wasting the court's time and taxpayer dollars."

For this survivor, her abuser was excused for violating his protective order on what was essentially a technicality (i.e., him lurking around her family member's house was not viewed as a threat to her), and she was not able to get the protection from the courts she needed because her perpetrator had threatened to kill her if she didn't drop the charges. The court failed her by not allowing her to speak with the judge in a way that would allow her to speak openly about her experiences and safety needs.

Some of the other ways that legal and court systems can fail to hold perpetrators accountable are as follows. We couple these examples with representative quotes from survivors who participated in our research:

- By having unequal policies regarding what specific actions constitute abuse and warrant protection ("One judge would not give me a protective order because my ex's behavior didn't rise to the level of domestic violence in my jurisdiction. In the court system of the jurisdiction where the event occurred, though, his behavior would have been considered domestic violence.")
- By failing to provide adequate legal counsel to victims ("Seeking legal counsel, I am left undefended because our legal system cannot accommodate me and does not want to know the truth.")
- By providing inadequate protections in the context of child custody issues ("An attorney suggested that I should stay with my husband for the sake of the children. Also, I once called the police, and not only did they not arrest him after he admitted that he had hit me, but they told me that I could not leave with my children due to the fact that neither of us had custody papers. So, I could leave, but my children would have to stay. They only warned my ex-husband that if

they had to come out again that night that they would have to arrest him then.")
- By failing to take violations of the law and protection orders seriously ("The police treat you like it's your fault the abuse is taking place. The courts say they are going to protect you, but they fail you when you really need it. My daughter had a protection order against the man who murdered her, and she would call the police; they would arrest him and then let him go. Almost 20 times, he was arrested for violating the court order and never spent 24 hours in jail.")

4. Professionals Reinforcing Stigmatizing Messages About Intimate Partner Violence

A fourth way that perpetrators can escape accountability is when professionals reinforce stigmatizing messages about intimate partner violence. This includes minimizing the abuse, implying or stating that victims are to blame for the abuse they experience, and perpetuating harmful stereotypes about victims and survivors. Consider how each of these stigmatizing experiences were reflected in the following survivor's story:

> "The attorney I had for the protective order case took both of us to the judges' chambers and left us alone while he went to get the judge to sign the order. As he was leaving me alone with my abuser, he smiled and said, 'You two try to get along for a few minutes, ok?' When I left my husband initially, the detectives who went back to my home with me and my dad told my dad that I would be back with him within a day or so because, 'They always go back.' Law enforcement was called out several times after I left because he would show up in the middle of the night; they could never find him and always asked if we were sure he was there. Then, they would say they didn't think he would bother me because he didn't have a criminal record."

This survivor's abuse was minimized when law enforcement conveyed that they didn't think her perpetrator would "bother" her, the attorney conveyed blame when he suggested that the abuse was a matter of the two people not "getting along," and harmful stereotypes were conveyed when the detectives told her dad, "They always go back." As such, the perpetrator's responsibility was minimized in all of these experiences—imagine how different this story would have been (1) if the law enforcement officers would have communicated that abuse was more than merely being "bothered," but rather a serious threat to her safety; (2) if the attorney had protected the survivor from having been alone with her abuser and conveyed belief that the perpetrator was abusive; and (3) if the detectives had asked her father if there were any reasons that she may have gone back, such as her perpetrator threatening harm if she left the relationship. In all of these experiences, the perpetrator either implicitly or explicitly was excused from accepting full responsibility for the extent of his abusive behaviors.

What Happens When Perpetrators *Are* Held Accountable?

In the earlier section, we saw what happens when community response systems fail to hold offenders accountable for the abuse they perpetrate. However, when social systems do work together to hold perpetrators accountable, the impact on victims and survivors is powerful. Consider the following two stories from Alana and Jody, two survivors who participated in our research, as positive examples of the power of holding offenders accountable.

Alana's Story

Alana's story demonstrates how people surrounding an abusive relationship can excuse perpetrators' abusive behaviors, but also the powerful change that can occur when even one person takes action to support victims and hold offenders accountable. At the time that she participated in our study, Alana was in her early 40s and had one adult child. A college graduate, she now works in a domestic violence agency, where she works to support victims and survivors of abusive relationships in her community. This work is near and dear to Alana's heart, in light of her own past abusive marriage, which involved physical, verbal, emotional, and sexual abuse. Her ex-husband, Pete, faced legal consequences against him as a result of this abuse, including a protective order and a guilty plea for domestic violence charges that resulted in a yearlong probation sentence.

There were a number of factors that led Alana to stay in her relationship, even after she realized the dynamics of abuse that were present in the relationship. She said,

> "Pete had a child from a previous relationship, who I had helped raise and loved like my own. This was a major way for Pete to maintain power and control over me: 'If you leave, you'll never see my child again.' I knew that leaving Pete meant losing this child. Though most of the abuse was emotional, I knew he was capable of seriously injuring or killing me and my own child; if he was hurting me this much when I stayed with him, how badly would he hurt me for leaving? And I felt responsible for him, for his happiness, for helping him change. I thought if I just loved him enough it would all work out. Isn't that what we are taught?"

Ultimately, the relationship led Alana to feel helpless and powerless: "I had no power. No control over anything in my life. I have never felt so helpless."

Throughout the relationship, Alana faced stigma in many forms. She was frequently blamed for the abuse and said, "I can't tell you the number of times I heard, 'Well, what did you do to make him so mad?,' including from his parents. People often said things like this. 'He's so nice; I can't believe he'd do that.'" Alana went on to say,

> "When we were married, I realized I had privilege suddenly. I was a wealthy housewife. When I left, some who were 'friends' while we were together would have nothing to do with me. . . . I had very little social interaction without him, and then only with married friends during the day."

As the relationship progressed, Alana became increasingly isolated from others. She said, "Pete eventually drove away most of my friends. He tried to separate me from my family as well." Others around her labeled and judged her as a result of the relationship: "I was 'crazy' for either making the abuse up or 'taking it.' He was wealthy, so I was a 'gold-digger.'"

In addition to the gradual isolation that Alana experienced, some people in her life excused the abuse and failed to hold Pete accountable for his actions. She said,

> "I actually had someone say to me, 'Wow, I would never have guessed you are one of those weak little women who allow themselves to be abused.' His friends thought I was crazy and making it up, other people looked at me with pity. It seemed like everyone had some idea about who I was based on my experience."

Friends and family members minimized the abuse when Alana reached out to them for support. She said,

> "Some of my friends said things like, 'Well, you made your bed, now you have to lie in it,' or 'If I had a husband that wealthy, I could take a beating now and then.' I was so embarrassed by the whole thing. My family would sometimes get very angry when I would not leave right away, and often looked at me as 'poor thing.' It was very frustrating to be treated like a child with him and then by my family as well. It often felt like all of these institutions thought of me as that 'ignorant, poor thing.'"

Shame and secrecy further kept Pete's abuse hidden.

> "Everything had to be a secret. I got so good at making up this fairy tale life that I think I believed it sometimes. It wasn't only fear of

him that kept things secret. It was that for the first time in my life I thought I had a chance at having that fairy tale, marriage, kids, house, security, love. I wanted that so badly. I feel like I lived in shame. Shame that my husband hurt me, shame that our kids could hear it happening, shame that I couldn't fix it, that I was unworthy of a loving husband, that everyone found out these things."

Pete's abuse also was downplayed when Alana sought professional help. She said, "My attorney was horrible. She treated me like I was ignorant and had little value. She didn't even pretend to understand why I married him." Within the court system, Alana said, "I did not feel believed; like the general belief was that I had exaggerated what had happened. The court blamed it on his alcohol abuse and 'hot tempers.'" She also faced discrimination in her career. She said, "There was at least one job I did not get because I was 'that crazy girl married to so-and-so.'"

Despite these experiences, Alana experienced a turning point when the abuse was taken seriously by a police officer. She said,

"Leaving was a long, slow process. I had left several times before, but had returned. The last incident of abuse (while we were married) was more terrifying than usual. I went to the police to make an 'informational' report. I didn't want him arrested, I just wanted there to be a record in case he did anything more serious in the future. However, once the police officer finished taking the report, he said 'I don't want you to feel guilty or scared, but *I'm* pressing charges against him.' It was frightening and also a relief. He was arrested. He quickly bonded out of jail and promptly came back to our home. A friend was there and called the police; he was arrested again. The next day I went to the local domestic violence agency, and an advocate helped me obtain a protective order. My family was extremely supportive. He continued to stalk, harass, and threaten me for months. He broke into my new house. He followed me everywhere, including to a police department one night. I was lucky in that I had an amazing support system. It was a great example of a coordinated community response that led to my safety and it included the police, my family, victim's advocates, and my friends."

Alana faced many challenges throughout her abusive marriage to Pete. For a long time, Pete's abuse was dismissed and not taken seriously, which allowed him to avoid facing any negative consequences for his actions. Finally, when that police officer believed Alana and took the initial steps to hold Pete accountable, the tide began to turn, and Alana was able to move forward in building a new life that was free from abuse. Holding perpetrators accountable is often a key step toward helping victims and survivors achieve safety and freedom from abuse.

Jody's Story

Jody was in her late 40s and had three children in their teens and early 20s. She had been in a committed relationship with her ex-boyfriend, Don, whom she had lived with. Jody experienced both physical and verbal abuse in the relationship with Don. She had known Don for many years before they entered their romantic relationship; they had been friends and worked together before they started dating. She said, "I had never ever seen that side of him." Judy thought that Don's violence was related to his abuse of alcohol. She said, "He started drinking daily and in playful moods while drunk would pinch me leaving bruises." Jody initially told Don that she was moving out, but that they could continue to date, as he had "begged me to stay and make it work."

A particularly violent incident led to the end of their relationship. The day before the event, Don got really verbally abusive, so Jody went to a friend's house and stayed there all night. The next afternoon, Don called Jody at her friend's house and said, "he was sorry and wanted to work it out." When Jody returned to the home, which they shared with his elderly mother, Jody says that he "immediately started verbally abusing me." She went into the room she shared with Don, and she found that "the room was destroyed and my belongings were strewn all over the floor."

The verbal assault continued: "I sat down on the bed, and he was screaming at me inches from my face calling me awful things and cursing at me." From there, Don became physically abusive, even stabbing her with a sharp object, although she said, "Thank the Lord was able to keep them from going deep into my arms. He then headbutted me." After that, Jody was able to get out of the room and find Don's mother, and she says that he "started verbally attacking his mother. Then, he would come back to where I was and start on me again. He went back and forth between the two of us for two hours."

Finally, Jody managed to leave the house and get to her car, but she found out as she tried to start it that he'd "disabled my car so it wouldn't start." As luck would have it, Jody was able to walk to a community center across the street, where a room full of police officers were holding a meeting. They called an ambulance for her and then arrested Don. Jody moved into the local domestic violence shelter. That day was a turning point for Jody, as Don faced several legal consequences stemming from the abuse, including having a protective order taken out against him, being arrested on a misdemeanor domestic violence charge, being sentenced to probation for over two years, and a yearlong inpatient rehabilitation program. In addition to the rehab, Don was ordered to participate in weekly substance abuse counseling as well as to pay restitution money to Jody. Jody ended sharing her story with us by saying, "Praise God, I am a survivor!"

How to Hold Perpetrators Accountable

As Alana's and Jody's stories show, a powerful shift occurs when systems work together to ensure that perpetrators are held accountable for their abusive behaviors. In the rest of this chapter, we suggest a range of strategies that can be used at different levels to hold perpetrators accountable. It's important to note that these strategies will be most impactful when multiple levels of accountability are engaged at once. For example, legal sanctions won't be as effective on their own as they would be if they were combined with strategies at other levels, such as friends and family members who personally hold offenders accountable, workplaces that do not excuse away abusive actions, and cultural and community groups who hold members accountable when they fail to engage in safe, nonviolent behaviors. The message that perpetrators should be held accountable will be stronger if it is repeated and reinforced at every possible level. To begin moving toward the shift of holding offenders accountable, we suggest the following three solutions to promoting perpetrator accountability for abuse at the societal and community levels:

1. Ask the Right Questions

Many people, when witnessing abuse from the outside, often ask themselves, "Why does the victim stay in the relationship? Why don't they leave?" It's understandable that people ask these questions, as it can be confusing to understand why someone would willingly stay in a relationship with someone who hurts them. However, we suggest that everyone—professionals, friends, family members, neighbors, coworkers, etc.—shift to asking another question in these cases. Rather than asking, "Why does the victim stay?," a better question to ask is, "Why does the perpetrator abuse and hurt his or her partner?" When we start reflecting on this latter question, we begin to shift accountability for the abuse to where it rightly belongs—with the perpetrator.

When we start to dig even deeper, by asking *how* they are abusing their partners, we can gain a greater picture into their actions that may be entrapping the victim in the relationship. It's likely the case that the victim isn't staying in the relationship completely willingly and voluntarily. Rather, victims who stay in abusive relationships often do so because they've been threatened that they will be hurt if they leave. Victims may also stay because they don't believe they have any other options for a life outside the relationship, especially if their perpetrators have restricted their access to financial or other resources that would allow them to leave the relationship. Or, the perpetrators may have threatened to harm or take away the children if they leave. When we start asking, "Why do perpetrators abuse?," rather than, "Why do victims stay?," we begin to paint a more complex picture that accounts for the various actions and threats that perpetrators use to keep victims trapped in their relationships. Then we can look at another important question: "What resources does the victim need to achieve safety?" Overall, we encourage all readers to maintain a self-reflective stance to ensure that, when it comes to considering the dynamics of abusive relationships, you are asking the right questions that will help you to be in the best position possible to hold perpetrators accountable and provide support to victims and survivors.

2. Friends, Family Members, and Community Groups Can Hold Offenders Accountable and Make Clear That Abusive Behaviors Will Not Be Tolerated

Through our See the Triumph social media campaign, we often focus on what people can do to provide support and help to victims of intimate partner violence. We know this is something that can be a big struggle for a lot of people, as it's hard to watch someone you care about be abused and not know exactly how to help them. Although supporting survivors is one of our main focuses at See the Triumph, we also know that people may, at times, need to know what to do if someone in their social network is an abuse perpetrator. This, too, can be a very challenging situation for many people. First, it can be hard to admit that people you know and care about could be abusive to their partners. They may seem like overall good people, and they may never have displayed abusive actions toward anyone other than their partners. Second, confronting anyone about problematic behaviors can be extremely challenging, and this is even more the case when those behaviors are violent and abusive. It's understandable why people would feel afraid, in these situations, that they may be victimized themselves if they speak out against the violence of someone in their lives. And third, people may feel loyalty toward the perpetrator, even if this person is engaging in abuse. Perhaps it's their son, daughter, sister, brother, coworker, or best friend, and they may not be as close to the victim. It's hard to feel like you're taking a stand against people who are relatives or close friends, especially when you love and care about them.

Despite these challenges, friends, family members, and other community members can play a powerful role in holding perpetrators accountable by conveying clear messages to them that abuse is not acceptable and will not be tolerated. Of course, when considering how to approach someone who is being abusive, it is essential to consider your own safety as well as the safety of the victim. It may be useful to consult with a domestic violence service professional in your community to consider the safest approaches for all involved as well as whether intervening at all is a safe and wise choice. However, if it is decided that intervening is appropriate, there are six main messages that people can convey to hold abuse perpetrators accountable:[2]

- "The abuse is wrong." It is important to take a clear stance that you don't support the abuse in any way, shape, or form.
- "You are hurting your partner." Abuse perpetrators often minimize or deny the extent of their abuse, so it is important to avoid validating the ways that abusers fail to accept responsibility for what they have done.
- "There are other negative consequences of the abuse." Perpetrators often feel like they can get away with their abuse. However, friends, family members, and community members can remind perpetrators of the possible direct and indirect consequences that could result from the abuse. This includes legal consequences, such as criminal charges, court-mandated batterer intervention programs, and other punishments, such as fees or jail time. Beyond legal consequences, there are other costs for perpetrators of intimate partner violence—which may include relational consequences (e.g., cut off relationships with friends and family or harm to involved children), economic consequences (e.g., job loss or legal expenses), and the loss of one's reputation if others find out about the abuse.
- "You are responsible for your own actions. You are also responsible for doing whatever you need to do to change them." Friends and family members can challenge victim-blaming statements that perpetrators make and remind them that they alone are accountable for their own choices and behaviors.
- "There are resources available to help you stop abusing your partner." As we'll discuss later in this chapter, there are batterer intervention programs in many communities, and these programs are specialized intervention services designed to change the thought and behavior patterns of perpetrators so that they will learn to stop engaging in violent and abusive behaviors.
- "If you do not stop abusing your partner, I will . . ." We encourage readers who are faced with a possible confrontation with someone in their lives who is abusing someone else to consider what actions they could take if the abuser doesn't stop. This may mean cutting off communication with the perpetrator or reporting the abuse to law enforcement.

All six of the aforementioned messages convey that perpetrators hold full responsibility for abuse. Now, taking the idea of these messages beyond individual interactions with perpetrators, let's consider how they might look in the broader community. Consider how these messages could be conveyed by religious and spiritual leaders, such as preaching sermons that emphasize that abuse is not tolerated or accepted in that faith community. Or, workplace leaders could develop policies for holding offenders accountable, such as terminating employment for perpetrators who are convicted of domestic violence or requiring all employees to be trained to understand the dynamics of abusive relationships and strategies for safe, nonviolent communication. Within neighborhoods, consider how neighborhood community watch groups could focus not only on preventing and reporting property crimes, such as burglaries, but also on communicating the importance of not committing acts of violence within one's own home. Think about instances in which couples are out at local stores, restaurants, or public parks and one partner threatens or hurts the other and people witnessing this routinely take action, such as calling law enforcement or, if it's safe to do so, by intervening to ask the victim if he or she is okay and to offer the support the victim needs to feel safe in that moment. Instead of turning away from talking about abuse in all of these contexts, what would happen if leaders and community members in all of these settings stepped up to send a clear message to perpetrators that abuse will not be tolerated in their communities?

Some readers may be wondering if the aforementioned actions might drive abuse further underground. For example, if someone "gets caught" abusing his or her partner in a public place, won't the abuser just be more careful about where the abuse happens? Won't he or she only abuse the victim in the privacy of their home? This certainly is a possibility, and is why it is so important to factor safety considerations into any decisions related to how to respond to known or suspected abuse. We certainly don't advocate for anybody putting their own safety at risk by intervening in a violent situation, and we also know it's important to consider how any responses might impact the safety of the victims involved. Again, if there are any questions about how to safely plan in the context of deciding whether and how to intervene with abuse perpetrators, we recommend that readers consult with trained domestic violence professionals in your local community, such as victim advocates or a domestic violence hotline.

Assuming all relevant safety considerations have been addressed, what is the potential impact of friends, family members, and community groups taking a clear stance that abuse is not accepted and holding perpetrators fully accountable for their abusive behaviors? This stance is critical to the overall safety of victims and survivors. When others remain silent about the abuse or excuse perpetrators as not responsible, this sends the wrong messages to victims and survivors—messages such as the abuse is not a big deal, that they themselves are to blame for it, and that they won't be helped if they reach out for help. Some victims are not immediately ready to leave an abusive relationship, but conveying that abuse is not acceptable and that the abuse is not their fault can plant a powerful seed that will later grow into a clear understanding that they don't deserve to be treated that way. We've heard from far too many survivors who participated in our research studies that the silence of others drove them further into their relationships. Conversely, many survivors also told us that, when someone close to them expressed their concern about their safety and told them they didn't deserve the abuse, this was a critical step in their decision to leave the relationship and move toward safety.

3. Community Response Systems Should Maintain a Clear Stance That Perpetrators Must Be Held Accountable for the Abuse They Perpetuate

In the previous section, we discussed the importance of strong community norms that hold perpetrators accountable for abuse and make clear that abuse is not acceptable. Beyond these social norms, however, it is important that there are tangible ways that perpetrators are held accountable for abuse within their communities. Some forms of intimate partner violence are not considered actual crimes, such as emotional/psychological abuse that occurs outside of the context of actual or threatened physical or sexual violence, and these forms of abuse are much more difficult to police at a community level. However, other forms of abuse *are* actual reportable crimes, although a vast majority of the abuse that happens in communities is never actually reported to any authorities. We do not advocate for mandatory reporting of all intimate partner violence, although readers are encouraged to follow relevant laws in their states regarding reporting intimate partner violence that involves minor children to child protective services as well as reporting abuse that involves elderly or disabled adults to adult protective services. Those reports are not only legally mandated, but they can provide a critical link to safety for children in those situations. In cases that don't involve mandatory reporting for children, we encourage communities to support and empower victims to make their own decisions regarding whether, when, and how to report abuse, although certainly any abuse in which there is an immediate risk of life-threatening injuries should be reported immediately to local emergency response organizations.

In order to hold perpetrators accountable for abuse, appropriate response systems need to be in place when intimate partner violence is reported to the criminal justice system. Sanctions and responses that may be in place may include the following:

- *Mandatory arrest policies for perpetrators*. These policies require law enforcement officers to make an arrest of the identified perpetrator during domestic violence incidents. However, it is important that these polices be implemented carefully, as they have been known in some cases to result in the arrest of both the perpetrator and the victim.
- *Protections that limit perpetrators' access to victims*. These include protective orders and restraining orders. Although these orders are

often viewed as "just a piece of paper," they also serve as a powerful tool for victims, as perpetrators can receive punishment for violating the orders. Several of the survivors who participated in our research studies described the importance of limiting perpetrators' access to victims. The following quotes illustrate this: "You also need a plan, and you need to get outside help, or you won't be free of your abuser. You need a safe place to go where your abuser has no access to you; cannot call you on the phone, and you also need to block the incoming e-mail, or send it to a folder, unread. This is the only way out, if you have children or not. The abuser must not have any access to you, through mutual friends, or even family members. I've learned this the hard way." "I moved away and threatened to place charges if I was contacted. It worked," and "I ceased all contact with the abuser." We can't view protective and restraining orders as the magic solution to intimate partner violence, but they can serve as powerful tools that provide an added level of protection for victims and hold perpetrators to a higher level of accountability for any efforts they make to harass or abuse their victims.

- *Safety-focused arrangements in the context of child custody cases.* Perpetrators need to be held accountable in family courts, especially in the context of custody cases involving minor children. Often, perpetrators continue to abuse their former victims after the relationship is over by using their children to maintain control over them. Custody exchanges can be dangerous and can become opportunities for abusers to hurt, threaten, and harass their victims. These arrangements can be especially complex for survivors, who are likely mandated to have this contact with their perpetrators, or they could be found in contempt of court for violating a child custody order if they don't have this contact with their perpetrators. Therefore, in child custody cases in which one parent is abusive toward the other, it is important to put protections in place, such as requiring the custody exchanges to occur at a neutral location or through another trusted family member, such as a grandparent. Supervised visitation may be warranted for parents who are abuse perpetrators if they are granted time with their children.
- *Court procedures that account for the dynamics of abusive relationships.* Earlier in this chapter, you read about a survivor whose perpetrator had threatened to kill her if she didn't drop the criminal charges against him, and she was not afforded an opportunity to speak privately with the judge so that she could safely tell the judge all the details of her situation. According to DomesticShelters.org,[3] witness tampering (i.e., when people charged with domestic violence threaten "survivors into recanting their stories in court or refusing to testify altogether") is extremely common in domestic violence cases and can hinder the criminal justice system processes from resulting

in a successful prosecution of a perpetrator. It is important for court personnel to be aware of this possible practice occurring in their courts and to take steps to ensure that victims and survivors are able to tell their full stories in a way that does not threaten their safety. Furthermore, if there is evidence of witness tampering, perpetrators should be held accountable for that, in addition to their accountability for the violence.

- *Appropriate legal consequences for perpetrators who are convicted of domestic violence crimes.* As we saw earlier in the case of the survivor whose abuser received a $2,000 fine for strangling her, when it comes to intimate partner violence, in many cases, the punishment doesn't fit the crime. Indeed, Olson and Stalans[4] stated that "more than three fourths of DV cases either never enter the criminal justice system or are dismissed or diverted before a guilty or not guilty verdict . . . Offenders convicted of domestic violence and placed on probation are likely to be the more serious and severe cases of battery." In order to ensure that communities hold perpetrators accountable for their violence and abuse, it is important that convicted offenders receive appropriate sanctions, which may include jail time, restitution to the victim, probation, community service, and participation in effective rehabilitation programs. Because batterer intervention programs are widely used as rehabilitation programs in communities across the country, the next section delves deeper into describing these programs to provide readers with an understanding of their format, effectiveness, and limitations.

Understanding Batterer Intervention Programs

Many perpetrators of intimate partner violence who enter the criminal justice system are court mandated to attend a batterer intervention program, such as during probation or as an option to avoid time in jail. In most cases, perpetrators who fail to complete these programs are supposed to face more severe legal consequences, although we'll talk later about how this does not always happen. Because these programs are used so widely as a legal consequence for perpetrating domestic violence and represent one of the major ways that communities attempt to hold perpetrators accountable, this section provides an overview of how these programs work and what is known about their effectiveness.

First, it is important to note that batterer intervention programs are not viewed as a form of psychotherapy, but rather they are a specific intervention programs designed to counter perpetrators' use of abusive behaviors. It is also important for readers to understand that couples treatment is generally not advised any time there is violence present in a couple's relationship. Couple therapy should never occur when one partner is afraid of another.[5] Some researchers have begun to explore the use of couples treatment for couples who have experienced violence;[6] however, these interventions are only appropriate for couples who are properly screened, are not at any risk that the violence will reoccur, and in which the perpetrator accepts full responsibility for the violence and has demonstrated an extended period of nonviolence.[7] Furthermore, this type of treatment should only be considered when the therapist is highly skilled and experienced in understanding and addressing the dynamics of abusive relationships. Generally speaking, however, any couple-focused interventions are not advised when violence has occurred in a couple's relationship, as this can present safety risks and implies that both partners share some responsibility for the abuse.

In the United States, many states have legislated standards for approved batterer intervention programs, although the research basis for these standards has been hotly debated among domestic violence researchers and practitioners.[8] Typically, these standards set forth the types of interventions that are allowed and those that are not permitted for court-mandated intimate partner violence perpetrators.[9] Many of these programs are grounded in a feminist approach that addresses how patriarchal societal norms underlie the power and control dynamics found in abusive relationships. A typical format for these batterer intervention programs is that they are conducted in groups, led by two co-facilitators, and last for a designated minimum amount of time, which may be anywhere from 12 to 52 weeks. One way that batterer intervention programs hold offenders accountable is by making them pay fees to attend the program. Because these interventions have been developed primarily for male perpetrators against female victims, they may not be appropriate for female perpetrators or perpetrators of either gender who abused same-sex partners. To date, very few intervention programs specifically for women have been widely researched, and more research is needed to determine the best strategies for interventions for female perpetrators of intimate partner violence.

Batterer intervention programs are not advisable for all perpetrators. For example, perpetrators with untreated substance abuse problems or major mental health disorders, as well as those who are not able to function effectively in the group format of many of these interventions, are likely not suitable for standard batterer intervention programs that are offered in communities across the country. In addition, the safety of perpetrators' victims should be paramount throughout the course of batterer intervention programs. This may be achieved by having open communication between program staff and victims throughout treatment and helping victims to create detailed safety plans to address the most critical safety risks they face. In addition, it is important for victims to understand the limitations of batterer intervention programs, as victims may hold out extreme hope that these programs will change their partners, which may lead them to be less active in taking steps toward safety while their perpetrators are involved in the programs.

High numbers of perpetrators drop out of batterer intervention programs. When perpetrators do complete treatment, the results are promising for a substantial number of perpetrators. However, anywhere from 40% to 60% of men who go to the first session of a batterer intervention program drop out before the program ends. And, to date, researchers haven't been able to pinpoint exactly what characteristics might make it more or less likely that a perpetrator will complete treatment. However, there is research that suggests that perpetrators with higher levels of mental health concerns are more likely to drop out of batterer intervention programs, compared with those with lower levels of mental health problems. Overall, however, despite the growing amount of research we have now about the different types of perpetrators, as we reviewed in Chapter 3, it's still too early for this research to provide clear guidelines for practitioners in how to classify individual perpetrators and assign them to different treatments based on their types.

Unfortunately, there is not a lot of research evidence suggesting that typical batterer intervention programs work.[10] In 2004, a group of researchers led by Julia Babcock,[11] a psychology professor at the University of Houston, did an extensive review of the existing research on the effectiveness of these interventions. They reviewed only studies that used rigorous research methodologies, and the interventions studied were mostly feminist-informed psychoeducational interventions or cognitive-behavioral intervention programs. Across all of the studies that Babcock and her team reviewed, they found that batterer intervention programs led to only a small reduction in recidivism, which they defined as any additional reports of physical violence, either by the victims or through police reports, during the follow-up period of the study. However, these researchers suggested that rather than taking these findings to imply that batterer intervention programs should be abandoned completely, more efforts are needed to figure out how to make these interventions more effective, such as moving away from one-size-fits-all models to tailor programs more to the individual characteristics of perpetrators. They concluded by saying, "Even the best court-mandated treatment programs are likely to be ineffective in the absence of a strong legal response in initial sentencing and in sanctioning offenders who fail to comply with treatment."

In 2005, Feder and Wilson[12] conducted a meta-analysis study in which they combined the results of 15 prior research studies that examined the effectiveness of batterer intervention programs. They found moderate effects in reduction in repeat offending, as measured by official reports (e.g., to law enforcement) for men who completed their full programs, although they noted that these findings may be influenced by other factors and not necessarily directly from the effects of treatment alone. For example, men who complete the programs may be different than those who don't complete them, and those different characteristics could be the source of the changes in recidivism. Furthermore, when they compared recidivism rates based on victims' reports of further violence, they found no difference between those who completed the interventions and those who did not. Feder and Wilson noted the challenges that arise from the body of research showing limited effectiveness for batterer intervention programs, especially in the context of state regulations that require court-mandated intervention programs. They said,

> The end result is that judges, prosecutors and probation officers continue to send batterers to these treatment programs, even if they have grave doubts about their effectiveness. Alternate programs cannot be implemented and tested even as evidence builds indicating that batterer intervention programs, at least as designed and implemented today, may not be effective.

One factor that seems to impact whether perpetrators can change is whether they *want* to change. Researchers have begun to study how perpetrators' readiness to change impacts their response to treatment, and, not surprisingly, this research suggests that those perpetrators who are more motivated to change respond better to treatment.[13] To truly hold perpetrators accountable, any batterer intervention program must occur in the context of strong, coordinated response systems in local communities.[14] These response systems must hold offenders accountable by ensuring that appropriate consequences occur when perpetrators commit the crime of abuse. As stated earlier, batterer intervention programs are court mandated for many perpetrators who are convicted by the courts as having abused, and they may be diversion programs that allow perpetrators to avoid other legal consequences if they complete the treatment. However, perpetrators who fail to complete court-mandated interventions actually do not face the legal consequences they are supposed to face for dropping out of the intervention.[15] In fact, in one research study with perpetrators in batterer interventions across four different sites, 52% of the perpetrators believed that they wouldn't face any sanctions for dropping out of the program.[16] Overall, batterer intervention programs can serve as only one aspect of communities' comprehensive efforts to hold perpetrators accountable, and they are not suitable for all perpetrators. Furthermore, their effectiveness is limited when perpetrators don't face significant consequences for failing to successfully complete the interventions.

How Holding Offenders Accountable Ultimately Supports Survivors

In this chapter, we've delved into the complexity of holding intimate partner violence perpetrators accountable for violence and abuse. There is a clear need for the development of stronger intervention programs that can help perpetrators who are able to change their abusive behaviors. As one participant in our research said, "Times are changing. Abusers are no longer heroes. They are damaged individuals who need help. We as a society need to develop effective treatments to help them stop being abusers." Even when more effective interventions are developed, however, there likely will remain some perpetrators who cannot or will not change their abusive behaviors, and for those perpetrators, it is important that they face other significant consequences, such as appropriate jail sentences. More broadly, however, societal shifts are needed to ensure that community discussions about intimate partner violence maintain a focus on the perpetrators as carrying the full responsibility for the abuse. As another survivor said in our research, "The conversation needs to focus on the culprit: an epidemic of violence in this country. No one wants to look at it, all media, courts, and families totally enable it, and more women are going to die." In order to make real progress toward ending intimate partner violence and promoting safety for survivors, the responsibility for abuse needs to fall squarely on the shoulders of perpetrators. For those perpetrators who will not accept this responsibility on their own, societal and community-level consequences need to do it for them.

Notes

1 For more information on this analysis, see the following website: http://everytownresearch.org/reports/mass-shootings-analysis/.
2 We first developed these messages in a See the Triumph blog post. The original post can be found at the following link: http://www.seethetriumph.org/blog/what-if-your-friend-is-an-abuser.
3 Please see https://www.domesticshelters.org/domestic-violence-articles-information/threatened-not-to-testify#.VnFEk16DPnh. The statement quoted is from paragraph 1.
4 Olson, D.E., & Stalans, L.J. (2001). Violent offenders on probation: Profile, sentence, and outcome differences among domestic violence and other violent probationers. *Violence Against Women, 7*, 1164–1185. The statement quoted is from p. 1170.
5 For more information on this topic, see the following resources:
   - Murray, C.E., & Graves, K.N. (2012). *Responding to family violence.* New York: Routledge.
   - O'Leary, K.D. (2001). Conjoint therapy for partners who engage in physically aggressive behavior: Rationale and research. *Journal of Aggression, Maltreatment, and Trauma, 5*, 145–164.
   - O'Leary, K.D., Heyman, R.E., & Neidig, P.H. (1999). Treatment of wife abuse: A comparison of gender-specific and conjoint approaches. *Behavior Therapy, 30*, 475–505.
6 For an example, see O'Leary, K.D. (2001). Conjoint therapy for partners who engage in physically aggressive behavior: Rationale and research. *Journal of Aggression, Maltreatment, and Trauma, 5*, 145–164.
7 Murray, C.E., & Graves, K.N. (2012). *Responding to family violence.* New York: Routledge.

8 For examples of perspectives on this debate, see the following resources:
- Austin, J.B., & Dankwort, J. (1999). Standards for batterer programs: A review and analysis. *Journal of Interpersonal Violence, 14*, 152–168.
- Dutton, D.G., & Corvo, K. (2006). Transforming a flawed policy: A call to revive psychology and science in domestic violence research and practice. *Aggression and Violent Behavior, 11*(5), 457–483.
- Maiuro, R.D., Hagar, T.S., Lin, H., & Olson, N. (2001). Are current state standards for domestic violence perpetrator treatment adequately informed by research? A question of questions. *Journal of Aggression, Maltreatment, & Trauma, 5*, 21–44.

9 The sources of the information about batterer intervention programs that is included in this and the following two paragraphs are as follows:
- Austin, J.B., & Dankwort, J. (1999). Standards for batterer programs: A review and analysis. *Journal of Interpersonal Violence, 14*, 152–168.
- Buttell, F.P., & Pike, C.K. (2002). Investigating predictors of treatment attrition among court-ordered batterers. *Journal of Social Service Research, 28*, 53–68.
- Campbell, J.C. (2001). Safety planning based on lethality assessment for partners of batterers in intervention programs. *Journal of Aggression, Maltreatment, and Trauma, 5*, 129–143.
- Dalton, B. (2007). What's going on out there? A survey of batterer intervention programs. *Journal of Aggression, Maltreatment, and Trauma, 15*, 59–74.
- Dowd, L. (2001). Female perpetrators of partner aggression: Relevant issues and treatment. *Journal of Aggression, Maltreatment, and Trauma, 5*, 73–104.
- Hayward, K.S., Steiner, S., & Sproule, K. (2007). Women's perceptions of the impact of a domestic violence treatment program for male perpetrators. *Journal of Forensic Nursing, 3*, 77–83.
- Huss, M.T., & Ralston, A. (2008). Do batterer subtypes actually matter? Treatment completion, treatment response, and recidivism across a batterer typology. *Criminal Justice and Behavior, 35*, 710–723.
- Jones, A.S., & Gondolf, E.W. (2002). Assessing the effect of batterer program completion on reassault: An instrumental variables analysis. *Journal of Quantitative Criminology, 18*, 71–98.
- Langhinrichsen-Rohling, J., Huss, M.T., & Ramsey, S. (2000). The clinical utility of batterer typologies. *Journal of Family Violence, 15*, 37–53.
- Lohr, J.M., Bonge, D., Witte, T.H., Hamberger, L.K., & Langhinrichsen-Rohling, J. (2005). Consistency and accuracy of batterer typology identification. *Journal of Family Violence, 20*, 253–258.
- Olson, D.E., & Stalans, L.J. (2001). Violent offenders on probation: Profile, sentence, and outcome differences among domestic violence and other violent probationers. *Violence Against Women, 7*, 1164–1185.

10 For more information about this topic, please see the following sources:
- Buchbinder, E., & Eisikovits, Z. (2008). Doing treatment: Batterers' experience of intervention. *Children and Youth Services Review, 30*, 616–630.
- Feder, L., & Wilson, D.B. (2005). A meta-analytic review of court-mandated batterer intervention programs: Can courts affect abusers' behavior? *Journal of Experimental Criminology, 1*, 239–262.

11 Babcock, J.C., Green, C.E., & Robie, C. (2004). Does batterers' treatment work? A meta-analytic review of domestic violence treatment. *Clinical*

Psychology Review, 23, 1023–1053. The statement quoted at the end of this paragraph can be found on p. 1049.
12. Feder, L., & Wilson, D. B. (2005). A meta-analytic review of court-mandated batterer intervention programs: Can courts affect abusers' behavior? *Journal of Experimental Criminology, 1,* 239–262. The statement quoted at the end of this paragraph can be found on p. 258.
13. For more information on this topic, see the following resources:

    - Alexander, P. C., & Morris, E. (2008). Stages of change in batterers and their response to treatment. *Violence and Victims, 23,* 476–492.
    - Babcock, J. C., Canady, B. E., Senior, A., & Eckhardt, C. I. (2005). Applying the transtheoretical model to female and male perpetrators of intimate partner violence: Gender differences in stages and processes of change. *Violence and Victims, 20,* 235–250.
    - Begun, A. L., Shelley, G., Strodthoff, T., & Short, L. (2001). Adopting a stages of change approach for individuals who are violent with their intimate partners. *Journal of Aggression, Maltreatment, and Trauma, 5,* 105–127.
    - Eckhardt, C. L., & Utschig, A. C. (2007). Assessing readiness to change among perpetrators of intimate partner violence: Analysis of two self-report measures. *Journal of Family Violence, 22,* 319–330.

14. Babcock, J. C., & Steiner, R. (1999). The relationship between treatment, incarceration, and recidivism of battering: A program evaluation of Seattle's coordinated community response to domestic violence. *Journal of Family Psychology, 13,* 46–59.
15. Resources for more information on this topic include the following:

    - Babcock, J. C., & Steiner, R. (1999). The relationship between treatment, incarceration, and recidivism of battering: A program evaluation of Seattle's coordinated community response to domestic violence. *Journal of Family Psychology, 13,* 46–59.
    - Heckert, D. A., & Gondolf, E. W. (2000). The effect of perceptions of sanctions on batterer program outcomes. *Journal of Research in Crime and Delinquency, 37,* 369–391.

16. Heckert, D. A., & Gondolf, E. W. (2000). The effect of perceptions of sanctions on batterer program outcomes. *Journal of Research in Crime and Delinquency, 37,* 369–391.

8 It's Not Your Fault

"I think that, for me, overcoming the stigma of being abused has been profoundly personal. The majority of the people who I encounter now perceive me as a strong person for overcoming my past challenges. I however had to overcome the cognitive dissonance of trying to understand myself as strong and independent AND a former survivor of IPV. I think the majority of the stigma I have experienced has been self-stigma, focusing on judging myself in a way that I would never judge another person, and a way that no one has ever judged me (to my knowledge)."
~ *Domestic Violence Survivor*

The quote speaks to the power of stigma that has been internalized. In Chapter 4, we explored internalized stigma, or the stigma that victims and survivors turn inward on themselves after hearing these negative messages from others. After experiencing stigma from so many other sources, the person begins to believe that these stigmatizing messages must be true. Also in Chapter 4, we discussed all of the consequences that can come from internalizing stigma, in particular the beliefs that the person doesn't deserve help from others, that ending the relationship isn't possible, or that others will judge and blame them for the abuse. Internalized stigma was the most common type of stigma that survivors in one of our research studies experienced, which tells us that it is a particularly important type of stigma to understand and eradicate. In this chapter, we explore how victims and survivors can overcome internalized stigma and know that they are not to blame or to be devalued because of their experiences with abuse. We cannot stress enough how important it is for victims and survivors to know that overcoming internalized stigma—and overcoming abuse itself—is possible. It sounds so simple, and to some it might seem obvious that victims and survivors should not be stigmatizing because of having faced abuse. But, as you've read throughout this book, the stigma surrounding abusive relationships is so pervasive that it can lead many victims and survivors to feelings of helplessness and hopelessness. In this chapter, we'll see that overcoming abuse and the stigma that surrounds it is not only possible, but that victims and survivors can achieve positive, satisfying, and nurturing lives and relationships.

In this chapter, we will describe strategies for overcoming internalized stigma as well as how victims and survivors can work toward countering the stigma they experience from perpetrators and within communities. In addition, we will see how survivors can become advocates who have a unique and important role to play in advocating for bigger, broader changes related to how IPV is viewed in society. We also will share examples of some of the inspiring stories we heard from participants in our research for how they managed to overcome the abuse and stigma they experienced. In addition, we'll describe the model we developed with another colleague about how survivors overcome past abuse. Our main goal for this chapter it to offer hope that overcoming abuse is achievable for victims and survivors, even if they feel that their past or current situations have left them feeling deeply wounded. As we've seen in our research, sometimes the deepest wounds turn into the greatest triumphs.

How Victims and Survivors Can Counter the Stigma They Face at Every Level

We firmly believe that victims and survivors can fight against the stigma that often surrounds intimate partner violence. This belief is grounded firmly in the countless stories of triumph that we have heard from participants in our research. We have also been inspired by our growing community on See the Triumph social media platforms, especially as we have heard from our community members on these platforms that they, too, have fought back against stigma and overcome abuse. This journey may not be easy by any means, but victims and survivors are able to rise above stigma and begin a new life free from abuse with enough inner strength as well as outside resources and support. To begin our discussion of how victims and survivors can overcome stigma, we'll first explore some strategies that they can use to counter the stigma they may face at various levels, including from within themselves, from their perpetrators, and at the community level.

Strategies for Overcoming Internalized Stigma

We begin this section with an overview of strategies that can be used for overcoming internalized stigma. Back in Chapter 4, we explained the IPV Internalized Stigma Model and how internalized stigma can develop. It begins with abuse of any kind. Then this abuse results in a variety of negative outcomes. These outcomes can be internal (e.g., negative emotions such as depression, shame, embarrassment) or external (e.g., isolation from family, decreased help-seeking). Then the victim experiences stigma from others—that is, someone else enacting stigma in a very overt manner—such as the question, "Why didn't you just leave him a long time ago?" Then the victim turns this stigma inward. For example, in response to the question of why the victim didn't leave a long time ago, the person thinks, "Hmm, why *didn't* I leave a long time ago? Maybe I did this to myself." This sort of thought magnifies and becomes embedded in victims' thought processes, which leads them to believe that the abuse is their fault, that something is wrong with them, or that they did something to deserve it. So, how can the person learn to turn these thoughts around and counter this internalized stigma? Drawing upon our clinical work counseling survivors as well as from what we have heard from the survivors in our research studies and the theories of cognitive-behavioral therapy, we suggest that changing one's self-talk can be used internally to challenge self-stigmatizing beliefs.

Self-talk refers to the things we say to ourselves. In other words, our self-talk reflects those internal conversations that we have with ourselves that influence how we think and behave.[1] These conversations can be both positive and negative, and they shape our feelings and behaviors. In our own clinical work, we have heard from many clients that self-talk has a very powerful impact on how we think about ourselves and others, and how we choose how to act in a variety of situations. Often, self-stigmatizing messages develop over a period of many years, so it does take some time and energy to identify and eventually replace them, and this is especially true for negative beliefs that have been reinforced by multiple sources, such as from abuse perpetrators and societal stigma.

Our self-talk reflects how we interpret situations, and the same situation can take a more positive or negative turn depending on how people talk to themselves about the situation. Here is a simple example to illustrate this point. Imagine that you are walking into work, and a car whizzes by you through a rain puddle, and it splashes you from head to toe with cold, muddy water. Negative self-talk in this situation may look like the following: "Geez, why did you stand so close to the street? You idiot. You knew that puddle was right there and that you'd get wet if a car drove past you!" On the other hand, positive self-talk would look more like the following: "Wow, I'm totally soaked now. I'm going to have to change clothes before I go into work. I'll call my boss and let her know what happened." Reading these two statements, do you see the difference? In the first case, you blamed yourself for the car that drove by and got you wet and called yourself a name, whereas in the second statement, you were upset, but not at yourself. You thought about what you'd need to do to resolve the situation and made decisions about next steps. To promote a more positive outcome in that situation, it would be critical to learn to say statements similar to the second statement rather than the first, more negative version of self-talk. In particular, it's likely that the negative self-talk would lead you to feel more upset about the experience throughout the rest of the day. On the other hand, the positive self-talk would help you to move forward and put the incident in its place, thus not allowing it to affect your outlook on the rest of the day.

Now let's apply this information to a victim of intimate partner violence. You might be able to imagine some of the negative self-talk statements that victims say to themselves. "Why did you let this happen?" "You will never get out of this relationship." "You deserved it since you're the one who stayed with him." These statements might sound similar to some of the internalized stigma examples we shared in Chapter 4. One of the biggest challenges from these negative self-talk statements is that they might continue for years and years, well after the abuse has ended. Even worse, they might grow into even more generalized statements about what the person believes to be true about her or his life. These types of negative messages might be, "You are not capable of a healthy relationship," or "You don't deserve to be happy."

An important step that victims and survivors can take toward countering internalized stigma is to be intentional about identifying and challenging negative self-talk. One of the first steps to achieving this goal is to begin by identifying times when they start to think something like this. For example, they could begin keeping a journal that tracks when they said those things, how often the thoughts occurred in a day, what else was happening around them when they noticed the negative self-talk, and what they were feeling before or after the negative self-talk occurred. Monitoring negative self-talk can be extremely valuable, even before people begin to intentionally work to change their thought patterns. In many cases, people don't even realize how often they are repeating negative self-talk statements in their minds. Developing awareness of these patterns is an important step toward unlocking clues for changing them.

Once a person has begun to monitor their negative self-talk, another important step that is especially relevant for internalized stigma is to examine the source of these beliefs. Once a person has listed out the negative self-talk statements that they experience, it becomes possible to determine sources of those statements. Let's consider the example of a survivor of a past abusive relationship who repeatedly asks herself, "Why did I let him do that to me?" This survivor can now examine other places where she has heard that message, either directly or indirectly. In considering this, she may realize that it's similar to what her perpetrator used to say to her, e.g., "If you were a better wife, I wouldn't have to hit you." And perhaps she also heard a related question from her mother when she told her about the relationship: "Why do you let him treat you like that?" In addition, she may have heard similar questions in the media concerning high-profile cases of domestic violence in the news, such as, "Why do women stay in abusive relationships?" Identifying these sources of internalized stigma can be extremely powerful. This process can help the person to expose these messages as false and reflections of the stigma surrounding intimate partner violence—rather than viewing them as "the truth" because they have become internalized as part of the person's belief system. Affirming the external source of negative self-talk statements can help victims and survivors realize that these statements are able to be changed.

Of course, constructing new, positive self-talk statements can be challenging. We have asked some of our past counseling clients to bring a list of negative self-talk statements into the counseling session. For each statement on the list, we worked with them to formulate new, positive statements that could replace the negative ones. Once new, positive self-talk statements have been identified, it can take time and practice to learn how to replace the negative statements with the positive ones. However, beginning to monitor one's self-talk and counter negative messages with more positive ones allows a person to feel a greater sense of control over his or her internal dialogue.

To illustrate how this process may apply to victims and survivors of intimate partner violence, consider Table 8.1, which lists some of the negative self-talk statements that participants in our research have described. Next, we offer an alternative, positive self-talk statement that could replace each negative one. Of course, it is important for each person to identify replacement phrases that will work best for them, so the exact wording of these statements might look different for each individual person who uses them.

In the process of replacing negative self-talk with new, positive self-talk, some people find it helpful to carry around an actual list of statements with them and to keep them in a pocket, purse, or somewhere convenient and easy to locate just so that they are close by and handy when they need to say them, or remember them when a more negative statement

Table 8.1 Negative Versus Positive Self-Talk Statements

Negative Self-Talk Statement	Positive Self-Talk Statement
"Why did I let this happen?"	"My abuser is responsible for all of the abuse."
"I will never get out of this relationship."	"It might take time, but I will get out."
"I am not capable of a healthy relationship."	"I am fully capable of a healthy relationship."
"I don't deserve to be happy."	"I deserve happiness."
"Maybe I did this to myself."	"I am not responsible for someone else's behavior."
"Why didn't I leave a long time ago?"	"I left when I was strong enough to leave."
"I was stupid to stay."	"I stayed for my safety."
"I attract losers."	"There is nothing about me that made him/her abuse me."

creeps in. Others go as far as to tape them on a mirror, or around the house, so that they are visible and easy to see in any room. Of course, people who are currently living with abusive partners should consider carefully if and how they can use such a list in a way that doesn't compromise their safety, and it may be helpful to practice memorizing one or two key positive statements rather than carrying a physical list in those cases. It takes a lot of practice, but over time and with enough rehearsal, negative self-statements can eventually change into more positive statements. Over time, these are positive messages can become embedded into a person's thinking patterns rather than the old, harmful ones that used to exist. Self-statements are important since these messages shape the way we feel, the way we behave, and the choices we make.

Some victims and survivors of abuse may be able to work through the aforementioned process of changing self-talk on their own. However, many others may find it necessary to work with a counselor or therapist to provide additional support as they work through this process. A trained mental health professional can be extremely helpful throughout the processes of seeking safety and overcoming past abuse. However, it is important to find a counselor who has the training and competence to work with clients impacted by intimate partner violence. We recommend that victims and survivors seeking to work with a counselor in their own community ask any prospective counselors about their levels of training, knowledge, and experience related to intimate partner violence, as well as the extent to which they consider the impact of trauma in their counseling work.[2]

Strategies for Overcoming Perpetrator Stigma

In addition to monitoring and changing ones self-talk to counter internalized stigma, victims and survivors can consider ways to challenge specifically the stigmatizing messages they receive from external sources, especially from their perpetrators and within their communities. In Chapter 3, we talked about stigma from perpetrators. We heard from countless survivors that one of the most significant sources of stigma was from their perpetrators. The stigma from perpetrators only reinforced the stigma that was present from all of the other sources. The types of messages delivered by perpetrators are the same as or similar to those the victim might hear from others, such as, "It's your fault," or "You did this to yourself." However, these messages from perpetrators are coupled with other abusive behaviors, such as manipulation, isolation, control, and physical abuse, so you can imagine how much they hurt and how powerful they are. Perpetrator stigma also can occur over a span of years, which further increases the intensity of perpetrator stigma. So how can victims and survivors counter perpetrator stigma when it is such a pervasive phenomenon? Three main strategies are to draw upon other sources of support, work toward ending the secrecy surrounding their abuse, and find closure for the collateral damage that the perpetrator has created.

First, survivors can challenge perpetrator stigma by connecting to positive sources of support. We heard from many survivors in our studies that they reached out to someone they knew, such as a neighbor, family member, or friend, and with this support, they eventually started to see more clearly what was occurring and that safety and support were possible. Consider this quote, for example, from a survivor who spoke about the powerful impact of social support during her process of leaving her abuser:

> "I think that overcoming it starts by being open about it and letting people know what you have been through. Physical abuse is easy; you have the scars and bruises to invoke people's understanding. Other abuses are much more complicated, but if more victims speak out, maybe they too will be better understood. I also know taking care of myself and surrounding myself with true friends and dropping others is working for me."

To counter stigmatizing messages they receive from perpetrators, it is critical for victims and survivors to hear uplifting, supportive, and encouraging messages from other people in their lives.

Second, perpetrator stigma can be challenged when victims and survivors work toward ending the secrecy surrounding their abuse. Keeping secrets can prolong abuse and stigma, and we heard from many survivors that a large part of perpetrator stigma was secrecy. Their perpetrators made it seem as though no one would listen, that others would judge, and that no one would believe if they were to tell. However, we heard from many participants that once they felt brave enough (and, of course, safe enough) to tell the big secret of abuse, they were able to begin the process of eradicating the stigma that the perpetrator had placed on them. Here is a quote from a research participant that describes this idea:

> "Secrecy, it must be kept a secret. For many years, this is what I believed. No one could know what I was living with. I had to make excuses for him, his behavior, my absences, to family, to friends, to our children. Secrecy sucks. I now live my life wide open. I do not keep secrets anymore, of any kind. I live out loud these days."

Perpetrators often use secrecy as one of their weapons of abuse, and this secrecy also serves to isolate victims and survivors. By eliminating this secrecy—when it is safe to do so—victims and survivors can reclaim their right to connection and support from others.

Third, victims and survivors can counter perpetrator stigma by finding closure and acceptance with any collateral damage that their perpetrators have created in their lives. Leaving a perpetrator also often means leaving old friends and family. Others who are close to the perpetrator might not be aware of the abuse, depending on what the perpetrator is telling them, so friends and family unknowingly make it even more challenging for victims to feel supported in their decision to leave. One participant said this about her decision to break free from perpetrator stigma and abuse:

> "When I left him, it meant leaving all of my friends, the people I came to know as family. And they wouldn't let me leave without a fight. They tried everything: guilt, blame, reminders of loss of status. But, being approximately my 7th attempt at leaving and with the incredible support of new friends, I stuck it out and resisted the threats, the guilt trips, the literal offerings of monetary gain (I found $1,000 cash in my mailbox as incentive to return)."

Also, as we've seen throughout this book, there are often ripple effects of abusive relationships that can continue long after a relationship has ended—such as custody and family court processes when children are involved, career and economic consequences, and ongoing mental and physical health challenges. These factors can be very difficult when a victim is contemplating leaving the relationship and throughout the recovery process. It is indeed a great injustice that victims and survivors of abusive relationships have to experience all of these negative consequences and outcomes as a direct result of how their perpetrators have treated them. Simply put, it isn't fair that victims and survivors should have to pay such a steep price for the abuse they have experienced. However, one theme we have seen time and again in our research is that survivors are much more able to recover from their past abuse and the havoc that perpetrators have wreaked upon their lives when they are able to accept their circumstances, develop a sense of closure and forgiveness (of themselves and others), and develop a sense of peace about moving forward from the abuse. In this way, survivors reclaim their lives and do not permit their abusers to maintain a stranglehold over the rest of their lives, from this point forward.

Strategies for Overcoming Stigma in Communities

Let's talk now about how victims and survivors can overcome the stigma that is often found in communities. One experience that survivors shared with us in our research was the notion of being labeled as a victim of abuse. Many participants talked about how being labeled as a victim was a large part of the stigma they experienced and that this label was difficult to face. For many survivors, shedding this label is a key part of the process of embracing a more complete identity and reframing how they view their experiences with abuse. Consider the following quote about how one survivor embraced the label of survivor:

> "I no longer see being labeled as a bad thing. I own my label of survivor with pride and tell my story to help others either in their own journey of recovery or in knowing they aren't alone and can get out of their abusive situation."

Of course, some people will prefer to avoid the label of survivor or another identity that defines them in relation to the abuse. Therefore, it remains important to support victims and survivors in determining their own identities, and the extent to which they will identify their experiences with abuse as central to their identities.

Another large part of the experience of stigma that victims and survivors face in communities is the shame that others place on them for staying in the relationship. Releasing these feelings of shame was a large part of what we heard from survivors regarding how they were able to overcome stigma. Take this quote, for example, in which the survivor explains how much overcoming shame was part of her process of overcoming stigma in her community:

> "I was ashamed that I had lived so long in an abusive marriage. I was ashamed that I had let my children see the things they had. Shame that I had pretended to be something I wasn't and shame that I hadn't been honest and asked for help."

As this survivor began to release her feelings of shame about her choices in her past abusive relationship, she became freer to embrace her new identity and to live a life free from abuse.

Releasing fear of being judged by others in one's community is another important task for many victims and survivors in overcoming stigma at the community level. One survivor had the following to say about stigma from her community and how to overcome it:

> "Victims fear what others think of them. Surviving abuse has meant getting past my fear of other's opinions of me and caring more about what God thinks of me. Pursuing my dreams has also given me new paradigms in which to measure my worth and replace the negative messages I received from my husband."

We heard similar experiences from many survivors. Accepting ones choices, feeling empowered to talk about them, and learning to care less about others' opinions are core aspects of overcoming the stigma that victims and survivors face within their communities. Another survivor said the following about how to use one's experience to educate others in the community:

"Once you are out of the relationship, claim your power. There's no sense in pretending it didn't happen, just use your experiences to educate others that there's no shame in having been in an abusive relationship."

Survivors as Advocates for Social Change

What role can survivors play in creating broader changes to how victims and survivors are viewed and treated in society? Thus far in this chapter, we have talked about strategies that victims and survivors can use to counter stigma that occurs internally, stigma that comes from perpetrators, and stigma from one's community. We also know that stigma is a large-scale social problem that needs to be eradicated at the broader level. We will go into detail about how agencies, policy makers, and other leaders can assist with this in the following chapters, but in this chapter, consider opportunities that survivors may have to create change in society. Of course, becoming a social advocate is not a necessary step for a person to be considered "healed" or "recovered" from a past abusive relationship. We believe strongly that the decision whether and/or how to become engaged in large-scale advocacy efforts should always be up to individual survivors. There are many reasons that a survivor of past abuse may choose not to become an advocate, including simply being disinterested, not having the time or energy, not feeling far enough along in one's own healing process, wanting to move forward and avoid future reminders of the past abuse, and not feeling equipped with the skills or knowledge to do so. Safety risks also may arise, such as survivors who believe that sharing their experiences publicly could put them at risk of future abuse. For all of these reasons, it is important to avoid engaging in advocacy as an optimal outcome for survivors, and the choice to abstain from these activities is a perfectly valid one that should be honored and respected.

For survivors who do want to engage in social advocacy efforts, this type of engagement can become a powerful experience in their own healing journeys as well as help them to feel that they are turning their own past challenges into a source of hope, encouragement, and support for others. In one of our recent research studies, we asked survivors about advocacy efforts they engage in, both large and small, in order to make an impact in society for how survivors are viewed and how survivors can be supported. In this section, we'll share some ideas that we heard from the participants in that study.[3] One of the major findings of that study was that survivors can be involved in advocacy efforts in a variety of ways, ranging from large-scale efforts that have a vast potential reach, to less intensive efforts that have a powerful impact on a smaller scale.

Large-Scale Advocacy Efforts

Large-scale efforts by survivors included speaking engagements, sharing their stories with others, participating in professional and/or volunteer work to address IPV, and engaging in advocacy via long-term social media initiatives. The following is a list of some examples of the ways that survivors can advocate for making large-scale changes at the community and societal levels.

- "I share my story with women and teens to give them hope. I was a volunteer for a domestic violence agency until I became disabled."
- "I sponsor women in 12-step programs who have been abused and share my experience."
- "I am taking classes to become an advocate. I want to help change the system that is so broken."
- "I volunteer with kids who have been through abuse, and I educate people around me about abusive relationships."
- "I lecture around the country about the dynamics of intimate partner violence, surviving abuse, the generational cycle of family violence, and many other facets of this societal and criminal problem. I have assisted law enforcement in writing policies for effective law enforcement response to domestic violence, testify as an expert witness in civil and criminal cases."
- "I now head up a group within our church. We will be working within this group for family violence and adding programs for them also."
- "I have helped other women already, and am going to trainings at my local shelter. My goal is to speak locally and statewide to churches and other organizations that commonly misguide women who are seeking refuge and help from abusive relationships."
- "I have been an advocate in my role as a nurse educator in a large women's clinic, mostly providing information and referrals."
- "I definitely feel that I am an advocate. I am a counselor and use my experiences in many ways. One way I have found myself as an advocate is with women and men leaving abusive relationships."
- "I am a full-time paid court advocate for a DV shelter. I had always worked in the legal field and discovered that I really enjoyed working with victims of crime, specifically DV. I have been doing direct services for 5 years and plan on making a career of it."

Smaller-Scale Advocacy Efforts

Survivors also participated in smaller-scale efforts to advocate for and support survivors. Although these activities may not have the impact on a larger society that the aforementioned efforts might, they still have significant potential to impact victims and survivors. One example that participants in our study shared was using social media to raise awareness about intimate partner violence (e.g., "I share information on Facebook that has helped others and made many uncomfortable, but it is a reality that people need to face" and "I share posts, articles, etc., on Facebook and Twitter and Pinterest").

Another advocacy activity that participants described included simply being available to listen to others. For example, one person said the following about how she thinks about herself as a good listener,

> "I have told several younger girls that are just starting out in relationships about what I went through, and if they ever have anything at all they can come tell me and I can help them. I can listen without a judgmental ear. I can understand what they are going through."

Another participant said, "Speaking about my abusive past is something that I have done with close friends that were experiencing the beginning phases of partner violence." Others said that they shared advice with others who were involved in abusive relationships (e.g., "When I hear the relationship stories of my friends, I immediately notice the warning signs of abuse. I speak to them clearly and let them know they deserve better and that they should end the relationship," and "I've given people advice sometimes but only if they ask. I know what they are going through, the fear, the pain, the disbelief in their self. I always try and help someone out of a situation if I can"). Participants also voiced that they consider themselves spokespersons about abuse and speak about their experiences in order to assist others. For example, one survivor said, "I speak out against abuse," and another said, "I don't know if it is being an advocate, but I talk about my experience every chance I get, in the hopes that someone within earshot will be encouraged to get help and get away."

Turning Points

We have discussed strategies for victims and survivors to counter the stigma they face at a variety of levels. For the remainder of this chapter, we'll turn our focus to the broader processes involved in how survivors overcome abuse and stigma. We will start with the idea of turning points, or moments that survivors know it is time to get out of their abusive relationships. We will also dive deeper into how exactly survivors manage to overcome abuse. We will tell two particular stories of Ava and Mona, as we believe both are powerful stories of overcoming abuse and stigma.

In another research study we conducted,[4] we investigated the key moments in victims' experiences of their relationships that lead them to making a choice to work toward ending those relationships, which we called "turning points." These turning points didn't always translate into the victims immediately leaving their abusive relationships, and in fact, it often took a significant amount of time for them to plan out how to leave safely. However, these turning point moments occurred when victims realized that they did want to leave the abusive relationships, once and for all.

In our research, we identified themes in the different types of circumstances that led to these turning points. One theme was severe violence.

When the abuse escalated to severe violence, these survivors knew that they had to leave. Here is one example of this sort of turning point from a participant in the study:

> "He threatened to throw me off a balcony—something just took over in me and even though I was really scared he was going to do it and I wouldn't be able to stop him I said, 'You will not do that to me. I don't deserve to be treated that way.'"

A second theme in the turning points research study was that survivors were able to change their perspective about the relationship, abuse, and/or their partners. In other words, these survivors had a shift in their thinking. For example, one participant shared that her abuser had isolated her from all of her friends and family. One day, she decided to go out with them anyway. She had a huge realization about how nice everyone was to her and just how cruel her abuser actually was. A third theme we heard from those who described their turning points was related to learning about the dynamics of abuse. Once survivors learned information about abuse, and the dynamics related to abuse in particular, this helped serve as a catalyst toward leaving. For example, one person mentioned that she read a book about abuse and realized that she wasn't crazy or stupid (these were the messages she'd been hearing from her husband) and that they separated for a final time later that year thanks to her really learning more about abuse through the book.

Sometimes, the fourth turning point stemmed from an intervention from an external source, such as child protective services or law enforcement, which assisted the survivor with countering the stigma. A fifth turning point that we heard about from participants was realizing the impact of violence on children. We heard from some survivors that when a child witnessed their abuse, they realized how impactful it was, and that had a direct impact on their decision to stand up to the abuse and leave the relationship. One participant said, "I left with my daughter when she began exhibiting anxiety at the age of six and when he began to throw things at me and yell in front of her. I had family pick up my belongings." Some survivors also had turning points when they saw their perpetrators direct any form of violence toward their children. The following survivor poignantly described this in the following quote:

> "He did exactly what the therapist predicted: he hurt my daughter. NOTHING is more important and precious than my children and the day he hurt my daughter, it was like someone threw aside a curtain and I saw for the first time what the therapist did (probably because I was watching him do to her what he usually did to me)."

Overall, turning points are an important part of victims' and survivors' processes of seeking safety and recovering from past abuse. Although sometimes turning points may occur over an extended period of time, they also may reflect moments in which they have some new realizations or insights into their own lives, their relationships, and their perpetrators. These new insights can then translate into decisions to work toward changing their circumstances and moving toward safety and recovery.

Overcoming Abuse and the Stigma That Surrounds It

Once victims or survivors begin moving toward safety and recovery, they start a journey that may take time and intensive effort that allows them to rebuild their lives free from violence. All too often, societal stereotypes would lead people—including many victims and survivors themselves—to believe that victims are destined to replay cycles of victimization and abuse throughout their lives. However, we know that recovery from an abusive relationship is possible. To illustrate this point, we now want to share some powerful stories from participants in our research so that you can read a few examples of how they were able to overcome abuse, and the stigma that surrounds it, and rebuild lives free from abuse. After we share the following stories of Ava and Mona, we'll talk more broadly about the processes that may be involved for survivors as they overcome past abuse.

Ava's Story

When she participated in our research, Ava had just turned 30. She is a mother to an elementary school-aged child and has an associate's degree and works in the health-care field. She was in one prior abusive relationship, "the first relationship I was ever in," for about five years, and she and her partner were engaged and lived together. In the relationship, she experienced physical, emotional, and sexual abuse. Although Ava took out a protective order against her abuser, he violated the order multiple times and was arrested for that. She reported that after she had left the relationship, her abuser also found where she had moved and was arrested for damaging property at her new residence and to her car. Ava faced grave danger to herself and her child in order to escape the relationship:

> "My baby was three months old, and the abuse was only getting worse. One night after Ethan (Ava's perpetrator) finally passed out, I grabbed what I could and threw it in the diaper bag, and we snuck out in the middle of the night. We stayed at a neighbor's until I found a family member who took us in until I could save enough money to get us on our feet."

Ava's ex tried to kidnap her baby multiple times. He would find her in public or come to her job and threaten Ava and the people around her.

She finally got a protective order, and things still didn't get better until he violated it so many times he landed in jail. Unfortunately, over the past few years, Ethan has come back into Ava's life, wanting a relationship with their son. Ava said this about it:

> "It is certainly unsettling. He still tries to break me down with verbal and emotional abuse, but now that I've been out for so long and grown so much, I recognize his attempts and can ignore them. I just don't want him to EVER get close enough to my son to hurt him."

We asked Ava about stigma and how the various components might have impacted her in her experience with abuse. Ava experienced isolation both during and after the relationship:

> "Isolation was due to the fact that, for years, my abuser worked to come between and break down all relationships with people I was close to, either by his own means or by threatening me and physically making me 'pay for spending time with them' to a point where I felt like I had to be isolated from my people just to keep the peace with him. Once I left, that feeling of isolation was strong, and I had to work through that to realize that all my loved ones still accepted me. However, there were some friends and people in my life that were also friends with him that would not associate with me once I left. That was a very isolating feeling as well."

Ava also felt that others judged her negatively on account of the abuse:

> "I had relinquished all power over myself, my feelings, my emotions, my needs, and my strength. It was almost as if I had to give it all to him. Once I left and was getting back on my feet, it seemed as if people around me thought I had no power over my own life. I felt like I had to work hard to prove to them and to myself that I was the one in control of my life, and I did have the power to make good decisions. I definitely proved that to everyone around me. It was frustrating sometimes the way people looked at me and thought I had no ability to make good decisions because I had stayed in such a bad situation for so long."

The abuse was also shrouded in secrecy:

> "I hate secrets. I felt I HAD to keep what I was going through a secret. 'What would people think? I don't want to be judged; I don't want them to be mad at me. He's going to change. I don't want them to not accept him. People will think I'm stupid and weak if they know I let him treat me this way. What if someone tells the authorities, then

he really will kill me? All thoughts that went through my head that made me feel I HAD to keep it a secret."

When Ava talked about secrecy as it applied to her experience after she left the abuse, she said that she still kept a lot of it a secret even after she left, because it had become a way of living that she became used to. "People in my life definitely labeled me as a big, huge secret-keeper for a long time after the relationship was over, which I understood, but it was still frustrating. Now, I can't and won't keep a secret for anything!" Ava reports that she changed the way she viewed herself and her situation in order to overcome the past abuse and stigma surrounding it. She said,

> "I changed the way I thought about things. People are always going to judge other people, but nobody knows what it was like in that house, and nobody knows how liberating it was to get out of there. So, eventually the judgmental statements or eyes filled with pity didn't affect me. I knew who I was and where I'd been and where I was going. You get to a point where looking ahead is all that matters. The past, the stigmas, you just make a decision, and you don't let them affect you."

Now, nearly ten years after that relationship ended, Ava expressed gratitude that she hasn't experienced abuse in any other relationships. She has maintained a life free from abuse by looking for warning signs early on. She said this about how she is able to maintain healthy relationships, free from abuse, "If I see the slightest sign that there is a potential for a person I'm dating to be controlling or possessive, which in my mind ultimately leads to abuse, I go running as fast as I can."

At the end of each survey we've asked survivors to complete, we ask for any thoughts or suggestions for other survivors who might be attempting to leave an abusive relationship. We were very touched and inspired by Ava's words. Ava encouraged other survivors to keep hold of hope for a positive future:

> "Please know that you can get out, and it will not always be an easy road, and IT will be lonely at times. *BUT* it only gets better; life is TOO beautiful to live it trapped and abused and hiding under the shame of it all. It's NOT your fault, and you don't deserve it, no matter what your abuser has tried to manipulate you into believing. Abuse can happen to everyone; it doesn't discriminate, but there are resources and people in your life who are ready and waiting to help you start over and live the life you deserve to live. I never thought I would get out, and once I did, I never thought I'd be ok without him. But I tried, and now I'm a new person, and life is incredible."

Mona's Story

Mona, like Ava, is another example of someone who has made it to the other side and had an inspirational story to share. Mona is a female in her early 40s, and she has three children who are teenagers or in their early 20s. She is currently enrolled in college and working toward a bachelor's degree. She was in one prior abusive relationship that lasted for nearly two decades and ended over four years ago, and she lived with her abuser, although she was never married to him. In the relationship, she faced emotional, verbal, physical, sexual, financial, and spiritual abuse. The legal sanctions her abuser received included a restraining order and misdemeanor charges. Mona's abuser perpetuated stigma as part of the abuse he directed toward her. He perpetuated blame ("Everything was always my fault, from finances to him hitting me"), isolation ("I was never allowed to see or visit my family, and I was only 'allowed' to be friends with his friends"), and loss of power ("I was never allowed to make any choices—then be shamed because I was told how I couldn't do anything right; he said he always had to make the choice because of my incompetence").

It was a long and arduous process for Mona to leave the relationship:

> "I ran away after he strangled me (for the last time) and broke my foot as I was trying to escape. My two teenage children lived in a local domestic abuse shelter for several months, and the advocates allowed my stay to be longer due to my broken foot and court proceedings."

Mona's experience of the court system was not positive.

> "The county in which my incident took place in, the appointed court system had very little knowledge of domestic abuse and seemed to be more empathetic to my perpetrator than to me. It still upsets me on how my court proceeding resulted. He was given a slap on the wrist and sent to ineffective counseling."

Her recovery process has been lengthy as well:

> "I was diagnosed with PTSD and received therapy for a few years. I still practice many of the relaxing techniques that she taught me and also re-read through handouts and worksheets we had to fill out during my stay at the shelter. Things seem to be getting better, but I have setbacks from time to time, just not as debilitating as they once were."

Fortunately, Mona had a good support system that surrounded her. She said, "My support network is very understanding, educated, and positive people. I knew who I could trust my story with." She urges other survivors to be cautious regarding with whom they share their stories, saying, "I only told those I knew I could trust, which is a few and select. I am not out to get special attention or to have people feel sorry for me—that has never been me." Despite the challenges in her past, Mona is proud of how far she has come in overcoming her past abuse:

> "It is a daily struggle but, just as with any other goal in your life, perseverance and confidence will get you through this. No step you take is an easy one, but well worthwhile once you stop and reflect on how far you have come and the obstacles you overcame. I do not see myself or think of myself as a 'victim' anymore. I am a survivor! And I am proud of that! My abuser was the worst of the worst. If I survived nearly 20 years of hell, I am very confident that I can survive pretty much anything else that comes my way!"

Over time, Mona has rebuilt her own life and the lives of her children in a safe, positive manner.

> "The changes in mine and my children's lives have been so dramatically different. I am watching my kids flourish by being nurtured in a safe, secure, and happy home. It makes our past 'almost' forgetful. We keep an open line of communication with them and I encourage them to always talk to me when the nightmares or flashbacks happen. I have also recently married to a very kind, sensitive, and supportive man, and he has been incredibly patient and understanding with me, my children, and our past. We are very, very poor, but still feel like the wealthiest family because we have each other, love, and the safety we have never had! Life is good now!"

She advises other survivors to seek help:

> "Get out while you can and if you cannot, find a way, make a safety plan, get your paperwork and finances in order, and most importantly—ASK FOR HELP! Because, from my experience, once the abuse starts it only gets worse. It is not easy but it is worth it!"

Mona encourages other survivors to learn to take life a day at a time in the recovery process. She said,

> "What I have done is tapped into my own special little talents. I enjoy art journaling and play an instrument. I am learning how to cook and bake and doing extremely simple crafts. I have also surrounded myself with positive and encouraging people who always seem to have an ear to listen and that shoulder to cry on.

I read that it takes 10 positive experiences to fade or phase out one negative one. This applied to children, so why wouldn't it for adults. I try to fill my day with as many, no matter how trivial, positives as I can. Each day I see as a manageable challenge or if it seems too overwhelming—I have been told that to just cry, is okay too."

The Processes Involved in Overcoming Abuse

You've had the opportunity now to read two inspiring stories from survivors who crossed over the hurdles of being abused and facing stigma and who are now well on their way in the journey of recover. Understanding stories like these is an important part of repainting the picture that those who have been impacted by intimate partner violence can, in fact, overcome this and go on to live without abuse in their lives. Far too many people hold negative, stigmatizing views of victims and survivors of abuse, but these stereotypes simply don't match the strength and courage that we have seen in the lives of real survivors who have shared their stories with us. Another aspect of our research with survivors of past abuse has been to explore the processes they experience as they move toward recovery and healing. Together with our colleague, Paulina Flasch, we studied these processes based on the narratives of the survivors who participated in our research. Through this research, we developed the Triumph Process Model, which describes the possible processes survivors experience as they move toward overcoming past abuse. To introduce this notion, consider Figure 8.1, which represents the Triumph Process Model:

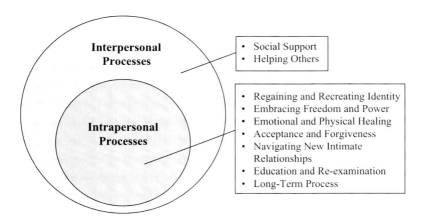

Figure 8.1 Triumph Process Model of Overcoming Past Abuse

As is depicted Figure 8.1, there are two main categories of processes involved in overcoming past abuse: interpersonal and intrapersonal. Intrapersonal processes are known to be internal to the person, while interpersonal processes refer to processes that occur in relation to others. Within each of these categories, we identified specific processes that were common among the survivors who participated in our survey, which we'll describe briefly in this section. Keep in mind, however, that our Triumph Process Model affirms that these processes may not all apply to every person, and they are not intended to be viewed as distinct "stages" or "phases" that must occur in some designated order. We have seen through the survivors in our research as well as through our clinical experiences as counselors that recovery from an abusive relationship is a very individualized process that may look very different from person to person. We have summarized this information and encourage readers wanting more information to see the full article.[5]

Intrapersonal Processes

Our research identified several distinct intrapersonal processes that may be involved in the abuse recovery process. The first intrapersonal process was called *regaining and recreating one's identity post-abuse*. When survivors became free from the abusive relationships, a major task was to rebuild their self-esteem and self-worth, which their abusers had damaged and depleted during the relationship. Participants also had to re-discover their old selves, or create totally new identities, although this often was very difficult to do after abuse. As one participant noted, "I felt like as time went by I slowly gained pieces of myself back. I slowly started to see myself as attractive again, loved being around myself, and just loving me."

A second common intrapersonal process experience that survivors had was that they *embraced the power and freedom to direct their lives post-abuse*. After perpetrators exert power, control, and decision making, survivors must re-learn how to make independent choices, small and large, about their lives. Small things, such as being able to wear perfume was a detail that one participant shared, since her abuser never allowed her to wear perfume. Larger choices, such as what career path to choose, or what friends to socialize with, could be made independently. Read the following excerpt from someone who wanted to share how it felt when she first moved out on her own:

> "Upon leaving my abusive partner, I felt more empowered than I felt in years, despite all the other challenges I faced. It was the one thing that made the isolation, the social exclusion, the blame, the shame, and becoming the black sheep of the family tolerable. Every little thing was appreciated. I moved into a tiny studio apartment and for the first six months was content in saying aloud to myself: This is my place, this is my shower, this is my bed, this is my chair, this is my

kitchen, so on and so forth, and I can do as I please without fear of being reprimanded. It was freedom, to be me again. To do without judgment."

A third intrapersonal process related to overcoming abuse was *recovering from mental and physical health symptoms of abuse*. Abuse entails so many types of physical and mental health consequences, and healing from these is a major need in the lives of those overcoming abuse. Many survivors spoke of the power of therapy or counseling with a professional as a large part of how this happened. Medical care from any physical traumas was also part of this process. *Becoming enlightened about abuse, control, power, and other dynamics related to intimate partner violence* was another large part of what participants described as part of the process.

Fourth, *finding forgiveness and acceptance with oneself and one's perpetrator* was another intrapersonal process described by those who took our survey. One person said that moving on meant, "to just quit asking 'why' and reliving the past every day for years. I have to let it go even though it is painful." Not everyone needed or wanted to forgive their abusers, but many survivors noted the powerful sense of release they experienced once they did achieve this forgiveness. Forgiveness of oneself offered a similar sense of release, as is reflected in the following quote from a survivor:

"Shame is something I am in the process of releasing. Today I accept that I did the very best I could with what I knew and where I was at, but that took a long while and a lot of therapy."

The fifth intrapersonal theme was *determining whether and how to enter into a new intimate relationship*. This included how to maintain a sense of health and wellness in new intimate relationships, with particular attention given toward not wanting to repeat old patterns from the abusive relationship. Sometimes this resulted in someone being overly cautious about signs of abuse, which may end up resulting in relationships ending, or this might have included someone being extra careful about checking into a prospective partner's background before going on a date. Others talked about their decision not to date because of feelings of fear related to the outcomes. The following quote speaks to this struggle:

"I remarried but it only lasted several years. I think that we divorced partly because I never got the counseling I needed to heal from my abusive relationship. Many times my second husband said he felt like he was my victim, just because I refused to let go of any of the control in the relationship for fear he would abuse me. I've not even attempted to enter into another relationship as I felt it was best that

I focus on raising my children, and learning to love myself. Maybe now that they are grown I may date again, but I'm perfectly happy with me and the fact that God isn't finished with me yet."

The sixth, and final, theme related to the intrapersonal process of overcoming abuse was *acknowledging the potential long-term time frame of recovery*. In fact, many participants said that recovery was an ongoing journey. Many used the term journey in both positive and negative ways—positive and uplifting, as well as painful and emotional. Many participants commented that the journey would never end, as if to say that recovery from abuse will be a lifelong process.

Interpersonal Processes

Two main interpersonal processes were found in relation to overcoming abuse in our study: *building positive supports* and *using one's abuse experiences to assist others who might be in abusive relationships*. For the first theme, building positive supports and relationships (other than intimate ones), study participants described how they built or rebuilt relationships with friends, family, professional helpers, support group acquaintances, coworkers, and other communities or people in their networks. To do this, participants had to regain trust toward others, repair or choose to end unhealthy relationships, and create a positive context for parenting. Some had to rebuild a social support system after realizing that their current social networks were not healthy or conducive to their recovery. A part of this also included setting boundaries in relationships related to what felt healthy and unhealthy. For example, one participant realized that even language she heard could be triggering and that she needed to communicate to others about what she would allow in her life. She said, "I set boundaries for myself in terms of the friendships that I kept and language that I allowed others to use in my presence." Social support was a huge part of the process of overcoming abuse. Building relationships with safe and healthy people was an important part of healing from abuse.

The second interpersonal process involved survivors using their own experiences to advocate for others and share their stories as a way to encourage both their own and others' healing. One person said, "I realized there were other people who were lost out there in the flurry of abuse. I had done good work to heal myself, now it was time to help others." In addition to helping others, becoming an advocate or spokesperson for survivors also assisted the participant in his or her own healing process. Here is one quote we heard that captures this: "I am now a domestic violence advocate, and this has been very therapeutic and has forced me to deal with some of my 'stuff' to better serve my clients." Similar to the information we shared earlier about how many survivors begin to engage in advocacy work to promote social change, many survivors find meaning and purpose in turning their experiences with past abuse into a positive mission to help, educate, and support others, and this can become part of the overall process of recovery following abuse.

Conclusion

Our goal for this chapter has been to offer hope that recovery from past abuse is possible. The challenges that victims and survivors of intimate partner violence face are numerous and very significant. Not only do they face the direct effects of the traumatic experiences of abuse, but these traumatic experiences are compounded by stigma at every level—including internalized stigma and stigmatizing messages they receive from their perpetrators, within their communities, and in the broader social context. And yet survivors need not be defined by these challenges and by the trauma they face. On the contrary, victims and survivors can become strong, courageous models of recovery. Victims and survivors can draw upon a vast array of internal resources to support them on their journeys to safety and to recovery. In the next chapter, we move toward considering ways that communities and professional response systems can help provide additional, non-stigmatizing supportive resources to help victims and survivors make the most of these internal resources.

Notes

1 Seligman, L. (2004). *Technical and conceptual skills for mental health professionals*. Upper Saddle River, NJ: Pearson.
2 http://www.seethetriumph.org/blog/finding-a-counselor-who-is-competent-to-serve-survivors.
3 Murray, C.E., King, K., Crowe, A., & Flasch, P. (2015). Survivors of intimate partner violence as advocates for social change. *The Journal for Social Action in Counseling and Psychology*, 7, 84–100, http://www.psysr.org/jsacp/murray-v7n1-2015_84-100.pdf.
4 Murray, C.E., Crowe, A., & Flasch, P. (2015). Turning points: Critical incidents in survivors' decisions to end abusive relationships. *The Family Journal*, 23, 228–238. DOI: 10.1177/1066480715573705.
5 Flasch, P., Murray, C.E., & Crowe, A. (2015). Overcoming abuse: A phenomenological investigation of the journey to recovery from past intimate partner violence. *Journal of Interpersonal Violence*, 1–29. DOI: 10.1177/0886260515599161.

9 Creating Responsive Systems for Victims and Survivors Who Seek Help

In Chapter 8, we looked at the internal processes that victims and survivors of abusive relationships experience to overcome abuse and the stigma that surrounds it. The intensity of the internal challenges they face underscores the importance of fostering positive, uplifting communities that will provide the optimal levels of support to help these people overcome the adversity they face. And yet in Chapter 5 we discussed a host of examples of ways that survivors may encounter stigmatizing experiences when seeking help, including help from friends, family, and professionals. We view this as one of the great tragedies surrounding intimate partner violence today. First, it is tragic that anyone should be abused in the first place. Second, it is a further tragedy that people who face abuse are often re-traumatized and stigmatized again in the process of seeking help and safety.

Despite this tragic bind for many survivors, we are confident that change is possible. Through our work, including through our partnerships and community with See the Triumph, we know that there are many, many people working in communities across the country and world who care deeply about changing and improving community responses to intimate partner violence. Professionals, volunteers, and community members from all walks of life are working—both in public, visible ways and behind the scenes—to continue to build new resources and strengthen existing resources so that communities can prevent future violence, provide support to survivors, and hold offenders accountable.

And yet we know that there is much work to be done to ensure that communities are fully equipped to support victims and survivors of abuse. In this chapter, we consider ways to work toward positive change at the community level to help ensure that we can create systems that are supportive for victims and survivors who seek help. We'll also address strategies for changing existing systemic barriers to offer more supportive resources and eliminate stigmatizing practices and reactions. We begin this chapter with three stories of survivors who participated in our research who talked about some of the hurdles they dealt with when seeking help. These stories highlight the challenges that exist in many current systems and illustrate examples of ways communities can improve these systems to offer better support to people impacted by intimate partner violence.

Lina's Story

Lina is in her early 30s. Her former husband, with whom she shared a relationship that lasted for over five years, was physically, emotionally, and verbally abusive to her. As a result of this abuse, her husband was arrested and had a protective order taken out against him. Lina's relationship began when she was very young:

> "I was in high school when the relationship started. He was my first boyfriend, and I was his first girlfriend. It was very sweet at first. The abuse started about a year into the relationship. It was something I had never seen at home. It was something that I never in a million years would have thought I'd experience. I hid it very well from my family. To this day, they don't know exact details."

The relationship had ended just over ten years before Lina shared her story with us:

> "It ended when he threatened to kill me. He was searching our apartment for weapons he had brought home the day before. When I found them, I hid them. He said if he didn't find them he'd kill me anyway. This was after he had already started hitting me and throwing me around the house. He left to go to another part of the house, and I grabbed for the phone to call the police. This was the first time I'd ever been brave enough to do so. He caught me and pulled the phone away from me. The police arrived shortly after, and he went to jail."

Blame was a prominent theme in the relationship. She said,

> "I blamed myself a lot of the time. I felt I was provoking him to hit me. Although my family didn't know what was going on, his did. I would have his mother tell me that I had to deal with it if I loved him. His family protected him, like they would a child, and I was often asked what I did to cause the argument. There were adults that knew what was going on because they'd see him push me around in school. I know friends told some of the leaders of our church. However, no one ever really did anything to try and get me away from him. I don't know if maybe they just didn't realize that a teenager can't make adult decisions. I felt that, since there were certain people that knew, and yet no one helped me, that they must think it was my fault. I was raised in a good home with strong religious beliefs and values. To come from a

home that doesn't believe in divorce and where my father would never even think about raising a hand to my mother, and then being the daughter that married an abusive man and then divorced him, well, all of that most definitely caused my 'black sheep' status."

"Just to clarify, my parents, though they didn't know details, were always very supportive of me. The people in school that would see him push me around looked at me like I was a loser. Later in life, I found out that people knew me as the girl whose boyfriend kicked the crap out of her. I was no longer one of the kids that hung out in the big, fun group like I did before my ex-husband. I was powerless and scared. I didn't think there was anything I could do to change my situation. I was most definitely ashamed, especially when I had to wear long sleeves and jeans all the time to cover up bruising all over my body. I stopped hanging around my friends because I couldn't stand their comments or judgments. There is a stereotype for girls and women who are in these types of relationships. People always assume it's the woman's fault because she stays. They also look at you like you're a loser, a piece of trash. I've heard so many people say, when they're unaware I have been there, that these women deserve what they get because they stay. They MUST like the abuse because they stick around. Ignorance."

"Friends, I'd hear, would often talk about how dumb they thought I was for staying. I'd constantly have to share my reasons, which were stupid, and constantly have to defend my relationship. Family didn't know the extent of the abuse I endured. I know that when relatives found out I was in this type of situation or had been, a lot of them avoided me, yet still said 'hi' to my ex-husband whenever they'd run into him. He was treated as if nothing happened. So it's safe to assume that they (a) didn't think it was a big deal, (b) felt it should be swept under the rug, or (c) felt I was to blame for the situation I'd been in."

Lina felt blamed and unsupported at work as well. She describes one notable incident as follows:

"There was one time I especially remember, regarding an employer. My ex-husband beat me pretty bad. I was very bruised all over my arms, legs, and face. One eye was completely bloodshot, and that entire side of my face was dark, dark purple. I was asked what happened, and I told them I had been in a car accident. They must have not believed me, because I was pulled to the side and asked about my situation. The woman asking me looked at me as if she was disgusted by me and proceeded to tell me that, if I was in a bad situation, I needed to be smart enough to get out. She also sent me home because I looked awful."

"After I separated, I spent about a year mostly indoors. I didn't want to go out, and I didn't want to face the world. Everything I'd been through left me lifeless. Plus, I really had no identity. He and I had been together since our freshman year in high school. I didn't know who I was. I didn't want to talk to anyone. I didn't want to reveal all the horrid details to my parents."

"Nearing the end of my first year away from him, I did seek help at a local domestic violence agency. I regretted with my entire being going there. I had finally worked up the nerve to seek help. I'd finally agreed to speak with someone. When I got there, I was nervous and scared and I was greeted by a cold receptionist. I was made to fill out paperwork. Then, when I met with one of the women that worked there she asked me about my situation; I'd begin to explain and she would interrupt. Then, she asked me what exactly I wanted or needed from them. I asked about counseling, and she said that they couldn't help me there and I'd have to go elsewhere. She was cold, lacked empathy, looked at me—more like through me—with an uninterested look on her face. Around me, I could hear other women speaking to other workers there, other workers with the same uninterested tone in their voices. I couldn't get out of there fast enough, but it was at that moment that I came to the realization that no one was going to help me. No one was interested in what had happened to me, and that I was going to have to get through it alone. I'd have to have faith in God and just push myself every day to live."

Despite all of the challenges she faced, Lina found the inner strength to move beyond her past experiences. She said, "I decided I wanted to be a strong woman. I decided I wanted to take care of and rescue myself and not wait on someone else to rescue me. I didn't want to end up yet another statistic." Since that relationship ended, Lina has not been in additional abusive relationships. She says,

"I always said I'd never allow myself to be in this type of situation again. I've done a good job at keeping myself from repeating the pattern. I have been in relationships where in the heat of the moment a boyfriend would curse at me, and I at him. However, I would stop and make sure they knew my feelings about mutual respect. I took two years after my divorce to start dating again. I wanted to make sure that I took time for myself to heal. Honestly though, even now I carry a lot of this pain and hurt with me."

In light of her past experiences, Lina believes strongly in the importance of community education about intimate partner violence. She said, "I think it's important for women and people in general to be better informed on the issue. Then, and only then, will people start to see domestic violence for what it is and how it truly affects people's lives." Lina offers the following advice to others who are experiencing abuse:

> "Remember that love is not supposed to hurt. Remember that there is life after that relationship. Remember that others have been in that situation, feeling as if there were no light at the end of the tunnel. Ignore the voice inside that tells you that you can't make it without that person. Ignore the voice inside your head that tells you they can't make it without you. It's not your responsibility to fix them or help them or save them. In the process, you're losing yourself, and you have to put yourself first. Especially if you have children. You can be strong, and you will survive. Once you're out of that mess, you're going to be so amazed at what's out there. When you're not living in constant fear and you're free."

Madeline's Story

Madeline is in her 40s and is the mother to two elementary school-age children. She has a graduate degree and works as a professor, and she is currently married. She was in a prior abusive marriage, which lasted for about five years and ended about five years ago. In that marriage, Madeline experienced physical, emotional, verbal, and sexual abuse, and her ex-husband had criminal convictions and a protective order taken against him related to the abuse. Madeline did not initially recognize that her relationship was abusive because it didn't fit the stereotypes she held about what abusive relationships look like. She said,

> "I did not realize I was a battered woman. After having been brainwashed for years before the physical abuse began, I thought that if he did not hit me with his fist or kick me, then I did not qualify as abused. Stereotypes and labels perpetuated this belief, as did the police."

During the relationship, Madeline became increasingly isolated. She said, "My husband chose to move to the most isolated locations possible, he took my car keys and phone when he was violent, and he worked to isolate me from family and friends." The abuse also threatened to hurt Madeline's career:

> "I was extremely worried about losing my job. I was new on the tenure track and working hard to build my career. My ex-husband stalked me and publicly humiliated me after I separated from him. My department members and chair were sent videos and emails. Luckily, they were very supportive."

Despite this support, Madeline says,

> "I am still in the closet whenever possible. My co-workers and professional colleagues are aware because of the stalking, but I try not to bring it up whenever possible. He told me it was my fault, and society confirms that every time."

Madeline escaped the relationship with help from her local domestic violence shelter. She said,

> "I left in the middle of the night and called a women's shelter. They came and met me and my children, and I stayed there for a few nights while I got my protection order. The police then went out and evicted my husband from the house. After a year of legal separation, I was able to get a divorce."

This was not Madeline's first attempt to leave the relationship, however. She said,

> "I had tried to leave him before. Once, I kicked him out for throwing something in the direction of our young child. The police told me that what he did was not illegal but that it was illegal for me to kick him out. I tried to leave him again once in the middle of the night. I lived in a rural area. When I called the women's shelter in the middle of the night, after finding my phone in the woods and piecing it back together, they told me they would have to call me back. I did not think of calling the police."

Madeline reported experiencing a high level of stigma from a variety of sources. Blame in particular was a prominent theme. She said,

> "My abuser blamed me, and so did the police when I called them. His family blamed me. My family also blamed me for getting married to him in the first place, even though they thought he was great before we got married. My parents blamed me for not having financial resources to provide day care and for my own attorney's fees."

Eventually, Madeline internalized this blame, and it became feelings of shame:

> "There is plenty of shame involved in being a professional woman who was deceived and ends up in an abusive relationship. We build our careers on our intelligence and professionalism. These are questionable when you marry an abuser and are afraid to leave."

Madeline also felt ostracized and discriminated against as a result of the abuse. She said, "My parents never thought I would amount to anything. They totally saw me as a black sheep. The rest of my family also treated me this way." She said that she noticed "discrimination against women by the police and court system. I think this includes the courts trying to ensure father's rights, despite the fact that they are abusers. I cannot imagine how this makes them good fathers in any way."

The court system in particular has been a source of frustration and disappointment for Madeline. She said,

> "The laws are not set up to protect women, and those few that are in place are not enforced. I had a terrible time leaving my abuser, getting my restraining order enforced (he violated it repeatedly), and in numerous criminal trials and divorce proceedings where his rights as a father were privileged over my rights as a human being. The courts allowed him to continue it indefinitely along with his criminal trials. I filed the motion years ago and it still has never been heard."

On the process of overcoming past abuse, Madeline said,

> "It takes time. As long as the abuse and stalking continue, you cannot escape the stigma. After five years, I still face it at my children's school and any time I have to give out my address because I am in the Address Confidentiality Program. All kinds of people feel perfectly justified asking me about it, from government officials to bank clerks."

She copes by trying to keep her focus elsewhere, on more positive aspects of her life: "You just have to ignore it and try to feel okay despite it." Madeline emphasizes the need for additional societal recognition of the dynamics and scope of intimate partner violence:

> "More education is required and that includes outreach. Women may not realize they are even in this situation, they may be afraid to leave, and they don't know the laws or where to turn for help. Frankly, even if they do, the likelihood is they will be killed, or stalked, or have to see their abuser regularly for visits with children that he uses to turn them against her. It is not a picture full of hope, but rather one of continued suffering and hardship."

Tiara's Story

Tiara is in her mid-20s and is mom to a toddler. Although she has completed some college, she is currently unemployed "due to lack of childcare and being dragged through court by my abuser." She was engaged to her former abuser, but they never married during their two-year courtship. The couple had one child. In that relationship, she experienced physical, emotional, verbal, and financial abuse at the hands of her abuser. The relationship ended badly. Soon after Tiara had moved to a new state, her abuser tracked her down, beat her, and held her captive in the home for nearly two days. Although she presently has full custody of her young child, Tiara reports that her abuser is "using [their child] against me in family court." She shared that, although her abuser is taking her to court for custody, he has missed several visitations with their child and hasn't complied with the court orders related to the custody.

It had been over two years since the relationship ended at the time when Tiara participated in our research. However, Tiara shared that she thinks she can apply the concept of stigma "to my situation, past and present." She said that her abuser "blames me, has isolated me from my family, and is trying to break me apart from my child." She also describes how she feels she faces stigma within the family court system as follows:

> "I am stereotyped by the courts and other agencies as angry, combative, emotionally unstable, greedy for welfare, typical single mother, uneducated, abusive towards my child, lazy, bitter. The courts and the agencies are quick to remind me that I slept with him, had a child and that he has rights, regardless. I feel that the judicial system only perpetuates abusive behavior and condones this."

She believes that survivors face challenges when it comes to sharing their stories. She believes that "society claims to want victims to speak up and out, but they want you to do it their way." Tiara's message to other survivors is as follows:

> "Fight like hell once you get out. Don't believe the hype about life being better once you leave. Things are totally different and often get worse once you enter family court. This is what shelters and other agencies don't tell you and often tell you to go with the flow. The judicial system is just another tool for your abuser to maintain control over you and they use it well. Get out, get a lawyer, and get educated about the laws in the state you live in and where you may want to relocate to. If a shelter offers you relocation, take it! And seek legal help right away!"

At the end of the study, she added, "Do not settle for food stamps and child support. Take classes to become a better parent, go to therapy, cry if you need to, tell your child and family you love them and stay strong."

How Communities Failed Lina, Madeline, and Tiara

Lina, Madeline, and Tiara each experienced unresponsive, unhelpful, and stigmatizing community systems as they left their abusers and sought help. Lina was enrolled in high school when her abuse began, and yet even though people around her saw her bruises and witnessed physical abuse taking place, no one stepped in. Even leaders of her church were told about the abuse, and still no one talked to her, asked what was going on, reached out to her or her parents, or asked her if she needed support. Friends stopped speaking to her, yet they still were friendly to her abuser, as if she were to blame and what he did was normal. Her family did not realize what was going on. Although his family knew about the abuse, they simply told her to "deal with it." At work, Lina was told that if she were in a bad situation she needed to be "smart enough" to get out. It's no surprise then to hear that when Lina had the strength to leave the abuse, she isolated herself for a year, not wanting to face the world. It is perfectly understandable that she would have come to believe that support would not be found, even if she reached out, after the experiences she had leading up to that point.

For Madeline, the police were the unresponsive ones. She was told that her husband's throwing of an object in the direction of her child was not illegal, but that her possible action of kicking him out of the house would be. When Madeline escaped from her abuser in the middle of the night, a domestic violence shelter staff member told her she would have to call her back at another time. Madeline also experienced discrimination in the court system and from various people when she had to explain that she was in the address confidentiality program so that her abuser could not find her. For Tiara, family court was a stigmatizing environment, leading her to caution other survivors to be prepared emotionally to handle this as another challenge once out of the abusive relationship. She also felt stereotyped, labeled, and devalued when seeking help from a variety of sources.

The problem that lies before us is clear—in too many communities, we have faulty systems in place that foster stigmatizing responses toward victims and survivors of abusive relationships. This problem is significant, but in the stories of Lina, Madeline, and Tiara, we also see clues for possible solutions, especially as we can identify links in the chains of help-seeking where people and organizations can become better prepared to support victims and survivors in non-stigmatizing ways. As we discussed in Chapter 5, we believe that many stigmatizing responses result not from an intentional effort to inflict harm, but rather on people and organizations being ill equipped to respond in appropriately supportive ways because of a lack of training and resources, burnout, and/or confusion about how to act. Assuming this is the case, the remainder of this chapter discusses strategies for improving community's capacities for supporting people impacted by abusive relationships. We begin by considering the important roles the informal social support networks can play—such as friends and family members. Later in the chapter, we will turn our attention to improving professionals' and organizational responses.

The True "Frontlines" of Community Responses to Intimate Partner Violence

When we think of people on the "frontlines" of community responses to intimate partner violence, we often think first of professionals, such as victim advocates, law enforcement officers, and health-care professionals. As we'll discuss later in this chapter, all of these professionals do play a critical role in how communities respond to and prevent intimate partner violence. However, we can think of these professionals more as a secondary line of defense. The real "frontlines" are made up of people from every walks of life who are the friends, family members, work colleagues, faith community members, and neighbors of people who have been abused.

There are many reasons why it is important to educate the general population within communities about the dynamics of abusive relationships. First, community members elect government officials who create and enforce policies that can impact how easy it is for victims and survivors to be safe and leave an abusive relationship. In many communities, these government officials also include judges, who are key to determining outcomes of protective order hearings and custody cases in family court that involve domestic violence. An uninformed public may elect officials who are not sensitive to the dynamics of abusive relationships or to the needs of victims and survivors. Second, when domestic violence cases go to the court system, trials may involve jurors deciding the outcome of a case. Because juries are drawn from the general population of a community, we need to foster communities in which potential jurors have a solid understanding of the dynamics of abusive relationships. Therefore, in addition to equipping the general population within communities to understand intimate partner violence and how to support victims and survivors, the readiness of a community to address this issue also impacts systemic resources available in that community. A well-informed community is far more ready to provide necessary support to victims and survivors than a community whose members simply do not know or understand the dynamics of abuse.

Beyond these more systemic reasons why it is important to educate the general public about intimate partner violence, this is important because virtually anyone in any community could become close to someone who is being abused. For a number of reasons, victims and survivors of intimate partner violence may feel more comfortable disclosing their experiences with abuse to friends, family members, and others close to them, as compared to professionals. In addition, even when people don't disclose abuse, friends and family members are often close enough to the situation that they can recognize or suspect when abuse is occurring. For many people, being on the outside of an abusive relationship in which someone close to them is involved is a difficult and confusing experience.

They may want to help, but not know how. They may fear for their own safety if they intervene. They may have tried to reach out, only to be met with defensiveness about the relationship. They may even have been told directly by the victim or perpetrator to "mind their own business." It is very normal for people in this situation to become frustrated and possibly distance themselves from the people in the abusive relationship as a result of this frustration.

When it comes to equipping community members to support a loved one who is in an abusive relationship, we believe that a little bit of knowledge goes a long way. In our See the Triumph Collection called, How to Help a Friend, we outlined five steps that are a good place to start for friends and family members who are concerned about someone they know who is being abused in an intimate relationship (see Table 9.1). Sometimes, the smallest responses can make the biggest difference, so we also believe that no response is too small and insignificant when someone is in need of support. We encourage readers to see the full collection on this topic by visiting the See the Triumph Collection at our webpage, as the following list has been adapted from this collection.[1]

1. Do Not Judge

When someone is being abused, your first reaction might be confusion, frustration, or disbelief. You may wonder, "How could you stay with someone who is hurting you? Why didn't you tell me sooner? How

Table 9.1 Five Ways to Help Someone Who Is Being Abused By an Intimate Partner

Way to Help	Explanation
#1: Do not judge them.	Show them that you respect their decision and believe that they are the experts in their own lives.
#2: Ask them what kind of help they would like for you to provide.	If they do not request any help now, let them know that you are available to help in the future.
#3: Know your limits.	If the help they need goes beyond what you can offer, help them locate services and resources in their community.
#4: Offer to provide practical support that will promote their safety.	This may include keeping an emergency kit at your house, offering to pick them up if they need transportation to a safe place, or knowing a code word that means that they need you to call the police.
#5: Tell them that they deserve to be treated with dignity, respect, and love.	Let them know that you are concerned for their safety. Make sure to let them know you think they are a person of value and worth.

could you let your child witness the abuse?" All of these questions might be swirling in your head as a victim or survivor discloses abuse, but rather than ask these types of questions, it is best to listen nonjudgmentally. Focus on supporting the person who desperately needs to feel heard. Keeping an open mind is of the utmost importance, because if victims or survivors suspect that they are being judged, they might decide not to talk or disclose the full extent of the abuse they've experienced for fear of being judged. If you are listening to someone close to you who is sharing experiences of abuse, you can remind yourself of the following statements to help you listen fully without judgment: (1) "I don't know the whole story." (2) "How would I respond if I were in his/her shoes?" (3) "The best help I can offer is to support, and not judge." These types of statements will assist with keeping you calm and focused so that you can stay neutral and refrain from jumping into a judgmental response. Staying nonjudgmental in this scenario is the most powerful stance you can take. It says that you understand and honor the person's experiences and perspectives and that you are trustworthy as a listener.

2. Ask the Survivor What Kind of Help You Can Provide

When someone who is being abused comes to you for help, it's difficult to know what that person needs. Every victim has a different situation and unique needs. For a variety of reasons, what one person needs from a friend or family member might be completely different than what someone else needs. One victim might need help with making an exit plan to leave the abuse. This might involve helping the victim with saving money in a private account that the abuser does not know about or making plans for when the victim will seek safety at a shelter. Another victim might not be in a position to make plans for leaving the abuse. This person might just now be considering the notion that the relationship is in fact abusive, so this person might just need a listening ear. What about the victim who hasn't yet realized that the behavior from his or her partner is in fact considered abuse? This might be particularly difficult for you as the support person, but we know that the victim must come to this conclusion on his or her own in order to be in the best position to seek long-term safety. In this situation, you can still support the person in ways that he or she views as helpful. For example, you could offer childcare so that she or he can interview for a new job. Perhaps through this new job (with perhaps a higher salary), the victim might begin to imagine establishing a life away from the perpetrator, which would be more possible with financial independence. For this scenario, you might struggle if you feel as though this is not the support the person needs, but remember that this choice needs to be in the hands of the victim or survivor. Of course, you can offer insights about the dynamics of abusive relationships and express

3. Know Your Limits When Helping a Friend in an Abusive Relationship

For anyone supporting someone in an abusive relationship, you must also be mindful of your own emotional, knowledge, and safety limits. Abuse can be exhausting for everyone involved, not only for the victim who is going through it but also for those who are close to someone who is experiencing it. You might feel sad to know that someone close to you is being hurt by someone. It is perfectly normal to feel sad and upset after you learn this information. You might feel confused about the fact that this person has just now disclosed this, or that your friend is choosing to stay with the person, even though he or she is hurting your friend. You might be afraid about his or her safety. When this happens for you, it is best to talk about your feelings with someone you trust. This might be a friend or family member, or a professional helper, such as a counselor or psychologist. Remember that you have emotional needs as well. Supporting someone in an abusive relationship is hard work for you, too. Exercise, meditation, journaling, or other relaxing activities might be other self-care tools[2] you can use from your toolbox. You should also consider the limits to your knowledge of abuse. Professional helpers—such as victim advocates, counselors, marriage and family therapists, or crisis counselors—have specific training that can help you when you reach the limits of your own knowledge. Checking in with yourself about where your knowledge ends is important so that you can refer your friend to someone with professional training when needed. Even professionals who work with victims and survivors would say that every story is complex and challenging to assist with. Rarely are answers easy to identify, and a suggestion or resource that works for one victim or survivor might not work for the next. Knowing just a few simple resources, such as a toll-free anonymous hotline for abuse, might be the answer for you and your friend when the situation seems more complex than you are comfortable handling.

An additional consideration regarding your limits is that of safety limits. When a friend lets you know that an intimate partner is abusing him or her, consider asking about access to weapons, especially firearms. This is for your own safety, in addition to your friend's safety. You should be especially cautious if the perpetrator has made threats toward you or others in your friend's life, if he or she has engaged in stalking, and if the person has access to lethal weapons. The Danger Assessment, for example, is a survey that examines the level of danger that a victim has of being killed by an intimate partner. This might be a valuable resource to use when trying to determine safety. It's a free resource that is available to the public.[3] In the event that your friend needs shelter, consider your own comfort level with offering your own housing versus assisting the person with finding a shelter, a hotel room, or another location unknown to the abuser. It is okay to consider your safety needs too, as you could be in harm's way if the perpetrator knows of your assistance. Reach out for additional supports when safety threats are present. You do not need to feel completely alone as you support your friend, but it is critical to know your own limitations in this situation.

4. Offer to Provide Practical Support That Will Promote Their Safety

The safety of someone involved in an abusive relationship should always be a top consideration. Although we recommend that thorough safety planning always be done in partnership with a trained professional, friends and family members also may have opportunities to help promote the safety of someone who is involved in an abusive relationship. Some of the ways that friends and family members can help include knowing the local resources that are available and how best to get in touch with them and keeping a packed bag for a friend in the event that he or she needs to escape from the abuser quickly. A friend can help the victim to gather useful supplies to keep in the escape bag, such as copies of identification cards, cash, food, prescription medications, supplies for any involved children, and other important documents. Friends also could help by taking in victims' pets to help keep them safe, especially because many domestic violence shelters do not allow pets on the premises. There are other ways that friends and family members can offer practical support for victims and survivors seeking safety from an abusive relationship, such as learning about technology safety and accompanying them to appointments and court appearances. We've heard from many of the survivors in our research how helpful it was to have a supportive social network that helped them to navigate the often-complicated networks of community resources. In addition, the supportive presence of a family member can help alleviate some of the anxiety that victims and survivors may feel when accessing resources to help keep them safe, such as when filing a police report or going to a doctor's office for medical care for injuries related to the abuse. Overall, friends and family members can play a key role in helping victims and survivors work toward safety, especially when they work in partnership with any involved professionals who are also offering support.

5. Tell Them That They Deserve to Be Treated With Dignity, Respect, and Love

This final step involves no formal training or knowledge about intimate partner violence. Rather, it only requires a genuine desire to support the person who is being abused. This step might sound simple, but consider for a moment what victims and survivors hear from their perpetrators. These messages contain hurtful, harmful words that can tear down a victim's self-esteem and belief that help is available. After hearing such harmful words, it is very powerful when victims and survivors can hear words that instead affirm the notion that they deserve to be treated with respect, that they are lovable, and that the abuse is not their fault. These words offer a powerful reminder that they have value and that a life free from abuse is possible.

Creating Non-stigmatizing Organizations and Resources to Better Serve Victims and Survivors of Intimate Partner Violence

As we saw in the previous section, friends and family members can play a critical role in helping victims and survivors of intimate partner violence get connected with supportive resources in their communities, including professionals and the organizations in which those professionals work. Now that we've explored ways that this first line of defense, or members of the general population in communities, can help provide support to victims and survivors, let's turn our attention to the secondary line of defense: professionals and organizations in local communities. Our aim in this section is to consider ways that these professionals and organizations can work toward creating non-stigmatizing organizations and resources to better serve those in need.

As we've shared throughout this book, far too many victims and survivors experience unsupportive and stigmatizing responses when they seek help to address their abuse from different types of professionals and organizations that are supposed to offer them support. How can we work to make this type of response a thing of the past and instead head toward a future that holds only helpful, positive, empowering services and resources for those impacted by intimate partner violence? In the expert panel research study that we conducted,[4] we interviewed national leaders of advocacy organizations that address domestic and sexual violence. In that study, we asked those leaders to share their thoughts on the top priorities for organizations and professionals who want to create non-stigmatizing responses for victims and survivors. Their responses and ideas for how to end the stigma toward intimate partner violence were incredibly inspiring. They discussed the social context of stigma and the impact of stigma on survivors, as well as strategies for ending the stigma. We summarize some of the findings that relate to organizations and communities and what these in particular can do to support survivors, and we encourage anyone wanting to read more to consult the full article.

1   We need proactive and responsive prevention and intervention services driven by a thorough understanding of the needs and experiences of victims and survivors.

2 Communities need to work to ensure that public and organizational policies hold offenders accountable, support survivors, address multiple layers of stigma, and don't add to the stigma that survivors face.
3 Communities need to celebrate survivors on their private accomplishments, such as calling a hotline or going to a counseling session.
4 Professionals who encounter victims and survivors in their work (including domestic and sexual violence service providers, law enforcement, medical professionals, and others) should be trained to provide multiple forms of support and resources that meet the unique needs of each survivor.
5 Professionals and organizations should address unique cultural issues in order to ensure that all people are treated with dignity and respect regardless of their background characteristics.

Each of these five priorities is an important goal, and they also offer a standard by which professionals and organizations can assess the extent to which they are already offering non-stigmatizing responses (e.g., are our services reflective of the unique needs of victims and survivors, and are we considering unique cultural norms and needs for the diverse populations we serve?). A careful self-assessment can help professionals and organizations identify potential areas for change to become even more responsive to the needs of this client population. In addition to this type of self-assessment, we suggest the following five strategies for professionals and organizations to consider for fostering non-stigmatizing resources and services for victims and survivors of intimate partner violence.

1. Developing Positive Collaborations With Other Professionals in Their Communities

Positive collaborative relationships that cross disciplines and professional categories are essential for supporting victims and survivors. Intimate partner violence is inherently an issue that crosses the boundaries of individual professional disciplines. Professionals and organizations from a variety of fields—such as law enforcement, medical and mental health professionals, social service agencies, elected officials and other policy makers, and school systems, to name a few—all do work that can impact the lives of victims and survivors. When these groups can work together at the local level, it helps to reduce the systemic barriers that victims and survivors can encounter when seeking services. One way to promote this type of interdisciplinary collaboration is for professionals to be cross-trained to understand the nature of each other's work better. For example, a local domestic violence agency might host a training for law enforcement officers on intimate partner violence, the stigma surrounding it, and how to respond to victims and survivors in non-stigmatizing ways. Likewise, the local law enforcement agency could train the domestic violence service providers to understand their legal obligations and criminal justice responses to intimate partner violence. Community-based collaborations also could involve working together for prevention initiatives, such as educating children and teenagers about healthy relationships. For example, one of the members of our expert panel study said,

> Educating children in our school system from an early age as to what a healthy relationship should look like and how we all can help support those impacted by domestic violence and sexual assault. Educating the community on what domestic violence looks like, what a healthy relationship is and what you can do to help if you know someone suffering from domestic violence.

In addition to collaboration through educational activities, other ways that professionals and organizations can collaborate include the following: (1) co-locating and integrating services, such as through the Family Justice Center model;[5] (2) developing inter-agency agreements for how to coordinate services for clients receiving services from both agencies; (3) sharing data and information to understand better the needs of clients impacted by violence and abuse in the local community; and (4) partnering together to advocate for changes to local policies and practices that may create barriers in the lives of victims and survivors.

2. Identify and Address Community-Based Barriers That Victims and Survivors May Face When Seeking Help

There are a wide range of barriers that can make it difficult for victims and survivors to access the services and resources they need. These include funding issues, criteria for receiving services, a lack of access to affordable childcare, limited options for affordable housing, and the time needed to access services, especially if that time is taken away from one's employment. Consider the following two quotes from our expert panel members, for example, which speak to the community barriers that victims and survivors often face: (1) "Survivors are less likely to seek help if they perceive the stigma, and this is even worse for men and marginalized women, or women from other cultures besides Euro-American. Even when they seek help, the stigma can still come from practitioners and the justice system or social service system." (2) "These can range from . . . how the court views them and even awards custody of children, to maintaining their housing if the landlord has already seen the domestic violence the survivor has endured in the past, to when she enters a new relationship and how their current partner may view them . . . Child Protective Services will get involved in their family and possibly remove their children from their care." We have heard many examples of these types of barriers, from landlords who do not want to rent to someone who is experiencing intimate partner violence, to the courts penalizing someone for intimate partner violence, to child protective services decisions that condemn survivors, even long after the abuse has ended. Professionals who work with victims and survivors are often in the prime position to learn about unique barriers in their own communities. When these barriers are identified, professionals can collaborate with others in their communities to respond to them, both by advocating for changes to the policies, practices, and limited resources that create them, by helping to create "work-around" solutions until these barriers are removed, and by educating the public and clients about these barriers so that they will be fully informed about the realities of their circumstances and can plan accordingly.

3. Create Supportive, Non-stigmatizing Environments That Reflect the Best Practices in Trauma-Informed Care

When survivors seek assistance for intimate partner violence–related issues, the environment of the organizations from which they seek services should reflect a positive, supportive, non-stigmatizing climate that is grounded firmly in best practices for trauma-informed care. A trauma-informed framework[6] involves an agency examining every aspect of its practices to make sure that it meets all the unique needs of clients who have experienced trauma. Adopting trauma-informed practices is an excellent way to ensure that survivors are met with supportive, appropriate services and with professionals who understand the role of trauma in the lives of people impacted by intimate partner violence. In particular, it is critical for professionals in those organizations to understand that survivors of abuse might demonstrate symptoms of posttraumatic stress disorder (PTSD), depression, or anxiety as a result of the traumatic experiences. As some of our participants indicated, some of the professionals they encountered did not understand the aftermath of abuse and how mental health symptoms impacted their functioning. As it applies to victims and survivors of intimate partner violence, an organization guided by best practices in trauma-informed care might make intentional efforts to celebrate the big and small successes of survivors who are seeking care. Even stepping a foot in the door of the agency or calling a domestic violence hotline might be a huge accomplishment for that person, and organizations can work to ensure that the strength and courage required to take these steps are acknowledged and celebrated.

4. Challenge Personal and Organizational Biases and Practices That May Directly or Indirectly Perpetuate Stigma and Make It More Difficult for Victims and Survivors to Receive the Help They Need

Perhaps one of the biggest ways that professionals can assist with eradicating the stigma that surrounds intimate partner violence is to challenge biases and practices that directly or indirectly stigmatize victims and survivors. These could include personal biases held by individual professionals in an agency as well as broader, systemic practices within organizations that make it challenging for victims to get the help they need. Laws and regulations at the local, state, and federal levels also might pose stigmatizing challenges for victims and survivors. For example, one member of our expert panel told us that,

> In some states, all domestic violence cases (when a survivor reaches out for help) are reported to Child Protective Services, and at times children are removed from the survivor as a result. I have been told by many survivors, this was one of the reasons they did not want to reach out for help.

Certainly, the safety and protection of children must be a high priority for everyone in our society. However, it is important to consider ways that policies such as these may hinder victims from leaving their abusive relationships. These policies that are designed to protect children may inadvertently keep some children at greater risk of harm, especially if their abused parent chooses to stay in the violent relationship out of a fear of having the children taken from them if they seek services. In instances where organizational and public policies and procedures hinder the ability of victims and survivors to be safe, professionals involved in the lives of survivors can advocate for changes to laws and policies that are not helpful. It takes knowledgeable professionals who understand the lives of survivors to advocate for these changes, as policy makers who have created them most likely do not understand the complexities of intimate partner violence.

5. Educate and Train Professionals to Understand the Dynamics of Abusive Relationships and Support Survivors, Examine Their Own Biases and Assumptions, and Seek Support for Themselves to Avoid Feelings of Helplessness

Finally, professionals can work toward non-stigmatizing communities through an ongoing commitment to education and training. Many professionals who interact with victims and survivors on a daily basis hold unchecked biases and assumptions about intimate partner violence, feel helpless or unsupported in their roles at work, and lack the training needed to understand fully the lives and needs of victims and survivors. Many professionals struggle with both personal and professional challenges when working with victims and survivors, and this can translate into negative attitudes and behaviors toward the clients they serve. Organizational administrators can assist professionals in their agencies by maintaining an ongoing commitment to promoting employee wellness and self-care.

In particular, it is important for supportive practices to be in place for times when employees begin to feel burned out or overly frustrated by their work. Recently, there has been much discussion about experiences of vicarious trauma, burnout, or compassion fatigue among professionals who work with traumatized client populations, including victims and survivors of intimate partner violence. Communities must take special care of their first responders, mental health professionals, and others who work in human service fields to make sure that they get the support, resources, and help they need to maintain their own mental health so that they will be most effectively equipped to serve victims and survivors.

The Power of Positive, Non-stigmatizing Support for Victims and Survivors

As we conclude this chapter, let's turn to the voices of survivors themselves to see the powerful impact that positive, non-stigmatizing support can offer to victims and survivors, both during and after abusive relationships. The following quotes from survivors who participated in our research demonstrate the ways that this type of support offers hope, encouragement, and comfort for victims and survivors:

- "Friends after many years gave up trying to help because I always went back and they didn't want him to go after them and their families. I cannot say enough great things about my family and the domestic violence shelter. The shelter changed my life and my children's lives forever! They understood, listened, and helped to get my life together again for four years of court, etc. I don't know what I would have done without them!"
- "It takes time. It was my family. It was my advisor and my professors, lawyer, and counselor who kept me saying it was not my fault, and it could have happened to anybody. That way of thinking helped me a lot, hearing it from others. Then, it was me later who believed that it was not my fault. Hearing it from others helps but it is self-forgiving that helped me a lot."
- "There is help available, even when it seems hopeless. Your local legal aid society is a great place to start. It is also good to call a crisis line because they have many resources to share."
- "Seek someone out, like a mentor, that has been through it. The domestic violence counseling group was amazing for me. There was a women who was my age, had a kid my age, and was nearly in an identical situation to mine. We leaned on each other and supported each other. Also, being able to have family and friends was amazing. I had to purge the poison of the years of abuse, and I'm still not done."
- "I would want to tell people who are currently in an abusive relationship that they deserve to be respected, but also that there is nothing

wrong with still loving the person abusing them. With regards to finding a way to leave the relationship, I would recommend that they find an understanding, supportive, and empowering psychologist, and that they also take advantage of other survivor support services, such as support groups, hotlines, and organizations."

- "Don't go through this alone. Get help from the domestic violence agency near you. Get counseling and get on with living your life. You are a beautiful person inside and out and you have a big heart."
- "Talk to someone. The whole time I lived in silence, and there are so many people who could have helped me. Do what you need to do to survive, but also look for a way out if you want to leave. Tell someone if you can. I lost my perspective and was not ready to leave at first but my mom helped me see what was really happening and that I needed to leave."
- "There is hope! You can survive and break free of the abusive chains. First, believe you are worth more, then seek and ask for help!"
- "Get a police escort. The day will come when you need to leave, and you will. Go back and get your kids and leave. Ask the police to stay while you gather your things. Drive to a safe location and call a friend or relative. Then go stay with them. Start rebuilding your life. Move to another state. Use social services to get back on your feet until you can re-integrate into society and normalcy."
- "Find support from anyone and everyone you can. This will give you the strength and the tools to get out of the relationship as quickly and safely as possible. A counselor that has experience with domestic violence can be very helpful. A domestic violence shelter can keep you safe until you get back on your feet. It will be hard, but once you get out, you can live your life freely and get back the control that was taken away from you."
- "Knowing others who have overcome and walked through abuse has been incredibly empowering. Real recovery takes place in community, not in isolation."

Throughout this book, we have shared many negative, stigmatizing experiences that we heard about from survivors who participated in our research. At the same time, we could have literally filled this entire book with quotes like the ones you just read. As much as stigmatizing experiences can be harmful, empowering experiences can have the opposite effect. When victims and survivors are met with supportive, uplifting responses, they have opportunities to have their dignity and worth validated. These responses offer a strong sense of hope and understanding that they deserve to be treated with respect. All community members—whether they are friends or family members or if they are professionals working with victims and survivors, have opportunities to offer this support, hope, and respect when people reach out for help related to an abusive relationship. To conclude this chapter, we ask you one final question: are *you* ready to provide this type of response to a victim or survivor in your own life?

Notes

1 To read the full See the Triumph Collection on this subject, please visit http://www.seethetriumph.org/collection-how-to-help-a-friend.html.
2 To read more about self-care, please visit See the Triumph's Collection on self-care http://www.seethetriumph.org/collection-self-care.html.
3 To read more about the Danger Assessment, please visit https://www.dangerassessment.org/.
4 Murray, C. E., Crowe, A., & Akers, W. (2016). How can we end the stigma surrounding domestic and sexual violence? A modified Delphi study with national advocacy leaders. *Journal of Family Violence, 31*, 271–287. DOI: 10.1007/s10896–015–9768–9.
5 To learn more about this model, please visit the website of the Family Justice Center Alliance here: http://www.familyjusticecenter.org/.
6 To learn more about a trauma-informed approach, please visit SAMHSA's concept of a trauma-informed approach here: http://store.samhsa.gov/product/SMA14–4884?WT.mc_id=EB_20141008_SMA14–4884.

10 Ending the Stigma Surrounding Intimate Partner Violence in Society

When we met for our interview, Sheila[1] was flustered and running a bit behind, and she said that recently a health condition "kind of threw my life in a tailspin." She and her husband had just reconciled after a separation, so it was a time of great transition for Sheila, her husband, Todd, and their children.

Sheila began the conversation by sharing her reasons for wanting to be a part of our study. She said,

> "A lot of things that have gone on in my life have to do with trying to straighten out things from my past, when they were already kind of messed up in the first place. Sometimes it takes a lot longer than I would want it to. Sometimes you don't realize how long things are going to be affecting you and in how many different ways, too."

Before her current marriage, Sheila was in an abusive relationship with the father of her two oldest children. Having grown up in a family in which abuse was prevalent, "It was normal. So, getting in the relationship with him was just, it was just normal." That relationship began when she was a teenager, lasted for over five years, and it ended shortly after the children were born. They were never married.

The abuse by her ex-boyfriend increased gradually over time. She described the progression as follows:

> "For the first couple of years, he didn't hurt me too bad. He might grab me real rough, you know, or there was this one particular time when we argued, and he pushed me. He pushed me really hard, and it knocked the wind out of me. And we didn't speak for like a month. This was a year into our relationship."

A few weeks after the incident, she experienced a miscarriage, which she suspects was related to the violence. For a while after that incident, she said that her ex-boyfriend didn't show any more physical violence, "except maybe grab me rough." She did say, "he would have sex with me rough. But I was sexually abused growing up. So, to me a man treating me bad like that or using me in any way, it seemed normal."

About two years into the relationship, Sheila and her ex began living together. She shared that, one night, her ex had gotten drunk and beat her up badly, all the while ranting at her and calling her a slut and other demeaning words, and then he raped her. She recalls,

> "I remember waking up the next day, and my body was hurting and aching so bad. I didn't know what I had done. I remember sitting there, trying to figure out what it was that I had done that was so bad so that I could just not do it again."

Even after such a violent incident, Sheila stayed with her ex. As she said,

> "I excused it away. He apologized. He was so sweet. He also said it was because of how I was with him when he was drunk, and that I needed to . . . that something I had done or said had, you know triggered. So, all I kept thinking was, 'OK, I'll just try not to do that again.'"

At that point, any time that Sheila considered leaving the relationship, "I would get a sick feeling in the pit of my stomach." But the abuse continued and got worse. Sheila said,

> "After that, it just seemed like eventually it just became a habit. It became, it just, it would happen more often. He drank more. I mean, it just progressively got worse and scarier. Wow, sometimes I'm amazed at what I allowed him to do to me."

Eventually, a particularly scary incident led Sheila to file a police report. She describes the beating as so bad that it led her to feel "like either I was blacking out or something, because I couldn't even feel it any more." Her abuser blamed her for that beating, saying, "Look at what you made me do." The damage from this incident was extensive. In fact, her face was so badly swollen and disfigured that she was practically unrecognizable. The incident also left Sheila with multiple concussions.

After that incident, Sheila did leave the relationship and went to live with a family member. However, it wasn't long before he pursued her to come back. She initially resisted the idea of reconciling with him, but even her family members encouraged her to get back together with him. So she decided to give the relationship another chance. But it wasn't long before the abusive and controlling behaviors re-appeared. At that point, Sheila didn't believe that leaving the relationship was a safe option. He had threatened that he would kill her if she left him.

Eventually, the "last straw" incident finally came. It was during an especially violent episode that, fearing for her own and her child's safety, she called the police, and she was able to leave, not even wearing shoes and carrying only her baby and the baby's diaper bag. From there, Sheila took up residence at the local shelter and began reading to learn about abusive relationships. She took out a protective order, which he violated and was arrested as a result. Shortly after that, she decided, "No more. I was over it, and he knew I was serious."

Sheila shared that, after the relationship ended, she "went through a lot of therapy and counseling and stuff like that just to make sure I didn't get back in another one." She found great validation after a meeting with a mental health professional who helped her realize that she wasn't "crazy" and who helped Sheila get on the path to recovery.

Sheila shared the sentiment that she wanted to help others, and that was one of the reasons why she came in for our interview. She said,

> "That's why coming here was just so important. It was just—it was just so important to do this, because I know that I couldn't have been the only one. I'm sure I'm not the only one. It felt that way. And went through that stuff. I was in a shelter. I saw other women. But I want them to know that on the other side there is happiness, and that you can be fulfilled, and that it doesn't take a man."

Far from being hopeless as a result of the difficult experiences in her life, Sheila remained hopeful and excited about the future. She said,

> "I'm excited. I'm excited about just the new stuff. And even just thinking about new things. It used to scare me. It used to scare me so bad. I remember. I was thinking about that today on the way here. I was thinking about there was a time when I wouldn't have done this interview, because it would have been just too scary."

In fact, Sheila's outlook on life became the inspiration for our See the Triumph Campaign, as you'll read in the following words:

> "One of the things that I loved so much is that coming into this part of my life I met a lot of people who are around the same age. And some of them feel like their life is almost over, or they think they can't change things. I feel like mine is just starting."

She went on to say,

> "I've had some conversations with my husband now about the abuse. And there were times when he and I would be talking, and he would say, 'Don't you feel embarrassed by that?' And I said, 'The only thing that bothers me about it is that other people can't see the triumph in it. Because to me, this is a treasure to be at this point in my life, in

this stage, and it be beginning. Some people don't even start to realize that they have the issues or start dealing with them until they get to this point.'"

* * * * * * *

Sheila's story, like the stories of so many other survivors—including the others you've read in this book—paints a very different picture of survivors of past abuse than the picture painted by the stigma surrounding intimate partner violence. That stigma would suggest that Sheila was bound to a never-ending cycle of abuse. After all, she grew up in a violent home and stayed with an abusive partner long after he initially showed signs of abuse, and even after his abuse toward her became extremely violent. Had Sheila followed the script written by the stigma surrounding abuse, she would have been destined to continue to become involved in abusive relationships—or even if she remained single, she would have been destined to be alone and damaged by her experiences of abuse.

And yet what we see in Sheila is a totally different picture. Instead of weakness, we see someone who showed tremendous courage in leaving her abusive partner, with virtually no worldly possessions to her name and still in the face of continued danger. Instead of isolation, we see a woman who surrounded herself with a network of friends, family members, and competent professionals to help her rebuild her life following abuse. And instead of hopelessness and despair, we see someone who is full of hope and excitement for the future possibilities that lie before her in her life.

In this final chapter, our goal is to present a road map for creating space for this more empowering, strength-focused view of survivors of intimate partner violence at the societal level. We underscore the rationale for prioritizing the goal of ending stigma surrounding abuse in order to prevent and respond to intimate partner violence in society. We then outline advocacy strategies for fostering positive social change to end stigma, support survivors, and hold offenders accountable. We conclude by summarizing our vision for a society that is absent of any stigma surrounding intimate partner violence, and how our research shows that this is not only possible, but achievable.

Rationale for Ending the Stigma Surrounding Intimate Partner Violence in Society

This book has been full of examples of the harmful impact of the stigma surrounding intimate partner violence—for victims and survivors; for professionals, friends, and family members of victims and survivors; for perpetrator accountability; and for the society at large. In this chapter, we summarize the points made throughout the book by suggesting that there are three main reasons why it is important to end this stigma: (a) to provide better support to victims and survivors, (b) to hold perpetrators accountable, and (c) to end the silence that allows abuse to continue to exist. In this section, we tap into the voices of survivors and professionals who work with them in order to underscore the importance of each of these reasons.

Ending Stigma to Provide Better Support to Victims and Survivors

This book has offered numerous examples of the ways that the stigma surrounding intimate partner violence makes it harder for victims and survivors to get the resources and support they need. This happens for many reasons, including internalized stigma that prevents them viewing themselves as worthy of support, stigmatizing responses from others when they do seek help, and societal messages—such as victim-blaming stereotypes— that keep abuse hidden at the community level. Therefore, one of the critical reasons that we need to work toward ending the stigma surrounding intimate partner violence is because ending the stigma will make it easier for victims and survivors to both *seek* and *receive* the help that they need.

How Stigma Impacts the Availability of Resources for Victims and Survivors

One of the manifestations of the stigma that has very serious implications for the availability of supportive services for victims and survivors is a lack of financial and other resources to provide adequate support to address intimate partner violence, both at the local and national levels. In many communities, services for victims—such as shelters—are stretched to the limit. It is not uncommon to hear from the domestic violence service providers with whom we talk and work that shelters are at capacity, and victims may need to seek services in other communities because resources in their own locations are maxed out.

Data from the National Network to End Domestic Violence (NNEDV) illustrate how great the unmet needs for survivors of intimate partner violence are. Each year since 2006, the NNEDV has conducted a one-day (i.e., 24-hour-long) census of how many adults and children seek the services of domestic violence agencies in the United States.[2] In the 2014 report, which is the most recent report available at the time of this writing, 67,646 victims of domestic violence received services from the 1,697 participating agencies, but there were 10,871 requests for services made by victims that were not able to be met due to programs not having substantial resources to provide them. Of the unmet needs, 56% were for housing. When asked why they were unable to meet these needs, the representatives of the agencies said that the main reasons were due to reduced funding from the government, private funding sources, and individual donors, as well as not having enough staff available.

As we will discuss later in this chapter, there remains a significant cultural silence even today about intimate partner violence and other forms of abuse. When people aren't talking about these issues, this can translate to a lack of financial resources to address them, such as if they are not recognized by political leaders, funding organizations, and individual donors as important issues to support financially. Services that cannot be supported financially can become obsolete, further leaving victims and survivors without the help they need to be safe.

Other Reasons That Ending Stigma in Society Will Lead to Better Support for Victims and Survivors

Ending societal stigma is critical for enhancing how victims and survivors are supported in our culture. As one survivor who participated in our research said, "Freedom is the most important thing. It is a basic human right." However, many people still today do not recognize that an abusive relationship involves a lack of freedom for victims, and therefore the needs of victims and survivors are often ignored. There remains a critical need for greater awareness that each victim and each survivor is unique, and his or her needs and choices should be honored and supported. Another survivor told us,

> "I think that as individuals and as a society we need to stop judging and patronizing victims in abusive relationships. The abuser is already making that person feel worthless and ashamed and dependent. We need to focus more on giving victims the power to make their own decisions and supporting them in their choices. Even if they decide to leave and go back again 8 times, the 9th time might be the time they leave for good. Just build them up, give them tools of empowerment, and give them education about the causes of domestic violence and the cycle of violence. Work on making them strong, and then they will be able to walk out of the relationship."

As long as societal stigma remains, it will impact the extent to which victims and survivors feel willing and able to get the help and support they need. One of the national advocacy leaders who participated in our expert panel study said,

> Survivors are less likely to seek help if they perceive the stigma, and this is even worse for men and marginalized women, or women from other cultures besides Euro-American. Even when they seek help, the stigma can still come from practitioners and the justice system or social service system.

This sentiment is also reflected in the following statement from a survivor in our research:

> "When you are stigmatized, you feel like a nothing. You feel like you don't deserve to live because other people are too lazy and judgmental so jump to their conclusions because of their bias, discrimination, or bigoted attitudes against women and children who need police and federal protection. It is very hard to overcome the stigma of being abused."

Across all of our research studies, the survivors we heard from emphasized the need to end the stigma in order to ensure appropriate support and resources for people who have been abused. As we discussed in Chapter 9, one way to achieve this is to ensure that professionals and others in the community receive proper training and education to ensure non-stigmatizing responses to victims. For example, a survivor told us,

> "I don't know if you ever get over the stigma. When you talk about it, you are always the person who was abused. To this day, people say to me, 'I can't believe you stayed. You should have just left.' I think that until there is more education in the police departments, the courts and the community, there will always be stigmas attached to abuse."

Another survivor emphasized that reduced stigma offers greater options so that victims can feel empowered to get the help they need: "I think there's a stigma because a victim internalizes the blame for their abuse. Information, literature, counseling, and outreach opportunities, all need to insist that the shame does not belong to the victim."

Finally, ending societal stigma increases support for survivors because it shifts the focus on victims and survivors from blame and judgment to respect and support. Far too many survivors today still face an uphill battle in getting other people to believe them and recognize their experiences as abuse. A survivor shared the following thoughts with us:

> "It's not always easy to tell. No amount of intelligence, degrees, salary, or accomplishment insulates a person. Victims may keep silent, thinking it will protect others. Abusers may be the most well-reputed, charismatic individuals you will ever meet—people you have known for years. Victims and abusers are people you know and see every day. We tell children to run and tell someone, to keep telling until someone listens and believes them. For women in domestic violence, we look away, or find some way to make it her fault."

A culture of believing and supporting survivors is critical for creating responsive social systems to meet their needs.

Ending Stigma to Hold Perpetrators More Accountable

Ending societal stigma also requires a shift in how perpetrators are viewed and held accountable. Perpetrators must be held accountable at the community and cultural levels for the abuse that they perpetuate. Victims simply should not be held accountable for their own abuse. One survivor told us,

> "I think progress has been made in the last couple of decades. The O. J. trial in the 1990s did a great deal to bring domestic abuse out of the closet and into the open, making it socially unacceptable. It does seem to me that the stigma is shifting from blaming the victim to blaming the abuser."

Despite some progress being made in recent years, many social forces remain in place that release perpetrators from being held accountable for their abuse.

It is possible to both view perpetrators as 100% responsible for the abuse while also considering the ways that the broader cultural and social contexts contribute to abuse. This is complex, of course, because by looking at cultural influences, including stigma, we run the risk of absolving perpetrators for their own accountability (i.e., by providing an excuse that "My culture made me do it"). Nonetheless, survivors who participated in our research expressed ways that they viewed cultural and societal contexts as contributing to their former perpetrators' actions and/or failing to hold them accountable for them. Consider the following examples:

- "To overcome the stigma of being abused you must first address the atmosphere that creates an environment of stigmatization. It was only when I rejected the culture and fundamentalist teachings of the social culture that promoted the male hierarchal teachings that I was able to completely overcome the stigma of abuse. I still battle the shame of being divorced twice at times. In our culture, it seems the stigma remains upon the woman who leaves abusive relationships. If a male is to divorce twice, we are less likely as a culture to frown upon him."
- "I can't say this is the best option, but I've stopped going to church. I was married in the church and have since divorced. I filed paperwork for an annulment and was denied, even though I know I had multiple grounds, domestic violence being only one of them. Having to justify my decision to leave my abuser, even years after the fact, to a bunch of religious leaders who don't know me and in a church that didn't support me, I just don't see it as healthy for me to keep trying to get some sort of validation from the church that what

I did was right, because I don't need them to tell me that. I already know."

A member of our expert panel of national advocacy leaders said that ending the stigma surrounding intimate partner violence would require "having consistent and clear penalties for abusers, such as jail time, fees, compliance with batterer treatment programs, and taking responsibility for their actions." This suggestion was reinforced by several of the participants in our survivor research studies, who noted the importance of ending societal stigma to ensure that appropriate community-level sanctions are in place to hold offenders accountable. For example, one survivor said,

> "I think working class women (as I am) are denied good educational choices and so do not see that they have any agency in the world. Therefore, they just don't see themselves as individuals with choices. This lack of perceived choice is underpinned by a society that constantly tells women that they are there to be used and abused by men. We need a sea change in how women are portrayed by the media and how they are treated by the judicial system. A strong message that domestic violence is not acceptable needs to be conveyed and backed up by punishments for the perpetrators that do not involve the women pressing charges. The assault should be treated in the same way that a stranger assault should be—automatic prosecution."

Another survivor said,

> "I did not know until after I left him that he had assaulted his first wife, and I didn't find out until the family court case that he had been charged with assaulting his second wife. I wish there had been a register of DV offenders that I could have checked before I started my relationship with him."

A third survivor shared the following thoughts:

> "I don't think there is any way to remove the stigma. As long as there are abusers and victims, and as long as there are not enough resources to really help victims escape permanently, and to bring the abusers to justice, there will be almost as much stigma attached to the 'stupid victims who choose to stay,' as there is to the abusers themselves."

Overall, ending societal stigma is a key to promoting the social changes needed to hold perpetrators accountable.

Ending Stigma to Stop the Silence That Allows Abuse to Continue

Another manifestation of the stigma surrounding intimate partner violence is the silence about this issue—as well as other forms of abuse—at the societal level. Even with growing attention to the harmful effects of abuse in recent years, there remains a powerful secrecy and silence related to abuse. Ending this silence is critical to make it easier for individuals, organizations, and society to overcome intimate partner violence. Victims and survivors feel the brunt of this silence. Consider, for example, the following statements made by survivors who participated in our research:

- "I would like people to actually speak to me about what happened, before they judge me, and believe what the abuser has said."
- "It's my belief that this will perpetuate forever until society stops with apathy. They stare it straight in the face and ignore it. Even continue to support these abusers. I'm thinking it's long, long overdue for people to wake up."
- "I'm just amazed at the blinders people wear while witnessing domestic abuse. They don't see it because they don't want to see it. They are much more apt to react defensively because of the rape culture that tells them victims are lying, when they should be stepping up and saying 'no more' to violence against women and children. It is disgusting."
- "It was only when I would share my stories of abuse and saw the 'no talk' rules in place and the minimization taking place consistently in the communities I was in did I realize that I had to leave that as well to grow and make progress. I think as long as these communities stigmatize and re-victimize abused people, mainly women, the women involved in abuse will be more intractable."

Thus another important reason to end societal stigma is to stop the silence that keeps intimate partner violence shrouded in secrecy. This is critical for several reasons. First, it will reduce the taboo around these issues and allow people to have more opportunities for open conversations and dialogue about the topic so that they will be recognized as the critical social issues that they are. As one survivor said, "I can't really imagine overcoming the stigma of having been abused. I suppose it would consist of having abuse become less of a taboo subject." Second, breaking the silence surrounding abuse is critical for educating people about abuse and preventing future abuse. Another survivor said,

> "It's so hard. I think education is key. It's something we speak in hushes about. Relationship violence should be talked about really young. And, we need to model good relationships for our children so they don't fall victim, give girls more self-esteem, and always encourage your children to say no."

Finally, as a survivor told us,

> "Abuse is something too many of us are dealing with these days. It's time we break the silence and secrecy surrounding abuse and reach out for each other. We can learn from each other's failures and triumphs. We need each other to grow and overcome. The only people that can truly understand what it's like to be abused are people that have been abused. Let the rest of the world form their opinions, and ignore the stigma."

Breaking the silence and ending societal stigma is a key to ensuring the survivors are supported—by one another and by the broader society.

Advocating to Promote Positive Social Change to End Stigma, Support Survivors, and Hold Offenders Accountable

Ending the stigma surrounding intimate partner violence is, in many ways, a huge task that lies before us. This stigma is pervasive and found at many levels—including within individuals, between people in relationships, among cultural and community groups, and within the broader social context. It is easy to become overwhelmed when thinking about this task—it can seem insurmountable. And, indeed, fully ending this stigma is likely to take a long time. Realistically, it will require many people and organizations working together to create a cultural shift toward positive social change.

Even as we stare in the face of the daunting challenge of ending the stigma surrounding intimate partner violence in society, we can be emboldened by the mission before us. Ending stigma is not easy, but it is necessary. It is necessary for supporting survivors, holding offenders accountable, preventing future violence, and breaking the silence that keeps abuse hidden and ignored.

Through See the Triumph, we promote an approach to advocacy that we call "everyday advocacy."[3] By *everyday advocacy*, we mean that we believe that everyone—regardless of their background, profession, education, or any other characteristics—can play a role in advocating to end the stigma surrounding intimate partner violence. Some people hear the term "advocacy" and get overwhelmed, or they say that they don't think of themselves as advocates. But we believe that advocacy comes in many forms—including both large-scale and smaller-scale efforts, as we discussed in Chapter 8 in relation to survivors engaging in advocacy efforts. Sometimes, advocacy does involve large-scale efforts, such as creating a public policy campaign or organizing a large awareness event in one's community. These efforts are great, but it's understandable that not everyone has the time, energy, resources, or even interest to engage in such large-scale advocacy efforts.

Therefore, we also celebrate smaller-scale advocacy efforts, which in fact can have a much bigger impact than anticipated at first. For example, a small-scale advocacy effort could mean sharing an article to raise awareness about intimate partner violence through a person's social media account. Even though this action doesn't require any money and only a small amount of time, it has the potential to reach a lot of people who may learn something by reading the article. More importantly, though, it sends a message that the person who shared the post cares about the issue of intimate partner violence and understands the dynamics of abuse. If one of his or her friends needed help related to an abusive relationship, it's likely they'd consider turning to their friend who has made a point to discuss this top openly using social media.

In the remainder of this section, we explore large- and small-scale advocacy strategies that readers can consider advocating for positive social change to more effectively prevent and respond to violence and end societal stigma. In particular, we focus on the following four strategies: (a) community-based advocacy for strengthening local response systems; (b) media advocacy; (c) creating space for survivors to share their stories in safe, empowering ways; and (d) challenging common stereotypes about intimate partner violence.

Community-Based Advocacy for Strengthening Local Response Systems

Every community is unique in the context it provides for its members who are experiencing abuse. Communities may differ in many ways, such as common attitudes toward intimate partner violence held by community members, the number and type of abuse-specific services available, and the general level of resources within a community. There can be many different configurations of these attributes. For example, in one community, there may be a strong sense of the attitude that abuse will not be tolerated in the community and a well-resourced domestic violence agency and shelter, but other resources that are important for the accessibility of services may be limited (e.g., a lack of public transportation and affordable housing in a rural community). In another community, members may be indifferent to the subject of abuse and therefore provide little support to their local domestic violence programs, but overall the community may have a lot of resources, such as accessible public transportation and quick access to law enforcement agencies in the midst of a crisis.

Every community's unique configuration with respect to these and other characteristics will determine the specific needs for strengthening the local response system's effectiveness at supporting victims and survivors, holding offenders accountable, and preventing future violence. Examples of specific needs that may be present in communities include more education and training for frontline professionals who work with victims and/or offenders (e.g., law enforcement officers, medical professionals, and court system professionals), greater access to housing and other economic resources, supportive resources for children who witness or experience abuse in their families, or community awareness about the services available through local domestic violence agencies. Whenever possible, we encourage readers to work with others in their local communities to identify the top priorities for their communities.

In this chapter, with our focus on ending societal stigma, we emphasize the need for increased broader, cross-community networks through which advocates across communities can share resources and learn from one another's successes and challenges. Several state-level and national advocacy organizations already work toward these goals. For example, one of the national advocacy experts who participated in our expert panel research study explained their advocacy approaches as follows:

> We work at the three levels of advocacy: individual advocacy, systems advocacy, and social change advocacy. The reality of stigma affects all three levels. At an individual advocacy level, we do a lot of work to help ensure that services provided to victims of domestic violence and sexual assault are survivor-driven, empowering, trauma-informed, and culturally-relevant. A part of this is about understanding how big a deal it is for many victims/survivors to tell anyone what is happening to them, and how culture, past experience with disclosure, current circumstances and resources affect whether or not they will and how they respond to the assistance domestic violence/sexual assault programs are offering (e.g., if you are only providing 'leaving' solutions and judge her for not 'being ready' to leave, then you are not reflecting any of the qualities of good advocacy). The same is true for our systems advocacy, where there is an additional challenge of conveying an appreciation that disclosure and safety planning are processes and not single acts or points of time, and that a decision NOT to disclose or fully disclose may be part of a safety plan and not 'denial' or 'fraud'). Similarly, on the social change level, how women and domestic violence and sexual assault victims/survivors are perceived and their experiences understood are big factors in how the problem of gender-based violence is defined and prevention and intervention strategies are articulated and implemented.

Therefore, many existing state and national advocacy organizations already engage in systemic advocacy efforts at many levels, and it is valuable for individuals to plug into these efforts when considering best practices for advocacy in their own local communities.

Media Advocacy

One of our national advocacy expert panel members told us that

> engaging celebrities, sports figures, newscasters, and political leaders in the conversation and ensuring they understand the influence their attitude, words, reporting has on our society is important to begin having the dialogue on what we can do to support survivors. Using talk shows and news that reach out to various cultural communities or those that might be isolated to inform them about what domestic violence looks like, that it is not victims' fault, and there is help.

This expert's views underscore the importance of engaging in the media in advocacy efforts to end the societal stigma surrounding intimate partner violence.[4]

As discussed in Chapter 6, various forms of media can perpetuate the stigma surrounding abuse. On the other hand, the media also can be a powerful tool for reaching large numbers of people to raise awareness about intimate partner violence and challenge stigma. We suggest the following considerations for engaging in media advocacy related to intimate partner violence,[5] and we use the term "advocates" in this section to refer to anyone who is interested in engaging in media advocacy to raise awareness about intimate partner violence:

1. *It is valuable for advocates to make connections with people working in media, even during times when the topic is not currently in the headlines.* Once reporters and other media representatives know of your expertise on the subject, they will be more likely to reach out for information when stories arise.
2. *Encourage media representatives to report the context in stories on intimate partner violence accurately.* Some media representations of abusive relationships imply that the abuse is an isolated incident. Therefore, advocates can work with media representatives to ensure that the typical patterns and power and control dynamics of abusive relationships are described.
3. *Encourage reporters to include educational information and local resources in stories about intimate partner violence.* When people see news stories about intimate partner violence, they may recognize that they or someone they know is in an abusive relationship. Therefore, reporters can provide a valuable service to the community when stories include information about local and national resources where people can turn for assistance. In addition, media stories can be presented alongside educational information, such as a description of warning signs of a potentially abusive relationship.

4. *Look for opportunities to engage in media advocacy activities to raise awareness about intimate partner violence.* This may include writing a letter to the editor of a local or national newspaper, doing a news interview for a story to raise awareness about abuse, and providing non-stigmatizing comments on social media or news websites when there are stories about intimate partner violence.
5. *Be prepared for last-minute media requests.* The reality of news cycles is that stories may develop at a moment's notice, and in many cases, intimate partner violence makes the news when there is a high-profile or especially severe case that grabs the headlines. Therefore, it can be difficult to predict when opportunities to raise awareness about intimate partner violence will arise, so it is important for advocates to be ready when the media does call. Some strategies for getting and remaining ready are to understand the resources available in your community and some basic statistics about intimate partner violence and to spend some time thinking about what message you want to convey about intimate partner violence. News stories often are reported with brief "sound bites" from experts and survivors, so it may even be beneficial to rehearse some important key messages so that you'll be prepared and confident to state these when the opportunity arises.

The media can be a powerful tool that can be used toward advocating for ending the stigma surrounding intimate partner violence. However, effective media advocacy requires some planning and preparation to ensure that non-stigmatizing messages are conveyed. The previously suggested strategies offer considerations to help advocates prepare to deliver those messages and ensure that media opportunities have the desired impact.

Creating Spaces for Survivors to Share Their Stories in Safe Ways

There is power in the stories of survivors of intimate partner violence: power to educate, inform, make people think, and help people heal.[6] There is a Native American proverb that says, "It takes a thousand voices to tell a single story."[7] We believe that this is particularly true for intimate partner violence. The overarching story that we aim to tell through this book is that people can overcome past abuse and the stigma that surrounds it. However, we know that within this larger story, there are countless individual stories of abuse and triumph, and each of these individual stories is unique, meaningful, and important.

Every survivor of abuse has a rich individual story to tell that is uniquely their own. However, just as each story is individualized to each person, it is also important to honor each person's unique views on whether, when, and how to tell their stories. This may be publicly, privately, and/or simply finding ways to tell their stories to themselves in new ways, such as through journaling or art. Even very private ways of telling and recounting one's stories are very valuable and should be honored. We do not believe it is a requirement that survivors tell their stories publicly in order to be fully healed or recovered from abuse. In fact, there are many reasons why it may not be in survivors' best interests to share their stories, such as if doing so would put them or their children at a safety risk or if they simply do not want to do so.

At a societal level, however, we have heard from many survivors and professionals, who work with victims and survivors, about the importance of creating spaces in society for survivors' stories to be told, heard, and honored. Some of the forms that these spaces could take include written stories by survivors, social media platforms and Internet discussion boards that allow survivors to share their stories, news stories featuring survivors, and research studies that embrace the complexity of survivors' stories, such as through the use of case study and qualitative research methods.

Our research has revealed several reasons why creating these spaces for survivors' stories is important. First, publicly available stories help other survivors know that they are not alone. As one survivor told us, "Talking more and reading the stories of others does help. Knowing that 1 in 4 women will understand what I'm saying from personal experience helps too." Having opportunities for survivors to share their stories publicly is needed "so that when survivors are ready to leave, and have made that decision for themselves, they will have role models to look to," as one survivor said. Second, publicly honoring the stories of survivors showcases their strengths and courage for all to see. As a member of our national advocacy expert panel said, "It's more than just sharing stories; it's supporting them to become leaders in their communities where they can become role models based on what they want."

Third, the public sharing of survivors' stories can create opportunities for them to be and feel heard by others. Unfortunately, survivors often feel like their experiences are not heard or valued. For example, one survivor said, "I feel as if people still look down on me when I speak of my experience. My ex denies everything, which makes me feel devalued by him still." Another shared with us that she continues to share her story, even though she felt that many people don't take her seriously:

> "I am in college and raising my children on my own. My goal is to be the sole provider for my children and prove to them all of their dreams can come true and we can do it on our own. I want to inspire victims to become survivors. So, my education will be used to advocate for women and children and hopefully start my non-profit to make a positive change in our community, even though I am told it will never change. I am already looked down upon, so the way I see

it will not hurt me any more to stand up for what is right, and who knows maybe my voice will be heard."

Fourth, creating spaces for survivors to share their stories provides survivors with opportunities to help others. One survivor told us,

> "Talking about it helps. Doing things like this research study helps. It makes me feel like I am helping others. I don't go around and share my experiences much. I don't carry a sign that says, 'I was raped and abused for years of my life,' but if someone shares that they are in a similar situation, I'll tell them. I feel it is my duty as a woman."

Another said,

> "I talk relatively openly about it. So, I don't have an issue with secrecy, because I feel like it would be better for people to know. I'm not like going around with an air horn or anything. But if somebody is talking about it, or they're asking about it, I don't mind telling them."

We have heard, time and time again, from the survivors who participated in our research that they want to use their experiences to help other people. The heart of many survivors is to give back to their communities and to help other people avoid some of the hurt and trauma they experienced.

To create these spaces, it is important to consider ways to honor each survivor's unique story and to give them freedom to share stories that highlight the complexity of abusive relationships in ways that are meaningful to them. One survivor said, "Society claims to want victims to speak up and out, but they want you to do it *their* way." Another shared,

> "I think I would feel like I had overcome the stigma if I could openly talk about my experiences and feel like people hear my story as just that, MY story, and not lump me in with all other abused people."

As survivors and professionals who work with them know, the experiences of being abused and recovering from an abusive relationship often do not come neatly packaged in a way that meets the stereotypical images of intimate partner violence. As such, survivors' stories are also important for challenging common stereotypes about intimate partner violence, as will be discussed in the next section.

Challenging Common Stereotypes and Biases About Intimate Partner Violence

Much of the societal stigma surrounding intimate partner violence remains wrapped up in the common stereotypes and biases that people hold toward abuse. Therefore, to end this societal stigma, it will be necessary to challenge these stereotypes directly and intentionally. At the individual level, this may mean countering stereotypes that arise during one-on-one discussions about intimate partner violence. For example, if you hear someone ask a victim-blaming question about someone involved in an abusive relationship, you can challenge the victim-blaming assumption and encourage the other person to focus on how the perpetrator is accountable for the abuse.

Stereotypes can be challenged within organizations as well. For example, if services in a domestic violence agency are geared toward only a specific type of victim (e.g., female victims only or victims only coming from a certain cultural or socioeconomic background), then agency staff can work to ensure that services are inclusive to meet the needs of clients from all backgrounds. At a societal level, these stereotypes can be challenged by using the media advocacy strategies described earlier or by advocacy organizations creating a public awareness campaign that counters common biases against intimate partner violence. One example of a national advocacy organization's campaign working to challenging stereotypes can be found in the NO MORE campaign,[8] which created a series of public service materials to say "No More" to such views as "Why doesn't she just leave?" and "She was asking for it."

We can further challenge the stereotypes surrounding intimate partner violence by consistently demonstrating how the actual lived experiences of survivors disprove the stereotypes. To provide examples of this, Table 10.1 presents a list of common stereotypes about intimate partner violence, along with quotes from survivors who participated in our research that counter each stereotype.

As Table 10.1 makes clear, survivors' lived experiences refute many of the common stereotypes about intimate partner violence. However, despite that being true for countless survivors, the stereotypes persist, and they likely will continue to do so until there are more clear and intentional efforts to challenge and counter them in society. From the stories and experiences of survivors of abuse, there is abundant evidence that the common societal stereotypes about intimate partner violence are false. It is up to each of us to continue to work together to replace these stereotypes with more accurate, empowering messages that promote a more positive and realistic view of victims and survivors of abuse.

Conclusion: A Vision for a Stigma-Free World

As we conclude this book, we highlight the story of one final survivor of past abuse who shared her story with us. Norma, who was in her mid-60s and has one adult child, holds a doctoral degree, and was phasing into retirement. She shared her experiences of her one past abusive marriage, which she experienced in her 20s. In that relationship,

Table 10.1 Quotes From Survivors of Intimate Partner Violence That Challenge Common Stereotypes About Abusive Relationships

Common Stereotypes About Intimate Partner Violence	Actual Experiences of Survivors of Past Abuse
Victims stay in abusive relationships because they like being abused.	"Many feel that women who stay in an abusive relationship enjoy it or have no self-esteem. I contend that's not the case at all for me and many others. Sometimes you fear for your life if he finds you, sometimes you have no visible means of support, and fear tricks you into thinking that you can't make it on your own. Sometimes, you simply want your child to have his father, which is a major part of the reason I stayed. I feared that he would find me and kill me, so I stayed until he hit me, and I believed our son would be next. Thank God, I had my education and spiritual strength which bolstered my will and self-worth to leave. I also had the support of my family and one close friend." "People asked me why I stayed. Well, at the end I couldn't leave because he made the house electrified. Even with that becoming public knowledge from the court, I still get asked if I stayed because I liked it. Who likes it? Really, who?"
Victims are at least partially to blame for their own abuse. It is easy to leave an abusive relationship, so if victims wanted to do so, they could "just leave."	"There is nothing worse than hearing people say, 'Why did you put up with it?' 'Why did you let him do it?' And, 'Why didn't you just leave him?' Also, to have people say things to you about being a weak person, a fool, or naive. They do not seem to realize that in an abusive relationship, you are controlled and do not have those options. To know that people understand how tough it was and realize that you are actually a stronger person for having got through it means a lot. There are still many out there, though, who, when they find out you were a victim, back off and don't have much to do with you." "Society must get over thoughts that it is somehow the fault of the one who is abused. And, that they should just leave. It is not always that easy to just get up and leave." "We live in a society that blames the victim (sexual assault, poor, homeless, abused, etc.). Overcoming the stigma means people understanding how difficult it is for a victim to get out of an abusive situation and that the stigma makes it even harder to leave. People don't understand the subtle ways in which abuse occurs and so they may not know how to support a victim so that he/she can get out of the abusive relationship." "I think there is a lot of stigma by those who have never been there. Education is the key and people need to realize that it can happen to anyone. A lot of people blame the abused and ask why they didn't leave sooner. Most do not understand the complications that come along with a controlling or abusive relationship. They also don't understand the dangers. Overcoming the stigma to me means to learn from the experience, grow from it, do not repeat it, and allow it to make you a better person."

	"To overcome the stigma is to educate people about domestic violence. When people understand that the victim often has no way to leave or is too scared to leave, then they will stop blaming them. If people would understand that victims are smart, strong individuals that have been forced to not be themselves, then everyone would not place a stigma on them."
	"We live in a culture where the victim is blamed. Be prepared that people will say cruel things but also be prepared that some people will not. Some people will be very supportive, will believe you, and will not stigmatize you. In fact they will counter the stigma that you have received from others. And you can find a healthy relationship. I have."
	"I think it would mean that the world stops believing it is the abused individual's fault. Somehow, someway, it is my fault and there's not a realization that oh yes, there really are individuals out there who are just plain dangerous and can trap even a very smart, capable woman."
Only certain types of people experience intimate partner violence.	"ANYONE, from ANY demographic, ANY education level can be a victim of abuse. I was a volunteer teaching self-esteem and sex ed classes to at-risk teenage girls by day, coming home to an abusive relationship at night."
	"For me, it was getting over blaming myself, moving beyond that. In my culture, I feel that there is more stigma related due to stereotypes. As an educated, articulate individual, I realized that intimate partner violence can happen to anyone, regardless of gender, race, or socioeconomic status. I think more work needs to be done regarding stereotyping."
	"It means that people see me as a strong, powerful woman who can do anything I want to. It means that people no longer see me as a victim, but as a survivor."
	"The changes in me are evidence to others that stigmas are false. The aspects of my life that were not stereotypical of society's picture of abused women are talking points to help dispel myths and my ability to share my story is helping someone else abused or not abused."
	"I work hard to dispel myths, to challenge assumptions, to change others' perspectives regarding intimate partner violence. The stigma is what I keep trying to stay one step ahead of, or it's what I keep chasing, trying to capture and get rid of. It's like wearing a scarlet letter. I am faced all the time with the 'brand' of IPV survivorship, and I want to be the one to define what that means."
	"Being abused leaves you with two stigmas: the whore or the victim. Half of the people you meet who know treat you like a problem child who is prone to drama and trouble. The other half treat you like you're made of glass, and they tiptoe around you, like at any moment, you might fall apart. To overcome this is to show you can have a normal life after the abuse, to find the balance between survivor and fighter, not victim and black sheep."

(Continued)

Table 10.1 (Continued)

Common Stereotypes About Intimate Partner Violence	Actual Experiences of Survivors of Past Abuse
Relationships are only abusive if they involve severe physical violence.	"When people think of an abused woman, they don't think like screaming and like grabbing wrists. They usually think like full-out punches. And there are just so many more factors to it that people don't think about it. They just go with the stereotype and roll with it. So, I just think we need more information, more knowledge for people. I mean it's easy for me to know these things not only because I've been in it, but because of my classes. But not everybody is going to take a sociology class or all of that."
Abuse is caused by such factors as substance abuse or anger management issues.	"For me, it is reframing the experience, the questions. It is acknowledging the truth you felt and the decisions and actions your partner made. I think a big stigma is that intimate partner violence is the result of alcoholism or anger management needs, but violence is about power, control and conscious selfish decisions and actions."
Victims of abusive relationships are "damaged" and devalued.	"Ending stigma would mean that people would respond to my experiences with empathy, rather than stereotypes or attempts to shame me. It would mean that my opinions, thoughts, and feelings would be given the same weight as anyone else's, rather than being attributed to my status as a survivor. It would mean that I wouldn't have to hide my status as a survivor at school or in the workplace for fear of being categorized as too broken, damaged, or unprofessional. It would mean that I could stop seeing portrayals in books, movies, and TV shows that inevitably blame survivors rather than perpetrators for abuse. It would mean that people would stop talking about how weak and pathetic people experiencing intimate partner violence are." "Speaking out and putting a face onto the problem of intimate partner violence. Let the public know we are just normal people."

"Just as people have stereotyped notions of abusers, there is a stereotype attached to being a victim of abuse. People look at you differently, even after you are out of the relationship for some time. I feel like if I were ever out with a group of friends or at a work meeting, and I disclosed that I'd been in an abusive relationship, people would look down on me or think I was weak or had issues. Also, there is a stigma you attach to yourself because you are ashamed that you let this happen to you. For a while, I felt like a weak person. I think I overcame it just with time and reframing the situation to realize that it was just the opposite, that I was so strong for getting out and making something of my life and becoming a healthy person."

"Just because we were abused does not make us weaklings or unworthy. We just need to understand that what we do does not cause someone to treat us badly; we are not in charge of our abusers emotions, they are. We deserve love, a good job, a family, etc., just like the rest of society."

"I have tried for years to become financially stable, while raising a child with no financial or physical help. I have not become financially stable, despite my good education, my excellent resume, and working full time and professionally. So, many likely still stigmatize me. I, however, know how hard I work, and how well I raise my child, and have come to realize that our economy and our society is not designed for women, single mothers, and survivors to become successful. Thus, I have refocused what I consider to be 'success.' I live in a strong and vibrant community of parents and friends. I am providing my child with an excellent home and education. I prioritize living ethically and having time for my family over working. Once you redefine success outside of the traditional paradigms, you can abandon the stigma projected on you."

There is a clear path and definition of recovering from a past abusive relationship.

she experienced physical, emotional, verbal, and sexual abuse. Her ex-husband was controlling and possessive. Despite the abuse, Norma said, "I stayed and tried to work it out because I wanted my child to have a father. My father and mother had a great marriage, and I wanted the same."

Eventually, Norma left the abusive marriage following a very violent incident, especially because she feared for the safety of their child, as she suspected that her ex-husband would begin to abuse the child as well. In looking back on her experiences since that relationship ended, Norma described how she and other survivors often experience discrimination and loss of status as a result of their abusive relationships:

> "Once you share the experience, there are those who view you as a continuing victim or damaged goods. Once you share the experience, there are those who regard you as inferior because they believe they're better than you for not having gone through such abuse. I carried shame because I felt as if I was too intelligent to have made such a poor decision regarding a mate."

In the process of overcoming her past abuse, Norma relied on her inner strength and her faith. She describes this process as follows:

> "To overcome the stigma of having been abused, you must open your mouth and publicly share the experience and the triumph of coming out a winner. It requires inner strength, self-belief, and self-acceptance. There will be those who may shun me, but I am determined not to let their misinformed response keep me trapped in the past. I believe everyone goes through some trauma in this life. Mine just happened to be intimate partner violence, an issue that has more stigma attached to it than cancer or divorce. Intimate partner violence is ugly and makes people uncomfortable, but I will not be silenced or constrained by shame as opportunities are presented for me to share my journey, and more importantly, my triumph."

Norma told us that she has publicly shared her story of triumphing over abuse, and this had been met with mixed reactions.

> "Telling about my journey has been bittersweet. On multiple occasions in large faith-based group settings, I've shared my story as a survivor speaker for a community agency that advocates for domestic violence victims and their families. The reactions of most have been compassionate and empathetic. Others have responded in silence through actions, facial expressions, as if to say 'Why is she airing out her dirty laundry?' This collection of folks finds ways to avoid eye contact when our paths have crossed again. It was uncomfortable for

them, but I'm determined to overcome the stigma of intimate partner violence. It's life, and it's real. In faith-based communities, I believe it goes on much more than most of us think but it's kept secret because of the stigma. Joining an agency as a speaker has been a freeing experience for me. In turn, I have helped others, who hid this dark secret, acquire freedom. After two of my presentations, two women hugged and thanked me profusely, calling me a blessing and sharing that they too had been ashamed and felt more free just hearing my testimony of overcoming. I now mention, as the situation allows, that I'm a survivor. I never did that until after sharing my story publicly. I am a talented, strong woman, an accomplished professional, who experienced IPV and came out an overcomer. Why should any stigma be attached to that?"

Norma offers hope and encouragement to others experiencing abuse in an intimate relationship:

"The journey to leave begins on the inside when you realize that you deserve better, and that you will survive. You don't need lots of advisors—just one person whom you trust and respect serving as your cheerleader. There is life after abuse, and it's been wonderful for me. It's exhilarating to look back at how I left and what I did in the midst of great fear—I drew spiritual strength from love of myself, family, and one good friend."

Norma concluded her participation in our research by reflecting on what the experience of sharing her story with us meant to her. She said, "Thank you for the opportunity to revisit a very painful time in my life and realizing not only how blessed I am, but just how proud I am of myself."

* * * * * * *

Norma's question, "Why should any stigma be attached to experiencing intimate partner violence?," is a challenge to us all. In truth, Norma is exactly right—there shouldn't be any stigma attached to experiencing intimate partner violence. Experiencing abuse can be a traumatic experience for victims and survivors, but it shouldn't be one for which they are shamed and stigmatized by anyone or within society. As we've seen throughout this book, nobody is immune to the possibility of an abusive relationship, and it is perpetrators who should be held fully accountable for their abusive actions. Moreover, the rates of experiencing abuse remain so high that as many as half of all people have experienced some form of abuse within an intimate relationship.[9] Even though intimate partner violence is often viewed as a marginalized issue, it is likely that this issue has touched everyone in society in some way—either directly or in connection with someone they know who has been involved in an abusive relationship. The stigma that has kept intimate partner violence as a hidden, marginalized issue simply does not reflect the significant impact that this form of abuse takes on individuals and our communities and society.

Ending the stigma surrounding intimate partner violence is indeed a daunting goal. However, our research shows that this goal is not only possible, but it is achievable. We know it is possible to overcome stigma because we have seen the evidence in the stories of the survivors you've read about in this book as well as the hundreds of other survivors who participated in our research but whose stories we were not able to highlight individually in the limited number of pages of this book. Beyond our own research, we know that there are countless other survivors who live courageously each day in a society that provides them with only limited resources and support and validation.

In Norma's final statement, she thanked us for the research study as an opportunity to revisit a painful time in her life in order to consider how proud she is for how far she has come in her life since that time. We appreciate this gratitude, but we also know that we are the ones who have much to be grateful for, as we are honored to be the bearers of the stories shared by the survivors who participated in our research. The topic of intimate partner violence—and the stigma that surrounds it is, on many levels, a painful topic to address. And yet we hope that as we close this book, we leave you with a sense of hope and inspiration.

Whatever reasons brought you to read this book—if you have experienced abuse yourself, if you have a close friend or family member who has been abused, if you are a professional who works with victims and survivors, or if you are simply a concerned citizen who cares about creating safe, nonviolent homes and communities—we hope that this book has challenged your thinking about abusive relationships and provided you with a more nuanced view of the complex dynamics of abusive relationships. But even more than that, we hope that this book has offered you plenty of examples of the powerful and inspiring ways that survivors can overcome past abuse, as well as ways that you—in big and small ways—can become a part of the larger social movement to end the stigma surrounding intimate partner violence, with the ultimate goal of ending abuse altogether.

Notes

1 Portions of this survivor's story originally appeared in a See the Triumph blog post, which can be found here: http://www.seethetriumph.org/blog/whats-in-a-name-in-ours-its-a-story-of-courage-and-triumph.
2 To learn more and find statistics from the census from each year since 2006, please visit http://nnedv.org/resources/census.html.

3 To see our See the Triumph Collection on this subject, please visit http://www.seethetriumph.org/collection-everyday-advocacy.html.
4 Please visit our See the Triumph Collection on Intimate Partner Violence, Stigma, and the Media for more information on media advocacy here: http://www.seethetriumph.org/collection-intimate-partner-violence-stigma-and-the-media.html.
5 Portions of this list are adapted from See the Triumph blog posts, and the full posts can be found in the See the Triumph Collection on Intimate Partner Violence, Stigma, and the Media: http://www.seethetriumph.org/collection-intimate-partner-violence-stigma-and-the-media.html.
6 Portions of this section have been adapted from blog posts from the See the Triumph Collection, "Every Survivor Has a Story." Please see http://www.seethetriumph.org/blog/every-survivor-has-a-story-series-introduction and http://www.seethetriumph.org/collection-every-survivor-has-a-story.html for the original resources from this collection.
7 This quote can be found at the following website: http://www.nrcprograms.org/site/PageServer?pagename=ThousandVoices_home.
8 For more about this campaign, please visit the following website: http://nomore.org/public-service-announcements/nomoreexcusespsas/print-ads/.
9 This statistic is based on the CDC's National Intimate Partner and Sexual Violence Survey, which showed that approximately half of both women and men had experienced psychological aggression in an intimate relationship: http://www.cdc.gov/violenceprevention/pdf/nisvs_executive_summary-a.pdf.

Index

Page numbers in *italics* refer to figures and tables.

abuse: mental 189; overcoming 182–7; physical 189; stigma and 4
abusive relationships: blame and 192–3, 197; community education on 201–2; controlling behaviors 16–19; counseling and 116–17; couples therapy 162–3; cultural groups and 131–2; Cycle of Violence 12–13; development over time 15–16; dynamics of 12–25, 201–2; ending 23–4, 126–7, 197; impact of accountability 152–5; impact on children 24–5, 181; isolation and 196; male victims 46–7; open discussion of 129; overcoming 211–12; patterns of 8–9; Power and Control Wheel 13–14; recovery from 182–7; religious groups and 132–4; safety and 204–5; same-sex 41–5, 125, 135–6; secrecy and 175, 184; sexual assault 21–3; social support 75–6; stalking 24; stereotypes of 43, 124–9, 196, 231; turning points 180–2; victim-blaming 126–7; violence in 19–21; *see also* intimate partner violence
abusive tactics: blocking help 72–3; control tactics 62–4; "crazy-making" 71; humiliation 68–9; isolation 64–6; long-term 77–8; stigma and 69, 76–8; verbal denigration 66–8; victim-blaming 73–4
accountability: batterer intervention programs 162–5; escape from 73–6, 145–52; fear and 146–7; impact of 152–5; legal consequences and 149–51, 162; perpetrator 58, 73, 75–6, 145–66, 221–2; professional failure and 147–52; societal stigma and 221–2; strategies for 156–66
advocacy efforts: community-based 225–6; everyday 224–5; individual 226; individual stories 228–30; large-scale 178–9, 224; media and 227–8; small-scale 179–80, 225; social change 226; strategies for 225–30; systems 226
anticipated stigma 34, 93–4

Babcock, Julia 164
batterer intervention programs 162–5
battering perpetrators 59–60
blame 4; internalized 88–9, 91–2; perpetrator 69–70, 197; religious group norms and 132; stigma and 31, 38, 48; *see also* victim-blaming

centrality, defined 93
children: abusive relationships and 24–5, 210; custody issues 150, 161, 176, 201, 208; impact of abuse on 24–5, 181
communities 208, 220; barriers to services 208–9; collaborations 208–9; education and training for 201–2, 208, 220; failure to take action 199–200; overcoming stigma in 176–8; perpetrator accountability and 147, 158–60; response systems 160–1, 192–3;

safety and 147; stigmatizing responses 198–200, 206–7; support from 206–9
community-based advocacy 225–6
controlling behaviors: choices and 16–17; devaluing 17; isolation 17–18; physically trapping 18–19; social systems and status 18
control tactics 62–4
counseling: abusive relationships and 12, 116–17; indirect help-seeking and 93–4; internalized stigma and 174; stigmatizing responses and 116–17; victim and survivor 14, 44–5, 47, 171, 173–4, 189, 211–12, 220
couples therapy 162–3
court system: abusive relationship dynamics 161–2; child custody issues 161; discrimination and 198, 200; ineffectiveness of 198–9; minimal legal consequences and 150; perpetrator accountability and 149–50, 198; stigmatizing responses 112; witness tampering 161–2
"crazy-making" tactics 71
criminal justice system: loopholes in 145; minimal legal consequences and 149–51; perpetrator accountability 146, 149–51
cultural groups: intimate partner violence in 130–1; societal stigma and 129–32
cultural norms 130–2
Cycle of Violence, phases of 12–13

Danger Assessment 204
disbelief of victims 100–2
discrimination 38, 67, 84, 109, 154, 198, 200, 236
DomesticShelters.org 161
domestic violence *see* intimate partner violence
domestic violence agencies: availability of supportive services 218–19; stereotypes of 231; stigmatizing responses 113–14, 195
Domestic Violence Awareness Month 138
Drapalski, Amy 84

emotional abuse: cultural norms 131; rates of 11; stigma and 69–73, 95

emotional healing, stigmatizing responses and 119
employment and education: barriers to services 208; discrimination and 128; stigmatizing responses 114–16; victim-blaming 194
enacted stigma 35–7
everyday advocacy 224–5
Everytown for Gun Safety 147

Family Justice Center model 208
family members *see* friends and family members
fear: of being judged 4, 177; of perpetrators 146–7; stigma and 76–7
Feder, L. 164–5
Flasch, Paulina 187
friends and family members: perpetrator accountability and 157–8; steps for helping abuse victims 202–6; stigmatizing responses 105–8, 117; support from 105–7, 202–6; victim-blaming 192–4, 197–8

Gottman, John 59

health care 93; *see also* medical professionals
help-seeking: court system 112; disbelief of victims 100–2; domestic violence agencies 113–14; employment and education 114–15; friends and family members 105–8; health care and 93; indirect 93–4; internalized stigma and 92–4; law enforcement 110–12; medical professionals 110–13; professionals and 108–20; religious organizations 114; stigma and 102–3; stigmatizing responses to 103–20
Holtzworth-Munroe, Amy 59–60
honor killings 131
humiliation 68–9

immigrants: cultural norms 130; stigma and 135
impairment 128
indirect help-seeking 93–4
individual advocacy 226
Integrated IPV Stigmatization Model 32–3, 35, 84–5, 88, 170
internalized blame 88–9, 91–2

Index

internalized stigma: abuse and 82–4; blame and 88–9, 91–2; characteristics of 34, 47, 88; external sources of 86–7; help-seeking and 92–4; impact of 88–92; negative self-talk 85; overcoming 169–74; process of 85–7; professionals and 119; self-doubt and 94; self-esteem and 94–6; self-talk and 171–4; sources of 172; understanding 96–8; victim-blaming and 48, 87

interpersonal processes: advocacy efforts 190–1; overcoming abuse and stigma 188, 190–1; positive supports 190

intimate partner violence: community education on 201–2; community responses to 147, 192–3; cultural norms 130–1; defining 9–10; experiences of 14–25; gender and 11; law enforcement and 110; media and 136–9; medical professionals and 110–11; negative attitudes towards 48; rates of 10–11; secrecy and 223–4; sexual assault 21–3; stereotypes of 196, 231–5; stigma and 5–8, 31–49, 69, 217–24, 237–8; survivors of 6, 25–6; *see also* abusive relationships

intrapersonal processes: exertion of power 188; forgiveness and acceptance 189; long-term recovery 190; new intimate relationships 189–90; overcoming abuse and stigma 188–90; physical and mental recovery 189; regaining identity 188

isolation: as an abusive tactic 14, 17–18, 38, 62, 64–6, 69, 183; effects of 91; as a source of vulnerability *120*; stigma and 4, 31–4, 44, 58, 84, 86, 88, 107; stigmatizing responses and 109, 118

Jacobson, Neil 59

law enforcement: failure to take action 148, 200; intimate partner violence and 110; protective orders 148, 150–1, 160–1; response systems 160–1; stigmatizing responses 111–12, 151; training for 110

lawyers: failure to take action 147–8; stigmatizing responses from 38–9, 112

leadership positions: abuse and 133–4; abusive tactics and 71; overcoming abuse and stigma from 178, 222, 227; perpetrator accountability and 158–9

learned helplessness 76

lesbian/gay/bisexual/transgender/intersex (LGBTI): stigma and 135; *see also* same-sex relationships

loss of power 34, 38, 44

loss of status: internalized 89; powerlessness and 34, 38; stigma and 31–2, 47, 58, 88, 236; stigmatizing responses and 109

Lucky (Sebold) 116

male victims: abuse and 10; help-seeking 125; stigma and 46–7

marital rape 21–2, 131

mass shootings 147

media: intimate partner violence in 136–9; public awareness and 137, 227–8; social media platforms 137; societal stigma and 136–8; trivializing of abuse 139; victim-blaming 139

media advocacy 227–8

medical professionals: failure to take action 147; intimate partner violence and 110–11; stigmatizing responses 112–13; training for 111

mental health professionals, stigmatizing responses 113

mental illness: internalized stigma and 84; stigma and 31, 84–5, 135

Mickelson, K. D. 93–4

National Domestic Violence Hotline 61

National Football League 137

National Intimate Partner and Sexual Violence Survey (U.S. Centers for Disease Control and Prevention) 11, 21

National Network to End Domestic Violence (NNEDV) 218

negative emotions 31, 44

negative self-talk 85, 171–4

NO MORE campaign 231

Olson, D. E. 162
overcoming abuse and stigma: interpersonal processes 188, 190–1; intrapersonal processes 188–90; process of 187–91; recovery and 182–7, 191; social support 190; Triumph Process Model 187–8
Overstreet, Nicole 32, 84–5, 92–4

perceived stigma 93–4
perpetrators: abusive behaviors 60–1; abusive tactics 62–73; accountability and 58, 73–6, 145–66, 221; battering 59–60; "crazy-making" 71; defined 10; leadership positions and 133–4; legal consequences and 162, 165; protective orders against 114, 148, 150–2, 160–1; responsibility for actions 146, 152, 158–65; social support 75–6; types of 59–60; victim-blaming 69–71, 73–4
perpetrator stigma: challenges of 76–8; overcoming 174–80; perpetuation of 55–8; secrecy and 175
personal biases: challenging 209–10; stigmatizing responses and 118–19
positive self-talk 171–4
power: professionals and 119–20; sources of 120
Power and Control Wheel 13–14, 16
powerlessness 34, 38, 44
professionals: court system 112; discrimination and 38; domestic violence agencies 113–14; education and training 210–11; employment and education 114–15; failure to take action 147–51; help-seeking from 108–16; lack of resources and support 118; lack of training and 116–17; law enforcement 110–11; medical doctors 110–13; mental health 113; negative responses from 109–11, 119–20; personal biases and 118–19, 209–10; positive collaborative relationships 207–8; power and 119–20; religious organizations 114; stigmatizing experiences with 35–7, 39–40, 108–19, 151, 206–7, 210; support from 206–11; trauma-informed care 209

protective orders 114, 148, 150–2, 160–1
psychological abuse *see* emotional abuse
public awareness 137, 227–8

Quinn, D. M. 92–4

rape 21–2, 36, 83, 113, 116, 131, 223
religious group norms: justification of abuse 133; leadership positions and 133–4; societal stigma and 130, 132–5; spiritual abuse 134–5; stigmatizing responses 114; victim-blaming 132–3
Rice, Ray 137–8

salience, defined 93
same-sex relationships: societal stigma and 135–6; stereotypes of abuse 125; stigma and 41–5, 135
Sebold, Alice 116
secrecy 129, 175, 183–4, 223–4
See the Triumph social media campaign 49–50, 157, 170, 192, 201, 224
self-doubt 94
self-efficacy 84
self-esteem 84–5, 94–6
self-talk 85, 171–4
sexual assault: advocacy efforts 226; media and 137; by partners 11, 21–3; prevention initiatives 208; rape 21–2, 36, 83, 113, 116, 131
shame 39–40, 43, 177, 197
social advocacy 178–80
social change advocacy 226
social media: awareness-building in 179; societal stigma and 137–8
social support 75–6, 175, 200–2
societal stereotypes 125–9
societal stigma: availability of supportive services and 218–19; cultural groups and 129–32; media and 136–9; multiple levels of 135–6; perpetrator accountability and 221; religious groups and 130, 132–5; same-sex relationships 135–6; secrecy and 223–4; stereotypes and 124–30, 231; strategies for ending 217–31; support for victims and 219–20; victim-blaming and 125–7, 139, 221–2; victims and 122–4, 139–40

spiritual abuse 134–5
Stalans, L. J. 162
stalking 24, 100–2
stereotypes: of abusers 124–5; of abuse victims 39, 43, 125–9; of abusive relationships 196, 231–5; devaluing victims 127–8; impairment 128–9; secrecy and 129; societal 125–9; victim-blaming 126–7
stigma: anticipated 34, 93–4; aspects of 4, 58; blame and 4, 31, 38, 48; consequences of 47–8; defined 31; discrimination and 38; emotional abuse 69–73; enacted 35–7; experiences of 31–47; external sources of 89; fear and 76–7; fear of being judged and 4; internalized 34, 47–8, 82–98, 169–74; isolation and 4, 31, 38, 44, 183; learned helplessness 76; long-term abuse and 77–8; loss of power and 44; loss of status and 32, 38; negative emotions and 31, 44, 183; overcoming 48–50; perceived 93–4; perpetrators and 55–8, 174–8; professionals and 35–7, 151; same-sex relationships and 41–5; shame and 39–40, 43; societal 122–4, 219–20; victim-blaming 69–71
Stigma Internalization Process 85–7, 94
stigmatizing responses: friends and family members 105–8, 117; harmful nature of 119; internalized stigma and 119; lack of resources and support 118; lack of training and 117–18; overcoming 174–7; personal biases and 118–19; professionals and 108–20; types of 109
stories *see* survivor stories
survivors: availability of supportive services for 218–19; closure and 175–6; defined 10; devaluing 127–8; discrimination and 236; emotional healing 119; enacted stigma against 35–7; individual stories 228–30; internalized stigma and 96–8; labeling of 176–7; overcoming abuse and stigma 182–91, 216–17, 236–7; perpetrator accountability and 152–5; professionals and 35–7,

39; secrecy and 129; shame and 39–40, 177; shift in perspective 181; social advocacy and 178–80; social support 75–6, 175; societal stigma and 219–20; stereotypes of 39, 125–8; support for 96–8, 107, 120–1, 175, 192, 198, 202–12; trauma-informed care 209; turning points 180–2; *see also* victims
survivor stories 228–30
systems advocacy 226

tactics of abuse *see* abusive tactics
trauma-informed care 209
Triumph Process Model 187–8
turning points: external interventions 181; impact on children 181; knowledge of abuse dynamics 181; severe violence 180–1; shift in perspective 181

U.S. Centers for Disease Control and Prevention 11, 21

verbal denigration 66–8
victim-blaming: in employment and education 194; by friends and family members 192–4, 197–8; internalized stigma and 48, 87–8; perpetrators and 58, 69–71, 73–4; religious groups and 132–3; societal stigma and 125–7, 221–2
victims: availability of supportive services for 218–19; defined 10; devaluing 127–8; enacted stigma against 35; fear and 76–7; help-seeking 100–8; isolation and 88; labeling of 176–7; learned helplessness 78; male 46–7; protective resources and 88; secrecy and 129; steps for helping 202–6; stereotypes of 125–8, 193; support for 100–5, 202–12; *see also* survivors
violence: experiences of 19–21; towards children 181; as a turning point 180–1
vulnerability, sources of 119

Walker, Lenore 12
Williams, S. L. 93–4
Wilson, D. B. 164–5
witness tampering 161–2

Taylor & Francis eBooks

Helping you to choose the right eBooks for your Library

Add Routledge titles to your library's digital collection today. Taylor and Francis ebooks contains over 50,000 titles in the Humanities, Social Sciences, Behavioural Sciences, Built Environment and Law.

Choose from a range of subject packages or create your own!

Benefits for you
- Free MARC records
- COUNTER-compliant usage statistics
- Flexible purchase and pricing options
- All titles DRM-free.

Benefits for your user
- Off-site, anytime access via Athens or referring URL
- Print or copy pages or chapters
- Full content search
- Bookmark, highlight and annotate text
- Access to thousands of pages of quality research at the click of a button.

REQUEST YOUR FREE INSTITUTIONAL TRIAL TODAY

Free Trials Available
We offer free trials to qualifying academic, corporate and government customers.

eCollections – Choose from over 30 subject eCollections, including:

Archaeology	Language Learning
Architecture	Law
Asian Studies	Literature
Business & Management	Media & Communication
Classical Studies	Middle East Studies
Construction	Music
Creative & Media Arts	Philosophy
Criminology & Criminal Justice	Planning
Economics	Politics
Education	Psychology & Mental Health
Energy	Religion
Engineering	Security
English Language & Linguistics	Social Work
Environment & Sustainability	Sociology
Geography	Sport
Health Studies	Theatre & Performance
History	Tourism, Hospitality & Events

For more information, pricing enquiries or to order a free trial, please contact your local sales team:
www.tandfebooks.com/page/sales

Routledge Taylor & Francis Group | The home of Routledge books | **www.tandfebooks.com**